THE DIRTY DOZEN

How Twelve Rookies, The Shotgun, And
A Hail Mary Vaulted The 1975 Dallas
Cowboys Into The Super Bowl

Ryan Bush

Copyright © 2016 Ryan Bush

Ryan Bush Publishing

First Edition - All rights reserved.

ISBN-10: **0997982306** ISBN-13: **978-0997982305**

Ryan Bush Publishing

490 E. Cougar Lane

China Spring, Texas 76633

Web Site - Dallas Cowboys Vault at RyanBush.biz
Facebook Pages:
Dallas Cowboys Vault
Decade of Futility
Dallas Cowboys Dirty Dozen
Twitter - @rcbushCowboys

CONTENTS

	Acknowledgments	vii
	Introduction	9
1	MONEY, MONEY, MONEY!	13
2	THE COWBOY & THE LAME DUCK	30
3	POLITICS & DISCORD	39
4	THE DRAFT	47
5	THE PRANK & THE NO SHOW	62
6	SETTING A TONE	71
7	CALIFORNIA COWBOYS	84
8	THE FAREWELL TOUR	92
9	THE SHOTGUN	99
10	MAKING THE CUT	106
11	A SPARKLING BEGINNING	114
12	THE FORTUNES OF OVERTIME	124
13	DOME WRECKERS	133
14	ELEMENTS OF VICTORY	143
15	SHADES OF IMPERFECTION	154
16	THE WILL TO WIN	163
17	BLOOD, BLOWS & BITTERNESS	188
18	TAKING AIM	203

19	MONDAY NIGHT MADNESS	208
20	GETTING BACK ON TRACK	219
21	THE CURSE OF THE CAKE	231
22	A GIANT VICTORY	241
23	BLOWOUT	248
24	THE SWEETEST REDEMPTION OF ALL	254
25	RUMORS & REACTIONS	264
26	THE HAIL MARY GAME	270
27	WILD CARD WONDERS	286
28	THE BUILDUP	297
29	SUPER BOWL X	307
30	EVER AFTER	325
	EPILOGUE - SEASONS AFTER	328
	BIBLIOGRAPHY	333

ACKNOWLEDGMENTS

As a hand needs fingers to function, so too does a story need friends to develop into a book. No author can do it alone. I have been reminded of this fact at numerous intervals while writing this book, and will always be grateful to the individuals behind the scenes who helped to make *The Dirty Dozen* into a reality. It would be a gross injustice if I didn't take this moment to thank a few of these people.

Thanks foremost belongs to the Lord, for comfort during the hard days, for inspiration on those long nights. I'm especially grateful for the doors that You opened.

Thanks to Daddy for your belief in this project and your unfailing persistence in it.

Thanks to Mama for your encouragement.

Thanks to Leon Smith for giving me a chance so many years ago. You didn't have to, but I'm glad you did!

Thanks to Brent Bankston for providing invaluable research material. Without it, I don't know if this book would have ever been started.

Thank you to Mrs. Burke at the Baylor Library for your assistance and direction in researching this book.

A very special thanks is deserving for all of the "old-time" writers whose work I came across in conducting my research. Writers like Randy Galloway, Bob St. John, Carlton Stowers, Sam Blair, Roger Kaye, Patsy Leftwich, Andy Anderson, Rose Ann Roberts, Ken Richardson, Ted Colton, Frank Glieber, Jack Gurney, a young Rick Gosselin, Harry Atkins, Richard Shook, Dale Hoffman, Bud Lea, Scott Fowler, Jeffrey Denberg, John Crittenden, Melvin Durslag, Gene Williams, Charlie Nobles, Denne H. Freeman, Jaime Aron, Dink Carroll, Peter Golenbock, Leonard Shapiro, Ron Martz, Dave Anderson, Red Smith, Tex Maule, and Dave Nightingale. Your insight and conscientious detail is very much appreciated. And to the duo of Blackie Sherrod and Frank Luksa…what can I say? Even though you have departed from this world, your work remains classic, your verbosity timeless, and your humor priceless. May your shadows never grow less.

Ryan Bush

INTRODUCTION

Bequeathed long, long ago to the golden vale of days gone by, the brightest decade in Dallas Cowboys' history sits impervious to all denigration. Quite possibly the most dominant ten-year stretch by any single team in pro football's modern era, the 1970's was headlined by the hallowed presence of the silver-stained blue-starred helmets.

And what a standard they set throughout the decade. No team won more regular season games, playoff games, played in as many Super Bowls or stole as many hearts as the Boys from Big D. First Dallas' team, forever America's Team, the Cowboys were an organization that grew to respectability as the 1970's commenced, learning not only how to come out ahead on the scoreboard on Sunday afternoons, but how to do so with a passion and flair all their own.

The fourth-quarter comebacks...the clutch defensive stops...the eleventh-hour miracles...the "Man in the Funny Hat." These are the recollections that remain prevalent even to this day, magical moments and inspiring figures that transformed an ordinary football franchise into a collection of awe-inspiring folk heroes.

To the ignorant layman, of which there are many after all these years, it would seem as if this sunlit, bygone universe existed without so much as a tremor, a false step, or a faint breath. *Are not these the Cowboys of twenty consecutive winning seasons*? To many, the figures of head coach Tom Landry, quarterback Roger Staubach, and wide receiver Drew Pearson will always be football saints who held fortune and fate in their own hands, whose gridiron immortality rendered them immune to the imposition of circumstantial obstacles.

History, unfortunately, remembers no such thing, for in the infinite confines of its memory resides a moment that witnessed the Cowboys teetering on the edge of destruction, seemingly wavering between mediocrity and distastefulness. It's a story often overlooked because of the larger-than-life icons that captained the franchise at the time. It's a story long forgotten by the onslaught of water rushing under an indestructible bridge.

It's a season that general statistical analysis forty years removed reveals to be a simple case of Cowboy conquest. It's a season of ten wins, a miracle catch, and another deep playoff run the franchise was already renowned for.

Ho-hum.

But what numbers don't tell you are the stories of the internal struggle, the innovative genius, and the rallying point which made them first underdogs and then inspirational overachievers.

Yes, Father Time had finally caught up with the Dallas Cowboys in 1974, as age, apathy, and the clutches of greed reduced a perennial powerhouse into a shell of their former selves. The Cowboys, playoff participants for eight years running, found themselves rudely uninvited to the postseason tournament after a sub-par 8-6 record left them buried in fourth-place in the NFC's Eastern Division. Names much beloved were ripped from the team's roster, as gnarled crafty veterans were either headed on a ship bound for other employment, or the pleasant pastures of retirement.

From all appearances, the death knell was sounding loud and clear over the streets of Dallas. The end was here. It was time for Landry to rebuild, start over with a new pool of talent and come back strong in two or three seasons.

But rather than lay down and accept their fate as bygones, the Cowboys rose up in unison, shocking the entire football world by storming back in 1975 with an outlandish offensive wrinkle and a rejuvenated defense, and from an impossibly complex situation defined the fortitude of the franchise for years to come.

A front-office long on ground-breaking techniques in college scouting, rolled up their sleeves and produced their deepest rookie class ever. Landry found cause to roll back the clock and re-invent himself not only as a football coach, but as a patient drill-instructor. Proud veterans rediscovered the joy of playing a young man's game, while a host of raw recruits were all out to prove they belonged on the field too.

It was the perfect combination of surprise, enthusiasm, wisdom, and magic that ever a football team enjoyed. If it had been anybody else coaching than Tom Landry, any other quarterback under center than Roger Staubach, and any other cast of bright-eyed scruff-faced rookies coming out of training camp, the Cowboys would have been forever a footnote of the 1975 season.

Just when you thought the game was over, just when you thought their road had ended, the Cowboys were there ready to surprise and astonish a captive audience. Once. Twice. All the way to the Super Bowl.

Ryan Bush

CHAPTER 1

MONEY, MONEY, MONEY!

"A nickel ain't worth a dime anymore." - **Yogi Berra**

"Inflation is when you pay fifteen dollars for the ten-dollar haircut you used to get for five dollars when you had hair." - **Sam Ewing**

    Long before cash became king on American soil, it was considered by the majority to be a duplicitous enemy that cut to the soul of the pocketbook of friend, foe, and foreigner. Excepting Parliament and the powerful nobility across the stormy waters of the Atlantic, no carnal institution was more frustrating than those little square redeemable notes whose value could change from colony to colony, parish to parish, and even city to city. As one Englishman noted in 1742, "There certainly can't be a greater Grievance to the Traveller, from one Colony to the other, than the different Value their Paper Money bears."

    To Eighteenth-century Americans steeped in the Biblical wisdom of "just weights and measures," money was very much a moral matter, at times even religious. That the nation's accepted currency possess an unchanging value was as essential to Protestants and conservative Catholics as the unconditional love of God, and was supposed to be a distinctive component of the American dream. Anything less was considered to be legalized tyranny against the average citizen.

As sure as the mark of Cain is a symbol of political power, so too is paper money an unmistakable signature of a debtor nation. The most common example of the times was that of Great Britain, whose heavy-handed, nobility regulated economy, founded on a subject's allegiance to the king, was something that Americans were desperately trying to free themselves from. But not even an expansive ocean separating them could prevent the eventual legalization of a very British-like ploy. In tough times when the bills were due, colonial governments knew of only one way to pay off demanding creditors; print more of them.

This political tactic officially sanctioned to keep the government functioning was a driving force in a changing lifestyle that would shape the nation for centuries to come. The American peoples' inability to grasp the mindset of a fluctuating currency and its inherent demands drove many longtime business owners into debt, while the simple second-generation farmer suddenly found himself unable to make ends meet.

With just a small dose of concentrated inflation, the vision of Benjamin Rush was becoming a reality. The proud, independent individuals of yesterday were slowly being turned into "Republican machines" racing for a currency they could not be proud of and a social position they did not understand. The price of living was going up, up and away to only God knew where.

And when the demands of a costly Revolutionary War proved to be too much for the resources of the Treasury Department, the government pursued the only recourse available to finish freedom's fight. They printed money out of thin air.

It was this financial shot in the arm that sealed the fate of the British forces, and it was this same influx of paper bills that set a young nation's economy – and emotional equilibrium – on the verge of collapse. The sweet taste of liberty had been swallowed up by the realization that the nation was running on financial fumes, resulting in a social discontent which drew the ire of a prominent member of Congress.

"All the perplexities, confusion and distress in America arise not from defects in their constitution or confederation, not from a want of honor or virtue so much as from downright ignorance of the nature of coin, credit, and circulation," wrote John Adams to Thomas Jefferson in 1787.

This ignorance remained a constant part of the nation's social fabric as the years unfurled, past the War Between The States and Lincoln's Greenbacks all the way into the twentieth century and a catastrophe that had even the best of experts feeling confused.

"I have studied finance and economics and international trade all my life, and now, after these recent events, I have come to the conclusion that I know nothing whatever about any of them," remarked Paul Moritz Warburg on the Crash of 1929.

The Crash resulted in the Depression, an era in American life where poverty was too often the norm. But plain, everyday people weren't the only ones going door-to-door for alms. America was about to undergo a shift in economic theory that promised to draw millions together in a common bond of befuddlement.

Borrowing from the wisdom of British economist John Maynard Keynes, newly elected President Franklin Delano Roosevelt began taking measures to fight off the economic downturn by inflating the money supply. Like a housewife desperate to make ends meet, the government went out onto the streets to unearth hidden treasures that just happened to be in possession of the people. Before long, begging transformed itself into demanding.

To emphasize Uncle Sam's mode of desperation, Roosevelt ordered all gold coins and gold certificates in denominations of more than $100 be exchanged for other forms of money. This law, passed on April 5, 1933, required all coins, certificates and gold bullion to be delivered to the Federal Reserve by no later than May 1 for the set price of $20.67 per ounce. If a citizen was found to be hoarding gold and proved to be unwilling to join in the exchange process, that person, depending upon the amount discovered, was either fined or jailed.

By the time this involuntary collection process had run its course, the government estimated they had taken in $300 million in gold coins and $470 million in gold certificates. Several weeks later, a joint resolution of Congress very quietly abrogated the gold clauses in many private and public obligations that required the debtors to repay the creditor in gold dollars of the same weight and fineness as those borrowed.

During the following year, Roosevelt completed this bit of financial sleight-of-hand by increasing the price of gold to $35 per ounce, effectively increasing the gold on the Federal Reserve's balance sheets by nearly 70-percent.

From the citizen's viewpoint, the America under Roosevelt was still a relatively simple nation that concentrated mainly on solving domestic problems. International trade was accepted. Involving the nation in the rest of the world's problems was not. War was considered a pitfall to be avoided at all costs.

That all changed on Dec. 7, 1941 when the Japanese bombed Pearl Harbor. Not only did that fateful day signal the entrance of the U.S. into World War II, but led to the developments that made America the unquestioned big boy in global peace efforts.

Whereas before it had only been mentioned in newspapers and over radio airwaves, the terrible effects of Communism, Socialism, and despotism became a central part of the American fabric with the lives lost at Pearl Harbor. The definition of American activism was about to take on a whole new meaning.

And so started what turned out to be a relatively quick and decisive participation in World War II, with exhaustive gains in manufacturing and revolutionary advancements in
technology paving the way. Using financial aid from their British allies, the U.S. was able to employ a successful air raid on Germany, which, in turn, led to Harry Truman's defining moment as Commander in Chief when he pushed the little red button and dropped the atomic bomb on Hiroshima.

After winning a war they had wanted no part of to begin with, Americans were united in their desire to stop Communism outright, but before a muscular performance such as Nazi Germany could take place. They wanted diplomacy in action, as opposed to the indifferent complacency they had previously perceived in their government.

Americans were now out to change the world, an operation that would cost businesses on the home front in a dear way.

Merchants. Traders. Manufacturers. And especially owners of professional football franchises.

Gary Davidson was never to be confused with a moralist. Businessmen with deep pockets rarely are. He had yet to come to God, had yet to find peace with his Maker. That would come later in life.

The Davidson that America best remembers was a California cool introvert whose chief obsession was promoting the welfare of his family of rebel sports institutions. Davidson was a rare specimen of the self-made millionaire class. He undoubtedly had a special way with money, but money had no less an influential way with him, providing Davidson with a dream and a vision reserved solely for the bold and the daring.

Money, you see, appealed to him in the same fashion in which it appeals to every other personage on earth. Money meant security. But more than just that, it also spelled riches and fame. For a man such as Davidson, these latter attributes were of pre-eminence in his life. He wasn't looking for a mere local ripple provoked by a commonly obscure financial boon. What Davidson sought above all else was a big splash, and an even larger audience to applaud him. Here was a man who had definite ideas about turning the world upside down with vault, cash box and charm.

Having grown up on the abundant shores of the West Coast, Davidson knew what mountains a little capital and hard work could move. A law degree from UCLA had paved the way for his establishment in a well-to-do tax and finance company in Orange County. His time at college also allowed him to meet Barbie, a former Bruins cheerleader. Before long, the two exchanged vows and were starting a family. Yes, life was good. But for Davidson, who envisioned himself a cut above the average Joe, life was not good enough. Not nearly so.

The fact that he already had more money than he knew what to do with, and drove expensive, sporty cars wherever he went impressed him not. Davidson was after far more than what he perceived to be the common essentials of life. Davidson sought peculiarly distinctive honors that set him apart while in the midst of a crowd. He wanted to be recognized when walking down the street, given an especial respect while at dinner parties, and to see his name in the morning paper.

A man of strong desires and even more prevalent shortcomings, Davidson's distinctive fault may have been simply a by-product of his surroundings. He was, after all, a blue-blooded American, a member of that hallowed descendant of the human race distinguished by an unmatched ability to dream. What Davidson could not have realized was that his dreaming was, in fact, the spawning of the longest, darkest nightmare that he would ever encounter.

Blinded by the timeless allure of the big strike and bright lights, Davidson's name and business empire was destined to become defined by an unprecedented search for a rainbow and his very own pot of gold. When it was all said and done, Davidson would be broke, divorced and a man of shattered credibility. All because of a dream, a gold-painted football, and a heartless, lifeless economy.

The month was August of the year 1971. Summer was in full swing. Had it been a perfect world in which he was living, Richard Nixon would have smiled unequivocally. It's just barely possible that he did anyway. Such was the strength of his affection for football.

As the thirty-seventh President of the United States, Nixon was perhaps the game's most recognizable spokesman. He offered his opinion regularly on the best collegiate squads, he phoned Miami Dolphins head coach Don Shula to share a secret trick-play to use in a Super Bowl championship game, and devoted many unaccounted hours poring over the pages of Street & Smith's football magazine.

But Nixon's life and career was far too muddied with uncertainty at this time to concern himself with recreational entertainment. It had been roughly fifteen years since President Dwight D. Eisenhower had aided in the construction of the Republic of Vietnam, as part of the Southeast Asia Treaty Organization. What was supposed to be a quick-fix operation where American military, political, and economic aid would usher in a new age of democratic peace for a war-ravaged territory, had developed instead into a mud-slinging, life-consuming, never-ending stand-off that eventually, according to the New York Times, cost more than 3.1 million lives before it was all said and done.

With the economy fast turning sour, a war was the last thing the American public wanted to be concerned with. And with an election cycle fast-approaching, Nixon was looking for something extravagant to re-gain public favor.

Nixon's political ambitions paled when compared to the domestic discontent surrounding happenings abroad. On April 30, 1970 the United States invaded Cambodia, prompting protests across the nation, most notably at Kent State University, where protestors launched a pithy demonstration that included setting fire to their own ROTC building. Nearly five hundred colleges were shut down or disrupted by protests. More than a year later, the focus of the US military still remained on the grounds of Vietnam, fighting a war their supporters had long since tired of.

In the manner of your prototypical politician, Nixon perceived an opportunity to change the outlook for the nation and his own political campaign all in one swoop. All he needed to do was go out of his way and address the financial plight that so many Americans found themselves in. By golly, he needed to whip the demonic forces of inflation once and for all.

The inflation rate, which had been 1.5 percent at the outset of the 1960's, had risen to 5 percent. Unemployment was fast becoming a problem, having jumped from 3.5 percent in 1969 to 5 percent just two years later.

The only way Nixon saw to manage the inflation-unemployment trade-off in a way that was not politically self-destructive was to borrow ideas from Western European countries and impose an income policy whereby the government intervened to set and control wages, whether in hortatory words or legal requirements.

But a money shortage wasn't a blight only felt by the public. As evidenced by the catastrophe at the Treasury Department, it was also a very real problem for the government.

By late 1967 withdrawals of gold bullion from the US Treasury had become quite extensive, thanks in large part to suspicious British officials who undermined international confidence in the US economy. And when the pound sterling was devalued in Europe, pressure on the US dollar increased, as French and other central banks began exchanging their dollar reserves for US gold at an alarming rate.

It was only a matter of time, they believed, before the US would officially devalue the dollar against gold, so European nations went out to redeem as many promissory notes as they could while the getting was still good.

During the second week of August of 1971, the British ambassador walked into the Treasury Department and demanded that $3 billion be converted into gold. Treasury Secretary John Connally did the only thing that could be expected. He signed the check, and immediately notified his superiors.

To avoid the collapse of the US gold reserves, the Nixon administration decided to abandon the dollar-gold combination entirely on August 11, 1971. "Rather than risk damaging US credit, he changed the rules, or more accurately, he abandoned the rules," noted William R. Clark in his book *Petrodollar Warfare: Oil, Iraq, and the Future of the Dollar.*

Connally chimed in, admitting to the Wall Street Journal that "We have awakened forces that nobody is at all familiar with."

Without a gold standard in place, market forces would determine the dollar's value, which in turn, would lead to substantial inflation for the immediate future…if not longer.

This Nixon foresaw, so on August 13, just two days after closing the gold window, he and 15 advisors retired to the presidential mountain retreat at Camp David. From this pow-wow came the New Economic Policy, which would temporarily (90 days) freeze wages and prices to make a thorough check of the state of inflation.

The end result of it all was a government-regulated wage-price control system that did nothing to curb inflation and everything to spike unemployment and help the economy sour all the way into the infamous oil glut of 1974.

These bold efforts at fixing what Nixon had convinced the American people was indeed a broken toy helped win him re-election over George McGovern in November of 1972.

Eighteen months later, he did the only thing the public would understand; he dis-employed the system nearly altogether. However, any goodwill gained from this last gesture officially blew up in the wreckage of the Watergate scandal, which led to his resignation in August of 1974.

He departed with his career, and his country's economy, in a veritable state of ruin, while the game he would now have time to enjoy was faring little better.

Gary Davidson was out of this country, at an owners meeting for a league that he thought was out of this world. Seated in a crowded conference room in Vancouver for one of the primary off-season functions of the upstart World Hockey Association (WHA), Davidson was feeling comfortable in his own skin like he had never felt before. It was always this way when he was onto something that nobody else was.

He was only months away from relinquishing his role as the league's president. But that didn't bother him in the least. Nobody could ever rob him of his status as one of the league's founding fathers, nor put out the flame from the latest light bulb that had been turned on in his brain.

Of a truth, Gary Davidson was enjoying life in 1973, especially when poring over his ever-increasing portfolio. At 38, Davidson was both a successful and an accomplished businessman. That he considered himself as something of a modern-day inventor only enhanced what was an already inflated assessment of his capabilities.

Davidson had founded the WHA only a year before, and had watched it gain noticeable traction against the rival National Hockey League (NHL). With Bobby Hull and the legendary Gordie Howe having recently signed lucrative contracts, the league now had a pair of bona-fide stars that would attract fans to games. Davidson was equally confident that more top-tier hockey talent would follow their example. Money talked loudly. When backed by prestige, it was a voice heard 'round the globe.

The other half of Davidson's sports empire – the American Basketball Association – had also gained a notorious coup against the rival NBA by inking Massachusetts big man Julius Erving to a contract with the Virginia Squires. "Dr. J." was a high-flying entertainer who wowed crowds with his theatrics above the rim. To Davidson, he was the savior who would save the cash-strapped ABA from financial ruin.

Little did all the hockey geeks in the room know that Davidson, for some time, had been trying to get a piece of the fastest-selling sports pie in America. Davidson, the same man who had taken both the NBA and NHL head-on, was wanting to become an owner of a professional football franchise. His first inclinations were to join the National Football League and watch his wallet grow.

But the most accessible inroad, either purchasing an already existing franchise or becoming an expansion owner, were fraught with countless potential suitors who would be bidding on the same piece of real estate as himself. Stories of futile endeavors to gain access into this elitist group of owners had reached his ears too many times for him to carry any illusions as to his odds of succeeding. Bidding a hefty sum and then relying on the good favor of an invisible dictator or a board of snotty rich guys who would rather spend their time fishing on a yacht could not have been more contrary to Davidson's personality.

As befitted his maverick personality, Davidson decided he didn't need to be part of the National Football League. He found it much more challenging and invigorating to go out of his way to destroy it. His plan of attack was simple, while also providing a ring of familiarity. Davidson would attempt to beat the big, bad NFL by simply creating a bigger and badder football enterprise of his own.

Davidson turned to Ben Hatskin, the owner of the Winnipeg Jets, and stated his intentions of dropping the puck and picking up a football. *Ben, listen to me. This hockey thing has been great, but it's time for something bigger, something better. Here's what I'm thinking. We could conquer the world if we...* He made it sound so easy, insisting that room existed in major market cities (New York, Chicago, and Los Angeles) for another football franchise. The new league could then endear itself to fans by planting other teams in smaller-market cities that the NFL had passed over, such as Louisville, Indianapolis, and Mexico City. There was also a possibility, Davidson said, of putting a team in Canada, maybe even Hawaii.

Hatskin was one of the more respected individuals at the conference since it was his check that had lured Bobby Hull away from the NHL. He had deep pockets, but more importantly, he had the capacity to absorb Davidson's sometimes outlandish propositions. When others would have laughed, Hatskin listened. What others found silly, Hatskin viewed as intriguing. To listen first and react afterwards helped better his odds of making unemotional decisions.

Hatskin didn't need anyone telling him that it was a long shot to succeed in going up against an established sports league. He already knew all about that. What he also was aware of was the fact that what was a long shot could be improved to a calculated gamble with a little forethought and common sense.

It didn't take very long for Hatskin to toss his hat into the ring next to Davidson's. The NFL was growing in leaps and bounds, thanks in large part to the television boom that was sweeping the nation, but Hatskin felt confident that it was far from becoming a monopoly on the market. Americans were hungry for football. Davidson had the vision as to how to feed it to them. What Davidson also had for support was exquisite timing, as it related to the player-relations sector.

Whereas Richard Nixon used a struggling economy for the promotion of his own political ambitions, Davidson was using it as the means to infiltrate the seductive world of sports ownership. While the NHL players and owners were busy squabbling over pennies at the turn of the decade, Davidson and a group of wealthy businessmen had sneaked in the back door and created a league of their own.

The landscape surrounding the game of professional football looked just as promising in 1973.

A newly-formed NFL players union had accomplished little in reconciling the differences that existed between athletes and desk stooges. Salaries were a hot topic of discussion in locker rooms, as were pensions. After nearly four years of virtually fruitless negotiations, rumbles began to filter through the press about an impending strike.

This was the best news for a man in Davidson's position, who fostered hopes of stealing the NFL's clout in the public marketplace. A disgruntled environment would provide him the opportunity to negotiate contracts with popular players who, in a different climate, would have scoffed at the notion of joining an expansion league. If Davidson could rustle up a few prospective owners who would be willing to sink $3 million into a franchise, then Davidson was certain that it was only a matter of when – not if – the players started signing. If the money was there, they would come. Davidson could take that to the bank as one of the undeniable laws of attraction.

But some of the very same factors that promoted friction between NFL owners and players, inflation and rising costs, and allowed Davidson a chance to get his foot in the door, would be working against his attempts to maintain such a high-cost enterprise. The American economy was dying on the vine. The economic "Golden Age" which Davidson had enjoyed since he was a teenager seemed to be turning to dust as inflation and spiked energy prices helped drag consumer confidence into the gutter.

Inflation had sky-rocketed from three-percent in 1966 to six-percent in 1971. These were alarming figures for the time, coming on the heels of a seven-year period in which the annual inflation rate never exceeded 1.6 percent. The political maneuver of Nixon's that ended the fixed-rate convertibility of the dollar for gold only worsened matters.

While Davidson was getting to know the prime investors and shareholders in the newly erected World Football League, a dramatic four-fold hike in energy prices, due to a major "oil shock," was about to strike unsuspecting business owners and consumers smack in their wallets. And no wallets were more primed for the picking than were those in Davidson's corner.

Provoked from every corner of the world marketplace, inflation jumped to over ten-percent in 1974, one of many prominent factors as to why Davidson's new football league would suffer through its first, and only, complete season.

It was on the afternoon of Oct. 2 1973 that Gary Davidson first introduced himself to the professional football world. Exhibiting the necessary combination of charm and confidence, Davidson sold himself and his new league in front of a host of bright lights and television cameras at the official press conference to announce the founding of the World Football League.

His message to citizens of the North American continent was a simple one. Starting the following summer, the World Football League was coming to play in a city and stadium near them. Expect football at its passionate finest, only with more excitement and new twists than ever before. And even if you couldn't make it to the stadium, this new 12-team league was determined to bring the game to your very own living room.

Over the next several months, Davidson did a yeoman's job of living up to his word, making one major announcement after another. Along the way, Davidson, an outsider where NFL owners were concerned, proved himself an artful and imaginative football visionary.

First were the alterations to the football itself. Universally accepted in its traditional brown leather colors, Davidson had the WFL balls painted gold and the white stripes re-painted a peculiar orange. Next, in an effort to relieve congestion in goal-to-go situations, Davidson had the goalposts moved to the back of the end-zone.

Then came news of the league's new TV deal. Its package with an independent New York-based television network that reached 117 cities and eighty-percent of the nation's population was truly ahead of its time. Thirty years before NFL Network dared to venture into such an unknown galaxy, the WFL and TVS partnered to broadcast regular season football on Thursday nights.

Veteran sportscaster Merle Harmon, a well-known radio voice for both the New York Jets and Milwaukee Brewers, was slotted to handle the play-by-play duties. Joining Harmon in the booth to add the color commentary was former Baltimore Colts running back Alex Hawkins. Weekly guest commentators were promised as an added bonus to the telecasts, including former NFL stars Dick Butkus, Gale Sayers, Alex Karras, and Don Perkins.

The first eight weeks of the schedule, starting on July 11 with New York at Jacksonville and running through the Birmingham-Chicago matchup on August 29, were set in stone prior to the season. After that period the league would designate the TV game 10-14 days before the game, assuring the fans on television a meaningful game during the season's stretch drive. In today's world, this is known as "Flex scheduling," a formula the NFL adopted in 2006 to cater to NBC's primetime telecasts of *Sunday Night Football*.

Though criticized by the press at the time, the WFL rulebook proved to be just as revolutionary as their broadcasting methods were visionary. At one of the earliest Board of Governors meetings, WFL executives voted to eliminate the extra-point kick from their game and make touchdowns worth seven points, to be followed by a run or pass "action point" play.

Following a touchdown, the ball was to be placed on the two-and-one-half yard-line and the offense would have one play to score via the run or pass. No kicks were allowed.

"I think that the 'action point' will add more excitement to football," said Florida Blazers head coach Jack Pardee. "This should eliminate most of the ties." Said Bud Asher of the Jacksonville franchise: "I'm enthusiastic. It puts more suspense in the game."

The idea for this new rule came not from Davidson, or Advisor on Officiating John McDonough, but from a football fan in White Plains, New York named Bill Finneran. His occupation? An aero-space systems analyst, of all things.

For a league determined to bring a new brand of excitement to the game of football, addressing the extra-point try was of paramount importance. With the improvement of kickers over the past several decades, it was a wonder the NFL hadn't beaten them to the punch. "There has been no suspense in football with the traditional point after touchdown being successful 99 percent of the time," said Davidson. "Our 'action point' will provide an exciting new element to the game." More than forty years would pass before NFL owners would alter the traditional kick after touchdown.

Davidson was truly well ahead of his time. He had a peppy brand of football, a television company to broadcast it, and a golden ball to play with. Yet all of it was academic without players.

To fill this last need, Davidson instituted an all-out attack on his biggest rivals, raiding NFL rosters with such extreme importunity as to cause consternation to boil over into anarchy, resulting in a most gregarious of labor stoppages. In this instance, Davidson's bait was provocative, if not predictable. For certain stars of the NFL, he offered more money than they could earn in a lifetime while playing in the cash-strapped, penny-pinching NFL.

With this maneuver, the souls of the football world officially went on the auction block. And in a conflict where cash was king, Davidson knew that to be the lowest bidder was to be as the eternally damned. He had to get his league's foot in the door immediately, or find it forever closed to him. So out came the checkbooks and the promises of a better tomorrow.

Davidson's up-and-coming league now officially posed as a richer alternative to the traditional power, a source where fortunes were made, not merely wages. The timeless battle between cash and allegiance was now being fought on the football front with a California lawyer leading the charge against a group of northeastern office stooges.

Caught in the middle of the mayhem was Thomas Wade Landry, the genius, head coach and architect of the Dallas Cowboys who could only watch helplessly as this bitter feud between rival leagues flooded his team with a wave of discontent and bickering. It cost him a season. And nearly much more than that. But for the organizational fortitude founded in the minds of the Head Coach Tom Landry and General Manager Tex Schramm, the dynasty that Landry had been striving for since 1960 would have likely been washed away in the wreckage.

What follows is the true tale of how Tom, Tex, and a dozen rookies overcame innumerable obstacles to return the Dallas Cowboys to the NFL's circle of elite franchises. It's a story of the faith, character, and passion that transformed the Dallas Cowboys from an aging run-of-the-mill franchise into one comprised of youthful exuberance and uncommon cunning.

Surrounded by a world running its normal course of squabbling over spilt milk and loose change, the 1975 Dallas Cowboys' squad rode a contagious wave of selflessness, sacrifice, and enthusiasm that stands out above the crowd even more than forty years later. Mixed with the wonder of innovation and what could only be described as divine intervention, theirs is a story that speaks to every soul that ever found satisfaction in watching the impossible become a most improbable reality.

Founded on the bedrock of the blue-collar work ethic and a never-give-up attitude, this team lived the life of the over-comer. In some cases, even the overachiever.

This most magical of seasons gave way to the most unlikely of playoff runs, and a Cowboys berth in the NFL's bicentennial Super Bowl in sunny Miami. It's a time where heroes were forged in the heart, and memories forever etched in the mind and is the definite point in time when the professional football franchise from Dallas became something far more than mere Cowboys.

They became America's Team.

CHAPTER 2

THE COWBOY & THE LAME DUCK

"If [Tom] Landry had laser-vision, I would have suffered an immediate pre-frontal lobotomy."
- Cowboys defensive end Pat Toomay describing the discomfort that accompanied his announcement that he had signed a contract to play in the World Football League

Down in Texas, where the grass grows long, the prairies stretch wide, and where the hills reach nigh to the heavens, there is an inherent tendency toward exaggeration. Steeped in the gospel of independence and social indifference, the typical Texan is an exaggerated example of what every American believes himself to be: proud, bold, fearless, and loyal.

The personification of this temperament received an unprecedented promotion in the 1930's when Hollywood first introduced the cowboy onto the television screen. Portrayed as the ultimate hero to Western civilization, no figure cut more trails, settled more feuds, rode more broncs, and enforced more foundational law than those swashbuckling Stetson-sporting dudes who owned every street and fight in town.

In the old west, where the cowboy is alleged to have been spawned, the law became synonymous with the individual. In many a frontier town, the sheriff was the only law in the territory, and was therefore required to be a man of wisdom, temperance, a fast draw, and even harder fists. It took "a real man" to ramrod a town in those days, one that welcomed responsibility and wasn't afraid to stand alone.

Few Texans have ever represented these values better than Thomas Wade Landry. Once an ordinary boy growing up near a group of sweet-smelling citrus plantations in the tiny town of Mission near the Mexico border, Landry soon became a hero in battle, a legend on the sideline, and a faithful family man.

As a soldier in his younger days Landry was a stalwart, flying 30 bombing missions in World War II. At home, he was the committed husband to Alicia and their three children. As a football coach, Landry constantly worked on his craft, ever molding it toward a fuller perfection with a tireless hunger for knowledge that was pleasing to a nation that loved to promote the value of the forward-thinker. The motion-offense. The Flex defense. Zone-blocking. These were all inventions of Landry's, ground-breaking concepts that not only changed the game moving forward, but vaulted Landry and his team to the top of the football universe.

Since joining the NFL in 1950 as a defensive back for the New York Giants, Landry had gleaned bits of information from Paul Brown, George Halas and Vince Lombardi, three of the great coaching legends of their time. These men were the innovative force behind much of the shift in the style of offensive play across professional football. But what Landry did was to sample their knowledge and take it to an entirely new level, while making it palatable for the television age that was about to sweep across the nation. He proved to the entire league that his schemes and philosophies – complicated though they were - could not only function in professional football, but thrive.

As a player/coach with the Giants, Landry quickly realized that the road to the top went through Paul Brown and the Cleveland Browns. So he invented the 6-1-4 umbrella defense to stop Cleveland's vaunted quick passing game. From there, he modified it into the standard 4-3 defense of today, using four-down linemen with three linebackers directly behind. This gap-control style of play that had specific responsibilities for every member of the defense was in stark contrast to the style of the times, when eleven defenders simply chased the ball all over the field.

When he became the Head Coach in Dallas, Landry invented an offensive scheme designed to beat that same 4-3 defense that many coordinators copied from those great Giants teams. Rather than simply line-up and play football, Landry's Cowboys used a wealth of motion and pre-snap shifts from their running backs, wide receivers and even linemen to confuse opposing defenses and promote missed assignments.

Landry put so much pressure on the opposition as to compel them to come up with a few new tricks of their own. The Cowboys' signing of former Olympic sprinter Bob Hayes as a wide receiver in 1965 forced the opposition to come up with the fabled "Cover 2" defense, where two safety men stayed deep behind the play to prevent a speedster like Hayes from getting behind the secondary for long gains.

But Landry was far more than simply the ideal American blessed with an innovative leaning. He was more than just a good person who chose to dress dapperly in front of the world on weekends. For millions of people watching in the stands or on television, Landry's calm, stoic figure seen on the Cowboys' sideline each autumn Sunday posed as a living, breathing, walking icon that was easy to appreciate for the prototypical sailor, yet difficult to comprehend for even the most dedicated of religious zealots within the Bible Belt. Even though blessed with unquestioned success in his profession, Landry posed as a Texas-sized conundrum for the simple fact that he was anything but a typical American male engrossed with sports.

Despite his simple mannerisms, Landry could often confuse the distant onlooker with a rigid self-composure that seemed almost inhuman at times. Here was a man at the height of an ultra-competitive profession who didn't throw tantrums, didn't stoop to profanity, and never seemed to break a sweat. Cowboys' running back Duane Thomas once referred to Landry as a "plastic man." Aside from Thomas' extreme personal critique, the general public was inclined to use a far more reverential tone when speaking of Landry's qualities, likening the Dallas head coach to anything from football's premier intellectual giant to the next best thing to Billy Graham.

Though often perplexed by what they witnessed (or didn't, as was often the case with Landry), fascination gripped his audience the longer they watched, perhaps equally intrigued by Landry's hand-crafted team that won games in a style all their own. In a league renowned for brute strength and manly toughness, Landry's Cowboys had discovered success on the wings of cutting-edge football formulas and computer technology. The cloud of dust that hung over the eastern seaboard from the customary three-yard fullback run into a pile had been replaced in Dallas by an offense enthralled with disguise and a defense that was as strange as it was effective. The Cowboys were not only a team, but a brand that would leave its stamp upon the game of football forever.

But before the brand would ever become a reality, Landry had to settle upon a career choice. Would he settle for a desk chair, or just another office chair? Yes, even Landry wrestled with this decision.

It is truly ironic that the same Tom Landry we all remember for his brilliance on a sideline returned to Texas in December of 1959 as the newly-crowned head coach of the expansion Cowboys to get away from the game he loved. Landry may have been many things, but he was no illusionist. He knew the odds of lasting through an expansion process were even less than winning the lottery. Landry thought he would come to Dallas, get closer to his family roots, and when the Cowboys wanted him to leave after three or four years, he would fade off into the sunset and start a new life as an insurance salesman.

Having come to faith in Jesus Christ less than two years before he was contacted by Texas E. Schramm about the position, Landry was at a place in his life that he probably never considered possible. Football was no longer a necessity in his life. Landry enjoyed the job of coaching, but could live without it if he had to. Family, oddly enough, was far more important to him than a career drawing-up plays on a blackboard.

What he was about to find out was that the Dallas Cowboys and ultra-confident General Manager Tex Schramm could not live without *him*. Since being run off from the Los Angeles Rams by a meddlesome ownership group in 1956, Schramm's single greatest desire had been to build a championship football team from scratch. For that goal to become a reality, Schramm needed a head coach with the mind and vision of Landry.

Despite the Cowboys losing 38 of 56 games over their first four seasons, it was Schramm who convinced team owner Clint Murchison Jr. to award Landry an astounding ten-year contract. Landry, in turn, re-paid Schramm that vote of confidence by shelving his plans to be a businessman and dedicating his career to coaching football.

The results soon started to reveal themselves on the field. Spurred by a strong 1964 draft class highlighted by the signings of cornerback Mel Renfro and world-class sprinter "Bullet" Bob Hayes, the Cowboys soon developed into one of the NFL's elite franchises, playing in consecutive NFL Championship games in 1966 and 1967. Dallas lost both games to Green Bay in the final seconds, creating another obstacle for Landry to get past.

The challenge of building an expansion club into a contender having been completed, Landry now had to figure out how to get his team past the pressure of the big game. That pressure increased volubly when the Cowboys' locker room showed signs of emotional strain after losing back-to-back first-round playoff games to Cleveland in 1968 and 1969.

A change in offensive philosophy pacified some of the players, but failed to produce the desired results. The Cowboys, in one of the more bizarre championship games in the history of sports, lost Super Bowl V on a last-second field goal by Baltimore's Jim O'Brien.

The fallout from that defeat centered around Dallas' quarterback Craig Morton, who found himself benched in favor of Roger Staubach with the Cowboys sitting at 4-3 midway through the 1971 campaign. Three months later, Landry was carried off the field by his team after the Cowboys manhandled Miami 24-3 in Super Bowl VI. Staubach earned the game's MVP honors.

Though Dallas lost a pair of NFC Championship Games the next two seasons by a combined score of 53-13, the general consensus held that Landry and the Cowboys would experience another breakthrough in 1974. Instead, Landry watched his team simply break down.

The downward spiral began in the spring with an attack on his coaching staff. Forty-four year old Jim Garrett, a well-traveled assistant who joined Dallas as their special teams coach shortly after the 1973 season concluded, jumped ship without warning in April to Houston when he agreed to become the head coach and vice president of football operations for the WFL's Texans. Garrett was certainly no stranger to leading a football team, having coached at Susquehanna University from 1960-65 where he guided the school to three unbeaten seasons and a 22-game winning streak. He had also spent a short time as the top-man for the Orlando Panthers of the Continental Football League.

But perhaps his strongest commendation that convinced Texans owner Steve Arnold to hire him were the diversified set of positions Garrett held as an NFL assistant. During his first seven seasons in football's premier league, Garrett was a scout, an offensive coach, a defensive coach, and a special teams coordinator for both the Cowboys and Giants. Though it was well known that his first choice for the job was none other than Hank Stram (the Kansas City Chiefs head coach was reportedly offered a 10-year contract valued at $2 million), Arnold felt confident that Garrett's expert knowledge and his many connections with both NFL and collegiate personnel would soon yield a winner in Houston. (Ironically, it would be Garrett's third son Jason who, thirty-six years later during the 2010 season, replaced Houston native Wade Phillips as the head coach of the Cowboys.)

Not one to hand out positions on his staff to just anybody, Landry filled Garrett's former role with an in-house promotion, dubbing tight ends coach Mike Ditka as the Cowboys' new special teams coordinator for the 1974 season. Ditka earned the promotion as much for his tireless work ethic and unrelenting energy as his loyalty to the franchise, a particular trait that Landry was, understandably, quite sensitive to during this time of change.

When finished with the coaching staffs, World Football League owners then offered new, better-paying jobs to numerous NFL players, creating brand-new allegiances that produced a strong sense of internal division and alienation amongst NFL camps. This made for the longest of seasons for Landry, when the spirit and effort of the Cowboys became undermined not just by a traitor, but by a forgettable legend known only as the Lame Duck.

During the Christmas holiday season of 1973, several dozen Cowboys' players received a formal type-written letter referring to a potential business opportunity in the coming months. Here's what each letter said:

Dear Player:

The World Football League will begin play in 1974 with franchises in twelve areas, including New York, Chicago, Detroit, Toronto, New England, Southern California, Hawaii, and Florida. The remaining franchises will be awarded from some twenty applications for membership under consideration.

It is the intention of the World Football League to be Major League in every way, particularly in signing the top professional players available. We feel strongly that every player should honor his present contractual obligation. However, we would very much like to talk with you about the possibility of joining our League at the expiration of your contract.

In order for us to know your status and to contact you, please fill out and return the enclosed post card as soon as possible.

Wishing you a Merry Christmas and a Happy and Prosperous New Year!

Enclosed within each envelope was a post card addressed by rubber stamp to Steve Arnold Enterprises, and containing on the other side spaces which could be filled in by the player giving his name, the name of his current team, his off-season address, the amount of years remaining on his current contract (not including the option year), and whether he would be interested in making the jump to the World Football League.

What began as an honest business query soon developed into a set of controversial partnerships. Unbeknownst to Landry, several players filled out the cards and dropped them in the return box. Later that spring, the announcement dropped like a bomb that star running back Calvin Hill had signed a rich contract with the WFL's Hawaiian franchise, effective immediately after his contract was up following the 1974 season. Soon after, news dropped that fellow Cowboy teammates Craig Morton (QB), Mike Montogomery (RB), and D.D. Lewis (LB) would be leaving for the WFL at the same time. Veterans Rayfield Wright (OT) and Jethro Pugh (DT) also signed future contracts that would begin in 1976. Third-round draft pick Danny White was leaving to play quarterback for the Memphis Southmen immediately, since he had yet to sign a contract with Dallas.

Among defectors, Hill was regarded as the most significant loss. Since the Cowboys rid themselves of the troublesome Duane Thomas in the summer of '72, Hill had been the workhorse in a run-oriented Dallas offense, rushing for over 1,000 yards in each of the previous two seasons. Now, the Cowboys had to use the 1974 season to groom a replacement behind both he and Montgomery, while also wondering just how motivated Hill would be in his Lame Duck season.

Though not a starter, Morton was still considered a valuable piece within the Dallas offense, providing reliable depth at the quarterback position behind Roger Staubach. As with Hill, the Cowboys would have to scramble to locate a competent successor to Morton, who was now looked upon with disfavor by numerous people in the Cowboys' front-office. As a nine-year veteran, Morton should have known better than to make a deal with the enemy, especially one so lucrative (rumors had the deal as worth as much as $550,000).

The fact that both Hill and Morton had already cashed signing bonus checks from their WFL contracts caused their even-keeled head coach to boil over with frustration.

"When they signed with the WFL it created an almost impossible situation from my standpoint," said a somber Landry prior to the 1974 season. "As a team sport we must have a joint effort in a championship drive. There can be no doubts about any player putting out everything he has. Every player must be rewarded if we win, or suffer if we lose.

"I don't believe the three players (Hill, Morton, and Montgomery) who signed future contracts will suffer if we lose. They'll be rewarded regardless...

"...There's no way a man can play as hard as he did. The incentive isn't there...the dedication...the sacrifice. When money is promised elsewhere, they can't possibly perform as well."

Morton refused to acknowledge any lack of ethics on his part. "I don't know why it's a mistake," he said of his status as a prosperous Lame Duck. "I did it because it's a tremendous opportunity that few people have a chance to enjoy. What was I gaining in Dallas?

"I could be there another five years in the same position. The only reason I did it was for my personal advancement. I wish everything could have worked out in Dallas, but it took me nine years to find out it wouldn't. So it's about time I took care of myself. I don't feel there's any harm in doing that."

Despite the defectors, the Dallas Cowboys were still a very good football team on paper going into the 1974 season, with the potential to be great if the locker room pulled together. A bitter July labor strike provided all of the necessary ingredients to assure that would not happen.

CHAPTER 3

POLITICS & DISCORD

"We never really jelled as a team. But that's probably attributable to the strike. I certainly wasn't satisfied with my role on the team."
- **Cowboys linebacker Cal Peterson, looking back on the 1974 season**

    Among first encounters, the one Tex Schramm had with Ed Garvey in 1970 was certainly memorable for the 50-year old General Manager of the Dallas Cowboys. Schramm, as the unofficial commissioner of the NFL, was in his seat of supremacy trying to iron out the inaugural agreement between NFL owners and the newly-created Players Association. Garvey, as an up-and-coming attorney from Minneapolis, was seemingly trying to devise a formula of his own. At the time, Schramm couldn't see what Garvey was chasing after, but whatever that something was it certainly couldn't have been honest.
    "After we'd agreed on all points, [Garvey] was going to draw up the legal agreement for the parties to sign," recalled Schramm in Bob St. John's 1988 biography *Tex!*. "A couple of months later when I received the bargaining agreement, it did not represent at all what we had agreed upon. All kinds of things had been added, and changes had been made to benefit the players. So we went back for another meeting to tell them the

agreement had been altered, and there was no deal unless it was written just as we'd originally agreed upon. So there was another big fight before we got it straight."

For a man like Schramm, renowned for owning an unusually long memory, this was one incident that he would remember for a long time, and convinced him that Garvey was one lawyer well worth keeping track of. It wouldn't do to be caught unaware when Garvey was dealing the cards. If Garvey could be so bold as to renege on his own word, then he was capable of virtually anything of a diabolical nature.

Schramm watched Garvey at work over the next couple of years and couldn't have liked at all what he saw. Upon assuming the position of Executive Director and President of the NFLPA, Garvey began playing one side against another, and got enough players riled up to force Alan Miller's resignation as the General Counsel a year later. With Miller's voice out of the room, Garvey then had a free hand to discredit the league's controversial Rozelle Rule, which in turn would get back to the owners ears at the negotiating table.

Under the Rozelle Rule, whenever a team lost a free-agent, the team signing that player had to compensate his former team. If the two clubs couldn't agree on terms, then Commissioner Pete Rozelle would intervene and decide upon a fair compensation. More often than not, his definition of fair was extremely favorable for the team losing the player. Like in 1967, when Rozelle awarded San Francisco two first-round draft picks from the Saints after wide receiver Dave Parks, who caught all of 26 passes during his final season with the 49ers, signed a free-agent contract with New Orleans.

As a result, teams tended to shy away completely from signing free agent players for fear of having either their roster or their pool of draft picks ruthlessly raided. With this set of circumstances in place, it was little wonder that only 34 free agents were signed from the rule's inception in 1963 all the way through the 1974 season.

With constant needling from Garvey's corner, it didn't take long for players to start grumbling about low salaries and lack of negotiating power. The players claimed they were being treated like slaves, without the freedom to choose their own employer. This rule, surely, was un-American and certainly unethical. The Rozelle Rule must be abolished.

Somewhere along the way Garvey inserted the racial prejudice card into the mix, which only stirred the emotions even more. "Garvey always used the racial issue to solidify the blacks behind the union by continually charging that the management was prejudiced," said Schramm. "Anybody in the league or associated with it knew this wasn't true. The truth didn't matter. He wanted passionate support."

What came out of all the unrest was a mid-summer players strike that had picket lines as the primary focus in all 26 NFL training camps across the nation. The clenched-fist salute replaced the forward-pass, and protestors holding up signs that read "No Freedom, No Football" got more media attention than did the handful of rookies laboring on the field.

"Garvey tried to split groups, even blacks and whites," said Roger Staubach in *Tex!*. "He had many blacks feeling they were seeking social upheaval. Blacks hadn't been treated very fairly in our society over the years, and they certainly could relate to taking such a stand – a revolutionary stand. It was as though we were going into a kind of black separatism. The association even came out with the clenched fist to signify what we were doing. That's the symbol of a revolutionary country. There are areas in society that need changing, but to equate them to professional football isn't apropos. Garvey and the NFLPA officials led the players to believe this was necessary."

Though union members recognized the same enemy in the Rozelle Rule, they could not find a common strategy that would defeat it, creating friction in their own camp. The players sought instant gratification by going on strike, intending to bully NFL owners into dismantling the Rozelle Rule altogether. The 33-year old Garvey, on the other hand, was all out to obtain leverage.

Garvey was a visionary in that he realized the war between League and Union was not about interests, but of law. Ultimately, he needed Congress to rule that the NFL was a league of 26 separate entities, rather than a single entity with 26 partners. In order to appease the short-sighted money-grabbers breathing down his neck, Garvey had to do an about-face toward the players. To impart to them his long-term plans would result in his immediate removal as union president, which nearly happened anyway after several high-profile players became disgruntled during the negotiating process.

Garvey's primary goal upon entering the 1974 strike was a simple one. He was trying to force the owners to modify their restrictions on player movement. If the owners banded together in mutual resistance (which was more probable than not), the Players Association would then appeal to the courts and Congress. This, for the players, would be the beginning of a long and tiresome string of events steeped in fundamental legalese and due process.

As a first-rate labor lawyer, Garvey was completely aware that the union couldn't afford to give away at the bargaining table what they could win in the courtroom. The NFLPA could not sue over the ultra-restrictive Rozelle Rule as a violation of anti-trust law, if it reached a compromise agreement during the collective bargaining process. And even though Garvey had no reason to believe that an agreement would come to fruition, he still needed to put his best effort forth on this front, knowing full well that the union would have to prove in court that it had bargained "in good faith" on these issues. Only when bargaining failed could the union then resort to the judicial system. And fail it certainly would.

The underlying irony in what had been a very demonstrative standoff was that it couldn't be anything but a poorly-timed bluff. There was no way that the players would dare to miss the start of the regular season, because for each game missed they would forfeit $1/14^{th}$ of their salary, making for a simple game of waiting for the owners. And wait they did.

Not until the middle of August did veterans begin crossing over and returning to practice, with the understanding that negotiations would resume full throttle the following winter. Back in Thousand Oaks, it was Roger Staubach who led the parade of Cowboys' players back to training camp. But there was to be no return to normalcy for the Cowboys in 1974. The strike was to be the last straw that threw the Cowboys down and, ultimately, out of the NFL playoffs.

While Tom Landry and the Cowboys were dealing with defectors and Lame Ducks in their own camp, Gary Davidson and the World Football League were fast making strides in the public spotlight. Through the first ten weeks of the 1974 season, an average of nearly ten million people tuned into TVS' World Football League broadcasts on Thursday night. Though well behind ABC's *Monday Night Football* telecasts, the WFL was still outdoing NBC's National Hockey League coverage, and was only a stone's throw behind the NBA ratings on CBS. "Even if WFL ratings did not measure up to the NFL's, they demonstrated to potential investors that football is king," wrote Joe Marshall in *Sports Illustrated* magazine in October.

But not even competitive ratings could turn a dollar for what was fast developing into a cash-strapped league. With poor turnout at the stadium hampering the efforts of team owners to procure local support from sponsors, Davidson's football empire, founded upon the allure of wealth and a better presentation, was staring down the gun-barrel of an unpromising tomorrow.

"Any new league is going to have problems," Memphis Southmen team owner John Bassett told *Sports Illustrated* during the 1974 season. "The only thing that scares me is something I never anticipated, the general economic condition of the country. Money is tight, whether you're running a shoe factory or a football franchise. A couple of years ago people were lined up in droves for the chance to finance a professional football team, for ego or whatever purposes. Those people aren't around anymore."

Bassett was one of the few owners who didn't have financial difficulties. Others weren't so fortunate. Jacksonville Owner Fred Monaco managed to pay his players one week after borrowing $27,000 from his Head Coach, who he fired shortly after. Players and coaches from other teams were paid with hot checks, that is when they were paid at all.

It was with a cough and a whimper that the World Football League crossed the finish line on their first season of competition in early December. Before thousands of empty seats at World Bowl I, the Birmingham Americans and the Florida Blazers played a 22-21 thriller that was fittingly capped by an impromptu invasion of creditors seizing all assets in the building.

All of the media's preseason concern about salaries, strikes, and Lame Ducks were forgotten in the immediate aftermath of the Dallas Cowboys' 24-0 season-opening romp over Atlanta in September of 1974. But Tom Landry wasn't about to assume the worst was behind his team. "I just didn't believe after the strike we could be that good," said Landry. Landry kept a sharp eye on his team early in the season, as if in anticipation of seeing a crack in their armor. Much to his own disappointment, Landry didn't have to wait very long to find what he was looking for.

A bizarre set of early-season misfortunes seemed to dampen the Cowboys' spirits, and threatened to break their will. With Dallas leading 7-0 in Week 2 against Philadelphia on *Monday Night Football*, running back Doug Dennison fumbled inside the Eagles' 5 and cornerback Joe Lavender ran it back 96 yards for a TD. Dallas eventually lost 13-10. "If we had won, I'm convinced our entire season would have been different," Landry reflected after the season.

After a dismal loss to the Giants the following week, the Cowboys appeared to have snuffed out a late Vikings rally when they recovered a Fran Tarkenton fumble. But the referees never saw the fumble and awarded the ball back to Minnesota, giving place-kicker Fred Cox a chance to steal one in Texas. Cox's kick sailed high, and though players from both teams said the kick was wide, the referee awarded the points and the victory to Minnesota.

"We played too many games last year like we were looking for someone to give us something instead of us just taking it," observed rookie defensive end Ed "Too Tall" Jones. Fellow defensive end Harvey Martin concurred, even admitting to the media that his effort was far from the best during the 1974 season. "On some plays when I was tired for some reason, I would be loafing and just hoping the coaches didn't notice it in the films. They always did. Why did I loaf? Well, I got a bad case of food poisoning and that could have been a contributing factor. It seemed I was in a crash conditioning program all year trying to catch up."

While Landry busied himself in trying to rally the Cowboys from a woeful 1-4 start to the season, the locker room remained a place of tension and unspoken anger. Golden Richards, the young blonde-haired wide receiver who had supplanted Bob Hayes at the No. 2 spot, found himself shunned by Hayes and Calvin Hill. Despite sharing the same huddle, neither would speak to Richards except on game-day when it was absolutely necessary. Pat Toomay openly resented being replaced at his defensive end position on passing downs by rookie No. 1 overall draft pick Ed "Too Tall" Jones, and didn't hesitate to second-guess the coaching staff, specifically Landry.

Additional murmuring on the offensive unit had it that Staubach played favorites on the field with No. 1 wide receiver Drew Pearson. When Staubach kept his job even after throwing 9 interceptions in a four-game span, Craig Morton decided he had seen enough in Dallas, and stopped coming to practice altogether. Landry had no other alternative but to trade him, shipping Morton to the New York Giants in exchange for their No. 1 selection in the 1975 draft.

It came as no surprise to anyone in the Cowboys' building that the team lost their final two games of the regular season to drop out of the playoffs. The once-mighty Cowboys were an old, dysfunctional mess of a team, too busy wasting energy on selfish interests and internal sparring to win meaningful football games in December, and had received no more than they deserved. For the first time since 1965, the Cowboys would be home for the Christmas holiday season, a misfortune that allowed an extended meeting of the minds between Landry and Tex Schramm.

Despite their ninth consecutive winning season together, neither could claim satisfaction with the final outcome, and professed a shared frustration over the events that led to it. The defectors. The strike. The bickering. And perhaps most surprisingly of all, an overwhelming sense of complacency among the players.

Landry and Schramm found mutual satisfaction in the acknowledgement that, were the Cowboys to have any chance of competing in the coming years, all of that would have to be shoved down the exit ramps. So with pad and pencil, they each marked down the sequence of events and possibilities on how they planned to do just that. While the NFL playoffs were thrilling football fans across America, a plan was being put into action in Dallas. Names of popular veterans were secretly put on the trade-block. New formations were discussed and devised. And a renewed emphasis on the college draft was discovered. Working inside the same walls that had just come crumbling down on top of the them was a blueprint that would carry Tom, Tex, and the Cowboys on a spirited comeback trail that would define the organization for years to come.

CHAPTER 4

THE DRAFT

"The draft we had in 1975 helped point the team in the right direction again. I'm not sure what would have happened without it, but we'd have had a lot of problems."
- **Tom Landry**

    For all of the attributes that are laid at the feet of the willful, hard-working American, the race to the top of the corporate ladder is often decided, not by skill or intelligence, but by the simple act of a helping hand. This irony, which has bewildered the mind of avid individualists for centuries, has also held true in the realm of sports over the years.
    Even in the game of football, the power of proper connections can move mountains and open doors where they might otherwise have remained forever shut. Consider the case of Tex Schramm, whose destiny as a front-office mainstay in the NFL was due directly to this unfailing phenomenon of human advancement.
    As a young man fresh out of college, Schramm wasn't looking for a way into professional football, but he didn't hesitate to walk through the first door that opened to him. A Southern California kid with charm and a talent for telling a

good story, Schramm received his bachelor's degree in journalism from the University of Texas, whereupon he immediately assumed the job as Sports Editor of the American-Statesman in Austin. However, his blooming career in the newspaper industry took a sudden detour in 1947 on the merits of a chance encounter of his father's back home in California. The events that led to his introduction into pro football as a 27-year old were recalled vividly by Schramm in Peter Golenbock's 1997 book *Cowboys Have Always Been My Heroes*. Said Schramm: "My father, who was living out in California, was in the stock brokerage business, and Daniel Reeves, the owner of the Los Angeles Rams, had a stock brokerage company out in Beverly Hills, and my father met one of Reeve's partners, Charlie Jowitz, who mentioned to my dad that Reeves had gotten rid of their publicity man, Max Stiles, because he suspected Max, a longtime newspaperman, of leaking stories to favorite reporters.

"My father told Reeves' friend, 'My son, Tex Schramm, just graduated from college, and he's the sports editor of a newspaper down there in Austin, and he might really be interested in the job.' So the guy went back and told Reeves, Reeves called sports editor Paul Zimmerman at the *Times*, and he apparently gave me a glowing recommendation, so the first thing I knew, I got a phone call. At the time I was covering the Kansas relays for the *Austin American-Statesman* – the University of Texas had a team going up there, and I went from there out to California and interviewed with Reeves, and he offered the job, and I accepted it, and that's how I wound up the PR director with the Rams."

From the public relations department, Schramm soon found himself a key member of the Rams scouting staff and involved in a process that left him no end to frustration. Due to the marginal profits that many NFL clubs enjoyed in those days, scouting of college players was a very limited affair, with individual teams concentrating mainly on in-state and regional prospects. When coupled with the scarcity of game-film, selecting players in the annual college draft became little more than a high-stakes crapshoot.

To a man such as Schramm, who believed wholeheartedly in operating on the basis of informed decisions, the accepted form of the NFL draft was orchestrated madness and a process in need of an intensive makeover. That he was sure of. How Schramm could accomplish such a change while operating on a restricted budget was not so clear. No matter how much he dreamed of doing so, he still couldn't send scouts out all over the country to blindly chase rabbits. And he still couldn't get his hands on game-film that either didn't exist or lay in a drawer thousands of miles distant. How then could Schramm locate the players and information that he sought?

Where other league executives before him had reached a dead-end and simply accepted the hand circumstances had dealt them, Schramm believed he saw a way out that would give the Rams' organization a leg up on their competition. He had already struck out on the two most common lines of scouting queries, making one thing quite clear. From his perch on the western shores of the continent, there remained absolutely no way that Schramm could go out and find the undiscovered football talents across the nation while staying true to budget guidelines. The only alternative left to him was to create a line of business connections that would, in theory, bring the players and their credentials to Schramm in Los Angeles.

"In those days very few people fooled with the small schools," explained Schramm, "and so I got this idea to put out the Tom Harmon Little All-America Team. I thought of it. Tom had played with us on the Rams. I knew him very well, and I convinced him Tom Harmon's Little All-America Team would be a good thing for him. We had stationery printed up, gave them an entry form to nominate the players who should be considered for Tom Harmon's Little All-America Football Team, sent them to all the small schools, and told them to nominate players. They didn't know it, but the return address was us, the Rams! And it was great! We'd get the names of all the linemen who were 6'2" or over, and we'd put those on a list and start scouting them. We had a lot of small-college players with the Rams because of Tom Harmon's Little All-America. That's what we did. That way we got all of the names of all the players in the small schools!"

Before very long, the Rams were a walking caravan of star players such as Elroy "Crazylegs" Hirsch, Bob Waterfield, Norm Van Brocklin, Glenn Davis, Tom Fears, Andy Robustelli, and Tank Younger, helping Los Angeles to three consecutive NFL Championship game appearances from 1949-51. After falling short in their first two showings, the Rams finished the job in '51, defeating Cleveland by a 24-17 final. In 1955 they appeared in a fourth Championship game, but this time lost to Cleveland in blowout fashion 38-14.

A split ownership group with the Rams soon caused friction in the camp and, ultimately, led to Schramm's departure from football two years later and his arrival on the television scene as a well-paid member of the CBS brain trust alongside Bill Paley and Bill MacPhail. Yet, even in helping orchestrate a breakthrough in sports coverage for the 1960 Winter Olympic Games, Schramm never lost his passion for the game and secretly harbored a longing to have a crack at building a football team from the ground up, a fact which managers of long established franchises in the NFL, CFL, and NBA learned the hard way when Schramm, in turn, respectfully refused offers for available general manager positions.

In 1959 Schramm was approached by Texas businessman Clint Murchison Jr. about the general manager job for the new National Football League franchise from Dallas, which would begin play the following year. From their first conversation together, Schramm knew that he had found his new landing place in the Lone Star State. Murchison was everything that Schramm had ever hoped for in an NFL owner; good-natured, laid-back, and hands-off in football-related matters. The fact that he had deep pockets only sweetened the deal. Schramm had everything at his disposal to help turn an ordinary sports franchise into a global giant.

Upon assuming the position, Schramm implemented the same scouting process that he had instituted in Los Angeles, with particular attention to players from obscure colleges. Hiring Gil Brandt, a baby photographer from Milwaukee whose hobby was studying college game films to see why some players were better than others, to head the scouting department would prove to enhance its efficiency. Schramm had first heard of Brandt from one of his players in Los Angeles, and the two had visited each other from time to time.

Bringing Tom Landry, the revered defensive coordinator of the New York Giants, back to his home state of Texas to coach the expansion Cowboys would prove to be Schramm's best decision of all. Because of Landry's systematic mind that viewed the game through a complex mirror of angles and numbers, the new head coach was able to soak in Schramm's explanation of what the scouting department was striving for, and offer additional advice and a unique perspective that would streamline the scouting process even more and avoid the scouting of potential prospects that Landry had no intention of picking.

After the Cowboys' first draft class in 1961, Schramm found satisfaction in realizing that the organization, though certainly young, did not lack for information on prospects. His only concern was having too much information and not knowing how to process it in a timely fashion.

"We would start with, say, 2,000 players in their freshman year in college and steadily accumulate information on them," Schramm explained to Sports Illustrated in 1968. "By the time they were seniors the number was down to 500 or 600. That total was reduced to 300. Then each of the 300 was ranked from one to 300. Since it took a man at least an hour to read and evaluate the information on a player... I knew we had to find a quick, dispassionate judge. The computer was the answer."

To help rationalize the team's scouting reports down to its lowest common denominator, Schramm hired A. Salam Qureishi, a brilliant young computer programmer and statistician recently employed by IBM. After a series of meetings with Landry and Brandt, the young Indian scientist hit upon a formula that would be easy to understand and compatible to the dinosaur computers of the age.

"At that time, the most sophisticated computer system could work with something like only 80 variables," Qureishi told Sports Illustrated. "It was immediately evident that we would have to cut down. We reduced everything to five dimensions." Those five variables, Qureishi asserted, were character, quickness-and-body control, competitiveness, mental alertness, and strength-and-explosiveness. He also developed a detailed questionnaire on players that could be distributed to college coaches across the country.

It was easy, and foolproof, allowing virtually no room for emotion. All that scouts had to do was to give a player a grade in each category using a number scale from 1 to 10, punch the numbers into the computer and simply wait for the printout. This formula was completed in time for the 1964 college draft, a moment in time that witnessed the Dallas franchise gaining a leg up on their competition.

Over the next seven years, the Cowboys used this computer system to draft players such as Mel Renfro, Bob Hayes, Roger Staubach, Craig Morton, Rayfield Wright, Calvin Hill, Duane Thomas, and others, all of whom enjoyed successful careers while helping Dallas go from the gutter to the very top of the football mountain. The Cowboys and their computer also gained notoriety for finding basketball talents Cornell Green and Pete Gent and developing them into productive football players.

A difference in philosophy led to Qureishi's departure from the Cowboys in 1972. Ironically, it was a year later that Schramm was quoted bemoaning the fact that the rest of the league had caught up to the Cowboys' Space Age scouting process. The small-school players that had once been on the board for the taking in the later rounds were too often gone, as other teams, flush with information from their own scouting ventures, were there to snatch them up ahead of the Cowboys.

Schramm's frustrations, when coupled with a disheartening 8-6 season in 1974, led to an organizational re-commitment to drafting excellence. It made for long nights and detailed scouting breakdowns at the office, and ultimately led to the introduction of the Dirty Dozen onto the Dallas football scene.

Seven days had passed since Pittsburgh dispatched Minnesota in Super Bowl IX by a 16-6 score. Now, just hours before the kickoff of the Pro Bowl, the National Football League's version of an All-Star game, a small crowd had gathered on the patio of the Sonesta Beach and Tennis Hotel in Key Biscayne for an all-important opening ceremony to the 1975 season. With one flip of a coin from NFL commissioner Pete Rozelle, the order to the beginning of the 1975 NFL college draft would be set in stone.

The Baltimore Colts and New York Giants had each finished the 1974 campaign with identical records of 2-12. Since Dallas had obtained the Giants first-round draft pick in the Craig Morton deal, it was Cowboys' General Manager Tex Schramm who joined Baltimore GM Joe Thomas in flanking Rozelle for the ceremony.

In the event that the Cowboys came away with the No. 1 selection, they planned on using it to obtain Steve Bartkowski, the All-American quarterback from the University of California, who was the top prospect on their draft board. Should they lose the coin toss, club officials were still optimistic that they could get Bartkowski at No. 2, due to the fact that Baltimore already had a pair of quality quarterbacks in Bert Jones and Marty Domres. The Colts, so went the popular opinion, had their sights set on Maryland's All-American defensive end Randy White. Either way the coin fell, it seemed inevitable that the Cowboys would get the player they wanted.

Then the drama began. As Rozelle, with a host of cameramen poised for the occasion, flipped a 1974 Eisenhower dollar into the air, Schramm called "heads." The coin landed tails. Baltimore had won.

As part of his victory speech to the media, Thomas shocked everyone in the room by announcing that the top pick was officially up for auction. "We don't need a quarterback," acknowledged Thomas. "But we believe that we can make a good deal for Bartkowski and probably get two veteran players in return."

Thomas' talk heard 'round the football world was an indirect invitation to the quarterback-needy Atlanta Falcons, the owners of the No. 3 selection. Atlanta needed a franchise signal-caller, as much to turn the fortunes of a beleaguered franchise as to attract attention for their vacant general manager position, which had been offered in recent days to the Cowboys' own Gil Brandt. The Falcons, more than any other franchise, were on the hunt for a particular player, a fact which Thomas and the Colts were determined to take advantage of.

On the flip side, it caused a change of plans in the Cowboys' camp. Nine days remained until the draft was set to begin in New York City, a time in which the trio of Tom Landry, Tex Schramm, and Brandt spent numerous hours with an inner-circle of scouts going over film and notes of hundreds of college players. The age-old dilemma of pursuing team needs versus simply taking the best player was discussed to great lengths, prospects were picked apart to the minutest detail, and situational possibilities utterly exhausted.

Discussions on what to do with the No. 2 pick were intense as they were diverse. Landry, Brandt, and chief scout Red Hickey were high on Randy White, the winner of the 1974 Outland award winner as the nation's best defensive lineman. Hickey, in particular, marveled every time he turned on the game film of White. "I never saw him make an error, which a lot of veterans do, in his pursuit lanes," Hickey said. "Like Tom [Landry] was saying, he reminds me of Alan Page, except Randy might be a little bigger." Other scouts within the Cowboys' organization were not nearly so impressed, feeling that White had reached his potential in college and wouldn't be the same player at the professional ranks once he put on weight.

The running back position was one that received quite a bit of chatter, with much of the conversation centering around Walter Payton. Among the scouts, it was agreed that Payton, a Little All-American at Jackson State, was the standout at his position, and a far superior athlete to media darling Anthony Davis of USC fame. Whether or not Payton was the best prospect after Bartkowski remained up for debate.

Trading the No. 2 pick remained a possibility, though enthusiasm in the room was noticeably lacking when this option was broached. The Cowboys, once upon a time, traded away their top draft pick for Buddy Dial, a wide receiver who never lived up to his potential in three years with Dallas. Had they hung onto that pick, the Cowboys would have wound up with Paul Warfield, who went on to stardom with the Miami Dolphins. Hesitancy notwithstanding, the Cowboys still performed their due diligence on this front.

Schramm contacted the Colts about a possible trade up, but found the asking price to be too high. He then contacted several teams about trading down to accumulate a couple of veteran players or draft picks, using veteran defensive end Pat Toomay as bait. Toomay had signed a WFL contract the previous summer to play for the Birmingham franchise, starting in 1975. By the time he had played out his option with the Cowboys, the cash-strapped Birmingham franchise was uncertain to still exist for the 1975 season, leaving Toomay's football future in the hands of a franchise he had grown disenchanted with. One of the more outspoken personalities on the Cowboys' troubled 1974 team, Toomay had officially given up on the Dallas coaching staff in the days leading up to the draft and requested to be traded. Cleveland showed interest in making a package deal for Toomay and the No. 2 pick, but bailed out at the last minute.

As the days passed and Draft Day approached, the Cowboys' draft board changed several times as coaches and scouts processed additional information through their fabled computer. Falling down the board were top linebackers Rod Shoate of Oklahoma and Jackson State's Robert Brazile. North Carolina's Ken Huff rose steadily, distancing himself from fellow offensive guards Lynn Boden, Dennis Harrah, and Kurt Schumacher.

And while the whittling process continued in Dallas, the inevitable came to pass in Baltimore when the Colts traded the top pick to Atlanta for the No. 3 selection, a medium-round draft pick and offensive tackle George Kunz. With news of the deal came a certain amount of relief for Cowboys' personnel, who no longer had to concern themselves with the possibility of Baltimore, frustrated by small-time offers from the Falcons, actually picking someone other than Bartkowski with the first selection. From the Cowboys' end, the first steps of the draft had now been simplified greatly. Bartkowski, without a doubt, would become an Atlanta Falcon, leaving Dallas with all of their options open at No. 2.

By the time the morning of the draft rolled around, those options seemed just as endless as ever. After all of the discussions, extra hours of film study, and tiresome note-checking in recent days, the Cowboys were still undecided as to who their first pick would be. The room remained divided over two names: Walter Payton and Randy White. Whom to choose?

The case for each was compelling. Payton would undoubtedly fill the role of the departed Calvin Hill and serve as the Cowboys' featured runner out of the backfield. And White would be the heir-in-waiting to the starting middle linebacker spot, once Lee Roy Jordan called it quits in a year or two.

Just hours before the draft, team personnel uncovered an alarming fact that helped steer the vote away from Payton. While going over the recent history of the tailback position, scouts discovered that, out of all the then-current NFL runners, only two (O.J. Simpson and Rocky Bleier) had been in the league five years or longer. For a team looking for long-term solutions with their first pick, this was the deciding straw that resulted in White becoming a Cowboy later that morning.

After Louis Wright landed in Denver via the No. 17 selection, the Cowboys were on the clock again and facing a familiar dilemma. Running back remained a position of need, but their top two prospects (Walter Payton and Don Hardeman) were already off the board, Payton having gone to Chicago at No. 4 and Hardeman winding up with the Oilers at No. 15. Voices in the room were emphatic in stating that, were the Cowboys to find a franchise back for the upcoming season, it was now or never. Davis would undoubtedly be gone by the time that the Cowboys' next turn to pick came up at No. 44. Anthony Davis, so it seemed to some, was the obvious choice at this point.

Tom Landry couldn't have disagreed more. While Davis was certainly an intriguing runner with a certain amount of potential, Landry felt that his size (5-9, 183-pounds) made him a high-risk gamble. Davis, Landry believed, wouldn't hold up under the beating of a fourteen-game NFL season and would be but a battered shell of himself by the time the playoffs rolled around in late December. If the issue of longevity was to be the deciding factor in passing over a prospect such as Payton, then it certainly must be so in the case of Davis too.

From running backs, the conversation naturally drifted over to the defensive side of the ball, which was in desperate need of an infusion of young blood. Bob Lilly, the legendary defensive tackle who had never missed a regular season game in fourteen years, was contemplating the possibility of quitting at the age of 35. Linebackers Lee Roy Jordan and Dave Edwards had been in the league for twelve seasons, and were rumored to be leaning toward retirement after the upcoming season. The same was said to be true for Cornell Green, who had been a fixture at the strong safety position since signing as a rookie free agent in 1962.

For nearly a full calendar year now, the Cowboys had been actively trying to find a suitable cornerback to start opposite of All-Pro Mel Renfro in the defensive backfield. Charlie Waters had given it his best shot for two years, but gave up too many big plays, convincing coaches to move him back to his natural position of safety, beginning in 1975. Waters' projected replacement was none other than Mark Washington, a four-year veteran who had yet to earn his coaches trust.

An opportunity to land a bona-fide starter seemed to be presenting itself to the Cowboys once again at No. 18. In a draft class deep on above-average talent, scouts were only too happy to find defensive backs Mike Williams and Neal Colzie available in the latter stages of the first round. Colzie received particular attention for his ball-hawking skills. A three-year starter in college, Colzie had notched thirteen interceptions while at Ohio State.

But for every scout that mentioned a cornerback's name, Cowboys chief scout Red Hickey was in the ear of Tom Landry reminding him of another star defensive player from a tiny school in Oklahoma. Thomas Henderson was an NAIA All-American at Langston University and was the Cowboys' top-rated linebacker in the entire draft. More importantly to Hickey, a former coach of the San Francisco 49ers and a longtime NFL scout, Henderson was an NFL-ready talent who could step in and start as a rookie.

Having watched the aging Dave Edwards battle injuries at his strong-side linebacker position, and knowing that weakside linebacker D.D. Lewis would, in all likelihood, be playing in the

World Football League the following summer, Hickey viewed Henderson as a long-term answer at either position. Henderson, said Hickey, was a star in the making. But Landry had his doubts, preferring to spend a high draft pick on someone from a big-name school...such as a Colzie or a Williams. Yet even Landry had to admit that the big-school players had marks against them. "The big question we faced was whether to take Henderson, Colzie or Williams," said Landry. "We might have gone for Colzie if he'd allowed us to time him. He wouldn't. You get cautious when that happens. A guy might look awfully fast on films but you take him and he does 4.8 and you're in trouble."

Even with Colzie removed from their list on this merit, Landry still seemed determined to pick a defensive back. Only after what was rumored to be a heated discussion between the two, in which Hickey predicted that the mighty Rams would wind up with Henderson at No. 20, did Landry concede. Landry had no intentions of letting a possible gem land on an already loaded Rams roster, so he signed off on the decision to make Thomas Henderson the newest and most confident member of the Dallas Cowboys.

If self-esteem was an Olympic event in the 1970s, then Thomas Henderson would have claimed a gold medal in runaway fashion. No NFL player, incoming or long established, could lay claim to the confidence and personal awareness that Henderson possessed. He believed in himself far past the point of pride and boastfulness so that it was acknowledged by all who came in contact with him that he was, without a doubt, the very best promoter that Thomas Henderson could ever ask for.

The Dallas media learned this the hard way in the hours following Henderson's first-round selection by the Cowboys. Local reporters knew that they could catch up with Randy White at a press conference during the coming week. Until then, they would have to settle for sound bites from the Cowboys' "other" first-round draft pick.

When a member of the *Dallas Morning News* caught up with Henderson on the phone shortly after the Cowboys picked him at No. 18, he found not an ordinary, bright-eyed rookie, but an unblinking veteran of the impromptu self-promotional act. "My name wasn't in neon lights because I'm from a small school," said Henderson. "But I watched those all-star games and I think I'm better than those other linebackers. Rod Shoate didn't play well in any of the all-star games and [Randy] White played well in one of three."

When told that White had been the Cowboys' first selection sixteen spots ahead of him and that it might be "Randy White and Tom Henderson" at linebacker for the Cowboys, Henderson noted, "Or Tom Henderson and Randy White. If White's as fast as I hear, what 4.8, then we might be in a race for the ball-carrier."

A product of humble beginnings in Austin, Texas, Thomas saw first-hand while growing up the daily struggle that his parents went through to put food on the table. Too often for a youngster such as Henderson, it seemed like a losing cause. No matter how hard Dad and Mom worked, there was always a money shortage. It was a reality that frustrated Thomas with the coming of age.

As he grew older, Thomas began to understand the limitations there could be for a child coming from a poor black household in the South. Respect in the workplace was often hard to come by as job opportunities, while open to others, remained closed to his family. In a family fighting a sobering battle for cash and respect, young Thomas lost heart. When he lost his ability to dream soon after, it was only a matter of time until he sought out greener pastures.

At the age of 16, Thomas boarded a bus bound for his grandmother's house in Oklahoma City. While there he took up playing football and soon developed into a defensive star for Douglass High School. By the time he graduated, Henderson had 13 scholarship offers, including one from the University of Oklahoma. Henderson's enthusiasm at his prospective future was dampened by a recurring theme. The majority of the schools anticipated redshirting Henderson for his freshman year. After mulling his options over he chose Langston, a predominantly black school, because of its close proximity to home and a promise from head coach Albert Shoats that he could play immediately.

Shoats recalled the first time that Henderson showed his face on campus. "He showed up one day as a freshman," said Shoats. "We had four good defensive ends at the time and he looked them over and said, 'Coach, I'll be your No. 1 defensive end.' I said, 'Boy, it's yours if you're man enough to take it.'"

Thomas proved to be more than man enough, earning the starting job on the way to a magical run with the Lions in his junior season of 1973. On a Langston team with 14 all-conference players, Henderson was the shining force, earning NAIA All-American honors on a defensive unit that allowed just 93 points in 12 regular season games, giving the uber-confident Henderson all the excuse he needed to strut around campus.

Once, a reporter was conducting a sit-down interview with Prinson Poindexter, Langston's All-American quarterback. Henderson abruptly walked into the room and sat down, figuring the reporter would want to interview him too.

During a game in which Langston was blanking Southeastern 26-0, Henderson – in full football attire – walked into the press box late in the game to warn Northeastern scouts that the Redmen could expect more of the same the following week. Henderson was as good as his word, as Langston bowled over Northeastern 40-6.

Langston's magical run came to an end in the semi-final playoffs at the hands of Abilene Christian's potent offensive duo of Clint Longley, a future teammate of Henderson's with the Cowboys, and Wilbert Montgomery, who went on to star for the Philadelphia Eagles in the NFL.

Henderson played defensive end until his final year in college when coaches moved him to outside linebacker in order to give him more room to roam. Despite playing at a new position, and in spite of the many inefficiencies of a 1-11 team, Henderson was a standout player once again, cementing his place as a top-tier NFL prospect.

The draft rolled on past the first-round, with Dallas picking up Florida offensive guard Burton Lawless at No. 44 overall, and Arizona's Bob Breunig later in the third-round. Lawless was the team's No. 2 rated guard behind only Ken Huff, who went No. 3 overall to Baltimore. "He's the best pulling guard I saw last season and we like to pull our linemen," noted Red Hickey.

Breunig's draft-stock had plummeted after a rocky senior season in which the speedy linebacker bulked up to 245 pounds. Had he stayed at his normal playing weight, the Cowboys felt Breunig would have been projected as a first-round talent.

The rounds flew by, with Landry and his staff paying close attention to the defense. Seven of the Cowboys' first nine selections were on that side of the ball. Lawless and Oklahoma center Kyle Davis, a fifth-round selection, were the lone exceptions.

The team couldn't resist causing some laughs with their ninth-round selection. A year after taking 6-foot-8-inch defensive end Ed "Too Tall" Jones, the Cowboys announced they were taking 6-foot-1-inch defensive back Ed "Too Small" Jones (no relation) out of Rutgers.

Not until the tenth-round did the Cowboys address the hole caused by Calvin Hill's defection, tabbing Dennis Booker of Millersville with pick No. 252. Landry increased his chances of finding a starter in the draft by picking two more running backs on consecutive selections, starting in the fourteenth round with Scott Laidlaw and then later with Willie Hamilton.

When the draft reached its end late on the second day, Cowboys' coaches and scouts agreed among themselves that they had picked a good class. It wasn't until those same players hit the practice field in spring workouts that they began to have an inkling of just how good.

CHAPTER 5

THE PRANK & THE NO SHOW

"The [World Football League] operators and franchise hucksters were, almost without exception, scoundrels or fools or a combination."
- **Frank Luksa, Dallas Times-Herald columnist**

In two days representing the Dallas Cowboys at the NFL Draft in New York City, Joe Bailey had become quite familiar with a microphone. As the team's business manager, it was his voice that uttered such dramatic lines as "Dallas takes Charles Bland, defensive back, Cincinnati." He had also heard quite a few interesting announcements over the loudspeaker, like when Pete Rozelle told the world that "New England Patriots, with their first-round selection take Russ Francis, tight end, Oregon."

The room, filled with team representatives from all 26 teams and media personnel from as far away as San Francisco, was immediately abuzz with curiosity, with people checking notes and files in search of information on this mysterious name that had popped up. Seemingly no one in the building had ever heard of Russ Francis. Bailey brushed off the incident as just another draft-day shenanigan from the Patriots, a franchise renowned for football oddities.

As soon as the draft was complete, Bailey was behind the wheel in his car on a mission to sign a list of rookie free agents. His first stop was in Newark, Deleware where Gil Brandt was hopeful that the Cowboys could land another basketball prospect, like they had done in recent years with Cornell Green and Pete Gent.

6-5, 235-pound John Kraus, complete with a Paul Bunyan-like beard, had attended the University of Deleware on a basketball scholarship. After his sophomore season, he tried out for the football team, and proved to be a serviceable tight end.

Unknown to Bailey and the Cowboys, Kraus had been the victim of a tasteless prank only a few hours earlier. He received a telephone call from someone identifying himself as a Cowboys' representative and was informed that he had been drafted in the thirteenth round. Kraus was so excited that he purchased a bottle of champagne and invited a few friends over to celebrate.

One of his friends double-checked the story and told him the truth: the Cowboys had selected Virginia Union guard Herbert Scott in the 13th round, and nobody else. So when Bailey phoned him from a booth near Kraus' apartment, it was little wonder that the rookie was plagued by doubts and distrust.

"I couldn't figure out why he sounded so unfriendly," Bailey recalled. "'Where are you,' he asked. I told him I had just arrived in town and was calling from a phone booth. 'Yeah, where is it located?' he said. I didn't know it but he thought I was the same guy who had made that phony draft call. He was going to find out where I was and then try to keep me talking while he sent some of his pals to take care of me."

Bailey kept talking, and was fortunate that he convinced Kraus that he was a legitimate agent of *the* Dallas Cowboys. Still, Kraus showed no interest in joining him for a pizza, insisting that Bailey finish the last leg of his journey by coming on over to his apartment to talk business.

Kraus was very subdued during their conversation and gave every indication of wanting to play for the Cowboys, admitting he was well aware of the team's past successes with one-time basketball players. But he refused to sign a contract, pledging to keep his promise to listen to another team's offer. No deal was reached.

Amidst a general feeling of public optimism surrounding the Cowboys' newest rookie class, an undercurrent of concern surfaced in the days following the draft that Gil Brandt & Staff might have actually let a top prospect slip through the cracks. This, to a football town whose fans found joy in doing their own scouting, was a story well worth following up.

The narrative originated in New York, where the Jets made draft-day headlines when they "raided" the roster of the World Football League's Chicago Fire, by selecting wide receiver James Scott in the eighth round. Scott played collegiately at a junior college in Georgia, where he graduated in 1971. He spent the following year in the Canadian Football League and sat out the entire 1973 season before resurfacing with the WFL. In one game against eventual World Bowl Champion Birmingham, Scott tallied 11 receptions for 165 yards and three touchdowns.

The Cowboys, as the story went, were definitely interested in drafting Scott, but had trouble tracking him down via any of his three telephone numbers that reached from Gladewater to Dallas. "If you can get him and pin him down," said Brandt, "then you have got the elusive butterfly. I've never had such a hard time catching up with a guy."

Brandt said several of his scouts spent days before the draft trying to contact Scott in person before they finally got him on the line. "We asked him to come to our practice field and work out," recalled Brandt. "He was supposed to be there at 9:30 one morning, and Clint Longley was waiting there to throw to him. He called at 9:29 and said he couldn't make it, that he had to run an errand for his mom. I asked if he couldn't stop by the field first and he said no."

When Scott didn't show up, Brandt said the Cowboys gave up any thought of drafting him. "I'm not sure there is a James Scott," he laughed. "I just know there's a guy who answers the phone."

Shortly after the conclusion of the draft, Sam Blair of the Dallas Morning News phoned him and pulled the story out of the elusive wide receiver. "I got some torn knee ligaments last season in a freak accident on the artificial turf at Soldier Field," he said. "There was no contact. I reached back for a pass and my knee folded under me. It's okay now. I've been working out on it, but my agent told me I shouldn't go out and run for anybody if they didn't pay me some money. I told the Cowboys I'd come by and talk. Then the next morning I called and said I'd be a little late. They were unhappy because I wasn't going to work out and we just never got together."

Every football fan in Dallas agreed that selecting a healthy Mitch Hoopes in the eighth round made more sense than gambling on a nomadic wide receiver who, in three years as a professional, had yet to make a spot for himself on an NFL roster.

The fact that Dallas didn't draft a receiver of note should have served as big news for their own established wide-out, Bob Hayes. But Hayes, in the twilight of his career, had other things on his mind than making good on a second chance, much to the dismay of team management, who found themselves confronted with a rude reality that just would not go away.

Just weeks after the excitement of the NFL Draft died down, the Cowboys were thrown another curveball when one of their own big-name players appeared in federal court to testify against the organization. The NFL Players Association was preparing to sue the team owners to gain free agency. But to succeed, they first had to overturn the Rozelle Rule, an edict from the Commissioner which provided that if another team signed a free agent player, Pete Rozelle would decide what the proper compensation should be. The NFLPA sought a system that would give the player freedom to negotiate with the team of his choice, without punishing the team that signed him.

What better way to undermine the integrity of the owners than to have former Olympic gold-medalist Bob Hayes take the stand in front of God and man. Hayes was more than willing to risk his career in order to demonstrate just how duplicitous NFL management could be in telling players they were allowed to leave and play for another team while at the same time relying on a rule that effectively killed any chance a player had of doing just that.

A full-time regular in the Dallas offense for his first seven years in the league since being drafted out of Florida A&M in 1965, Hayes had fallen upon hard times with the Cowboys in recent seasons, even being relegated to bench duty for the majority of the 1974 campaign after losing his job at split-end to Golden Richards. Hayes' first response to his demotion had been to lash out at Landry, whose offensive system, he claimed, didn't take advantage of his world-class speed. Hayes then did his best to make life as difficult for his replacement as possible, treating Richards with cold disfavor. For a player who seemed to be trying his best to force the team to trade him elsewhere, Hayes' next step in his defiance of the entire organization led him to court, where he did his best to discredit the Cowboys' front-office hierarchy.

Under oath, Hayes testified that in 1969 he was making a salary of $23,000, and in 1970 he asked for $75,000, but was turned down forthright by Tex Schramm. Hayes said that he played out his option, taking a ten-percent pay cut, with the intention of signing with another team after the season.

Hayes said Landry informed him before the 1970 season, "You are important to our game plan." But, he said, once the head coach learned his top receiver was playing out his option, Landry sought to make him seem less attractive to other teams by keeping him on the bench for much of the season. According to Landry, Hayes was benched because he wasn't blocking like he should.

Even so, the Washington Redskins approached his agent to sign him for the 1971 season. But George Allen ultimately decided against striking a deal, fearing that Rozelle would punish him for not abiding by the hands-off-free agent rule by forcing the Redskins to give up young star receiver Charley Taylor as compensation. The Miami Dolphins also pursued Hayes, but backed out in fear they would have to give up Paul Warfield.

In 1971 Hayes signed a five-year contract with Dallas for $55,000 a year, plus a yearly $10,000 bonus, and a deferred payment of $60,677. In effect, Schramm had given him his $75,000, and a few dollars more.

But in the February 1975 hearing, Hayes' attorney, Ed Glennon, claimed that Hayes was only receiving the yearly salary and the $10,000 bonus. The Cowboys insisted that the minimum average for each year, after adding up all the incentives, was $87, 254, a claim that eventually was verified in court.

Hayes' day on the witness stand ended in a thud for the Players Association, as the former All-Pro wide receiver gave way to multiple contradictions under cross-examination. Hayes then made himself scarce on the practice field, which forced the Dallas front-office to quietly start seeking a trade partner.

One of the silver linings that emerged from all of the bickering, finger-pointing, and tedious courtroom arguments at the Rozelle Rule trial was a fact that many NFL executives and players were just gaining a new appreciation for. They, at least, had a league and a cash-box to fight over. The desk stooges in the World Football league offices weren't nearly so lucky.

Buried beneath a mountain of debts and embarrassed by a highly-publicized ticket scandal, WFL owners set about to orchestrate a fast-paced facelift that would re-ingratiate the league to football fans and business owners. The first order of business was to distance themselves from Gary Davidson, the high-profile showman linked with so many of the previous season's disasters.

Davidson was released from his duties as President in October of 1974, and walked away from football with the promise that he would be back on the American sports scene before very long. He already had plans, he said, to launch a professional bowling league. That announcement was received with blank stares of incredulity.

"Paying to watch somebody bowl," Fort Worth Star Telegram sports editor Bill Van Fleet once opined, "is like buying a ticket to watch somebody fish."

Davidson went back to California as a broken man, his marriage busted and his reputation in ruins. It would be a long time before Davidson would be able to convince people that he was something other than a fraud.

His replacement as President, Chris Hemmeter, proved to be equally as suspect during his short-lived stint with the World Football League. The Owner of the WFL's Hawaiians franchise, Hemmeter assumed his new role with all the cunning of a misguided Jesuit, while paying homage both to his birthplace in the epicenter of American politics in Washington D.C. and to the University of Cornell, where he steeped himself in Catholic philosophy and earned his degree at the top of his class in 1962.

Catholics, especially in the political realm, have a trademark move for satisfying the desires of a fickle public. Those steeped in the art of casuistry refer to this tactic as "blowing cover as cover," and find it extremely useful in maintaining order while staying true to patterns of social progression.

Cultural shifts are very often a product of reshuffling ornaments and repainting window dressing, rather than any significant foundational upheaval in philosophy. When neighborhood parents, out of concerns of safety for their children, request that the city council remove a certain poisoned apple tree from the middle of the public square, council members generally react by constructing a building around the tree of interest, and then slap a sign on the front window that reads, "Candy Apples. Children Welcome." What the public can't see won't hurt them.

During the winter and early-spring months of 1975, Hemmeter tried his own luck with this sleight of hand magic. But instead of "blowing cover as cover," Hemmeter seemed to simply blow the league's cover. What was thought to be a league on the rebound, with the intention of paying their debts and mending their ways, was discovered instead to be just another version of the same broken toy that America had tossed aside the previous year.

With Davidson out of the picture and a forgettable season finally in the books, Hemmeter sought to wipe the bad taste from the mouths of football fans by wiping Davidson's creation off the map altogether. Out the door went the old, despicable World Football League, which became legally known as the Football Creditors Payment Plan, Inc. The World Football League was, in fact, a relic of past history.

Very quietly behind closed doors, Hemmeter paid $10,000 to the Football Creditors Payment Plan for the rights of the "name, initials, service mark, and goodwill" of the old league. He then dubbed his new creation…the World Football League. Surprise! The footballs were the same. The rules were the same. The contracts were the same. The logos were the same.

Unfortunately, Hemmeter found that the problems were the same, too. Money was still tight, and perception of the World Football League a nagging problem. Investors shied away with religious persistence. The league's appeal for NFL players had tanked. The news stories coming out of certain cities only worsened the situation.

The Internal Revenue Service, in seeking to obtain $236,000 in back taxes owed by the franchise, formally offered the contracts of 59 Birmingham players on the public auction block for anybody or any entity who cared to submit a sealed bid. Included in this allotment of players were three members of the Dallas Cowboys. Pat Toomay, Jethro Pugh, and Rayfield Wright had each signed futures contracts with the Americans in 1974.

The Cowboys weren't concerned with the possibility of losing the rights to their players, for multiple reasons. For one, Toomay's WFL contract for 1975 had already been declared void. Pugh and Wright weren't scheduled to join the rival league until the following season. Secondly, Tex Schramm judged that NFL teams would stay away from the auction block out of fear of repercussions from the Rozelle Rule. Pete Rozelle had made it quite clear to each owner that any club buying a player at auction would come under the NFL's option compensation rule.

Representatives for a possible team in Jacksonville (replacing the defunct Sharks) sent a letter to players offering payment of "15 per cent of total monies" owed if the league came out of escrow. The letter also pointed out that if "all players" did not agree to this, "there will not be a league."

Rumblings off the mainland were just as ominous. The Hawaiians sent a letter to its players offering stock in the club in lieu of salaries owed. Calvin Hill even flew to Hawaii to try to drum up some support for this project. His eagerness to help was understandable. Hill had more to lose than anyone else if the league did go under. Hill's future football home remained a question of debate as WFL owners tried to sort out the mess in front of them. Would Calvin be a star on the island, or wear the star in Dallas?

Hemmeter put an end to all of the speculation when he emerged from a meeting with owners at a Philadelphia restaurant and declared that the World Football League was a go for 1975. He admitted that, thus far, the league had been the "biggest sports disaster in history," but said that a new collection of at least 10 teams under the same flag would play a twenty-game schedule during the upcoming summer and fall. The world would get the football that they deserved! He stressed that the new WFL was technically different than the old one, and unveiled a revolutionary profit sharing system to prove it.

With the league controlling the majority of each team's income, Hemmeter promised that the new league would pay off all of the remaining debts from the old one over the next 12 years by donating 1.5 percent of each team's net revenue to a special disbursement fund. The new sharing plan was guaranteed to sustain each team for at least the next three years.

Though few people realized it at the time, Hemmeter's promises of the league's long-term success were based upon the presumption that the Chicago Fire would sign Joe Namath to a free-agent deal, thus securing a TV deal with TVS. But when Namath stalled and eventually backed out of signing, Hemmeter's perfect world came crumbling down on top of him.

The World Football League was crawling toward a predictable end. And Calvin Hill was boarding a one-way flight to Hawaii, his Cowboys' days forever behind him.

CHAPTER 6

SETTING A TONE

"You've got to pay an awful price to win. You've got to pay the price to get ready to win. If you're not willing, you lose."
- **Tom Landry**

On the morning after a palpably miserable 1974 season had concluded with a Saturday night loss in Oakland, Tom Landry was at his desk working on a host of changes aimed at injecting some life into an aging, apathetic franchise. So engrossed was he in scratching out a rough guideline on a pad that Landry failed to realize that, according to the letter of the law, he was no longer employed by the Cowboys. That ten-year contract he had agreed to in 1964 had expired, making Landry a head coaching free agent for the first time.

The majority of head coaches coming off a sub-par season would have felt uncomfortable in this position, and likely would have been chomping at the bit to get a deal done. Not Landry, though. He had already been assured a couple of weeks before by both Tex Schramm and team owner Clint Murchison Jr. that they wanted him to continue to coach in Dallas. After this verbal promise was followed by a handshake, Landry put all thoughts of a new contract from his mind and focused entirely on righting the Cowboys' ship, adding alterations in the team's weight-lifting process and third-down offense, among other things. Just maybe, Landry thought, his example in negotiations with the ownership group would serve as an inspiration for the many cash-conscious players on the Cowboys' roster, and set a new tone moving forward for the 1975 season, with personal craft serving as the categorical imperative over personal security.

Even in the weeks after the draft when Murchison approached him about the possible terms, Landry assured the Owner that he wasn't worried about it, and would work on hammering out a new agreement at a date in the near future. What turned out to be an inordinately busy off-season in Dallas led to a longer-than-expected delay for the two parties, and eventually, into Landry coaching the entire 1975 season without a contract.

Another front-office luminary all-in on the Cowboys' comeback project was Vice-President Gil Brandt. During the week leading up to the Super Bowl, Brandt had been offered the General Manager position with the Atlanta Falcons. Rather than jump at the opportunity, Brandt remained non-committal and disappeared into his office to prepare for the Cowboys' upcoming draft. Shortly after the draft had concluded, Brandt announced that he was staying in Dallas and would be assuming some of the duties of former public relations director Al Ward, who had left the Cowboys to become the General Manager with the New York Jets. The expansion Tampa Bay Buccaneers then tried to lure Brandt away a few weeks later, but received the same firm denial. Explained Brandt: "I want to do everything I can to make sure we get to the Super Bowl this coming season and I think we will. I don't like to see the Dallas Cowboys finish 8-6…I do take it personally. Very personally."

What Brandt also took personally was the advice from sports agent Howard Slusher that resulted in Randy White being a no-show at the Cowboys' rookie orientation in March. Slusher was concerned that a bad showing from his client at the weekend practice sessions could be detrimental in contract negotiations, and thus encouraged White to steer shy of the Cowboys' practice field. Meanwhile, forty other rookies, including Bob Breunig and Kyle Davis who were represented by Slusher, showed up to the workout.

"Randy's failure to show has a very adverse effect on our coaching staff, the people of Dallas and everybody concerned with this team," said a visibly perturbed Brandt. "It just shows he's not concerned with the team. He didn't have enough pride in the team to come out and get to work."

Brandt claimed that Slusher's contract concerns were completely unfounded, while also tossing aside the notion that White was absent because he was visiting his ill grandmother. "It is a shame agents mislead players," said Brandt. "When you make a guy the second pick in the entire draft you know what he can do. He's been scouted personally by our staff fifty times. He's been timed, been sprinted, everything. We KNOW what he can do. But he wants to change positions. This really hurts him not being here. You figure he'll miss two weeks in camp because of the College All-Star game and not being here could be critical......I thought Randy had more pride than that..... He just didn't impress me as a guy who'd skip a workout. I talked to Randy. I talked to Slusher. Randy agreed to come. Then apparently Slusher talked him out of it. I've tried to phone him back since Thursday and it appears he's been avoiding me."

Even the normally calm head coach didn't waste time in pulling any punches, going hard after the team's No. 1 draft pick. "This is very disappointing when a guy with that much ability and drafted so high doesn't show up," observed Landry. "His agent is obviously behind this. Randy's got to make up his mind pretty quickly if he wants to play. He's interested in moving to linebacker. If he's going to try to do that he better get with it. Yes, he could always come in later to be looked at linebacker but you'd think he'd want to be here for me to see him because his future is somewhat in my hands."

Slusher poured more salt on the wound a few days later when it was reported that he had contacted the Philadelphia Bell about White possibly joining the WFL franchise. While contract terms were being discussed in Philly, Cowboys' management privately fumed behind closed doors, bemoaning another intrusion from the rival league.

Before any more barbs could be traded through the media, White himself saved the day by showing up at an April practice session and making peace with his Head Coach. The well-mannered barrel-chested rookie expressed himself eager to put on a Cowboys' helmet, and emphatically declined any interest in jumping leagues. And getting a deal done wouldn't be a problem either, he said, a promise from White that Landry was noticeably happy to receive.

    It didn't take a brain surgeon to discern where Tom Landry stood on the issue of Calvin Hill's defection to the World Football League. He didn't care for the move, not in an ethical sense, nor as it related to the team's depth chart at running back following his departure. Hill was on his way to Hawaii to cash in on his football abilities, while Landry stayed back in Dallas, burdened with the chore of locating his replacement. Or, that is, a pair of replacements.

Landry thought it unlikely that one of the Cowboys' remaining backs could singlehandedly replace Hill's production. In four seasons as the featured runner, Hill averaged just under 1,000 yards on the ground, in addition to his contributions as a receiver. Less than four years before, in Super Bowl VI, Landry figured his team might be set at the running back position for the better part of the decade, as two All-Pro runners (Hill and Duane Thomas) were sharing the backfield.

Inexplicably, both found cause for dissatisfaction in Dallas, and both left the Cowboys under controversial circumstances. To get back what the Cowboys lost with Hill's defection, Landry anticipated using some form of a platoon system for the 1975 season.

Landry's options to choose from were abundant in number, though markedly inexperienced. Charles Young, a second-year pro out of North Carolina State, had provided the Cowboys with a welcome speed threat out of the backfield as a rookie, rushing for 205 yards on just 33 carries, for a healthy 6.2 per-carry average. His 53-yard run against Houston in November was the team's longest of the season, and the longest by a Dallas tailback since their Super Bowl championship campaign in 1971.

Young was the Cowboys' No. 2 selection in the 1974 draft after Ed "Too Tall" Jones, and was viewed at the time as the heir apparent to Hill, in the event that the veteran Dallas tailback should, in fact, jump leagues. A year later, the Cowboys simply weren't sure where Young fit in, though they were quick to say he was the odds-on favorite to assume Hill's former role as starting tailback.

Landry admired Young's prowess as a pass receiver, and praised him for his tough running between the tackles. But Young's inability to get a grasp of the Cowboys' playbook prevented the head coach from awarding him with much in the way of Sunday playing time for the first half of his rookie season. Landry threw him a few bones during the season's latter stages, and Young certainly made the most of them. That, however, did not mean that Young's production would remain at, or near, the same level as the Cowboys' featured runner.

The coaches previously tried out Young at fullback in short intervals, but planned on avoiding the fullback option in 1975. The physique, coaches felt, did not match the results. Lining up closer to the line of scrimmage had seemed to compromise Young's vision as a runner, thereby hampering his effectiveness. His blocking from that position was equally unimpressive. No, Young was a halfback, and if everything worked out as Landry hoped it would, there he would stay. But would it?

Behind Young on the off-season depth chart was a 6-1, 195-pound bundle of inspiration. A rookie free-agent signee out of tiny Kutztown State in Pennsylvania, Doug Dennison had shocked many football locals during the summer of 1974 by parlaying a strong preseason into a roster spot. After seeing minimal action in his first season, Dennison was showing the drive and work ethic that would be necessary to challenge Young for the starting job.

While Young's best attributes were his speed and pass-catching abilities, Dennison combined a healthy dose of quickness and power that had many comparing him to – of all people – Calvin Hill. Though Landry didn't go so far as to draw that parallel, he did have high praise for Dennison before training camp. "Doug is a reckless type of football player," said Landry. "After our off-season program, he may be the best-conditioned athlete we have on the team. He has looked just tremendous – quick and explosive."

The front-office had addressed the positional uncertainty in January's NFL draft, selecting a trio of runners in the later rounds. Millersville State product Dennis Booker, a 6-2, 235-pound runner who averaged over six-yards per-carry in the Pennsylvania State College Athletic Conference was taken in the tenth round. Four rounds later, the Cowboys tabbed Scott Laidlaw out of Stanford. Laidlaw measured out at an even 6-feet in height, weighed 206-pounds, and according to his college backfield coach, Dave Curry, was "better prepared for professional football than any player in our conference (Pacific Eight)."

The only other player drafted by Dallas with potential as a running back was Willie Hamilton who, in his final season at Arizona, tallied 1,400 yards, 11 touchdowns, and averaged 5.8 yards-per-attempt. The Cowboys selected him with the intention of moving him to wide receiver, yet still planned on giving him a tryout as a back. Until Landry could see these rookies during simulated game-action in training camp, he couldn't be sure of how well they would fit into the Dallas offense. It wasn't in Landry's makeup to open up the starting running back job to three rookies. But circumstances left him no choice.

And, speaking of circumstances… The situation in the Cowboys' backfield became even more alarming when, in late spring, it was reported that 205-pound starting fullback Walt Garrison had undergone knee surgery after sustaining an injury while taking part in a rodeo. According to the medical prognosis, Garrison would not be able to play football until September at the earliest, more likely in October. Now, the Cowboys were not only in need of a halfback, but a fullback besides.

In the nine seasons since being drafted out of Oklahoma State, Garrison had piled up more than 5,500 yards from scrimmage, and scored 39 combined touchdowns rushing and receiving. Garrison's willingness to take on linebackers who were thirty pounds heavier than himself, coupled with his set of soft receiving hands, made him a valuable asset in a Cowboys' offense that loved to use multiple formations as a method of deception. Garrison was officially listed as a fullback, but could also play halfback, and even split out wide as a receiver.

The team wasn't as desperate to fill this hole as the former, though Garrison's injury would certainly hurt their depth at fullback. Even before Garrison was busted by a bronco in the ring, Landry was planning to insert Robert Newhouse into the lineup solely as a fullback, starting in 1975. Newhouse would never be the receiver that Garrison was, but his old-school, tough-as-nails temperament around the line of scrimmage made him an invaluable asset on running downs.

A short, tough runner who moved with the force and low center of gravity comparable to a bowling-ball, Newhouse was an up-and-coming player in the Cowboys' system. He rushed for over 500 yards in 1974 while splitting time at halfback and fullback, but Landry thought he would be even better when settled into one particular position. His short, stocky frame made him an ideal blocker, as Landry could attest to from going over game-film from the previous season.

Newhouse was also a natural at understanding blocking assignments and anticipating where running lanes would open up. The transition from Garrison to Newhouse as the full-time fullback would be smoother than it could have been. Landry knew what Newhouse would provide the Dallas offense. He was a starting-quality player, a fourth-year professional who could be relied upon to carry a load when needed. The performance of the Dallas offense would certainly not suffer with him on the field. Landry only wished he could say the same about any one of the Cowboys' five competing tailbacks.

The month was May, and the Dallas Cowboys were hard at work to shake off the rust, and escape the demons which haunted them from a season ago. The strife, the bickering, the little petty jealousies that had undermined the team's 1974 campaign had officially been swept into the dustbin of history. There was no longer any talk of strikes, of Lame Ducks, or of contract disputes. There was no complaining behind the coaches backs about playing time, or lack thereof. The racial tensions that had permeated the locker room had dissolved as well. At long last, the Cowboys were taking on the shape of a football *team* again.

On the practice field, Drew Pearson ran his pattern perfectly, a normal occurrence for him, caught yet another in a long series of passes from quarterback Roger Staubach and decided it was time for a break. He headed for the bench at the west end of the field and had just sat down when Staubach, channeling the ex-Naval officer within himself, challenged his favorite wide receiver.

"Pearson, what are you doing over there?" demanded the veteran quarterback. "You're not helping yourself or the team sitting on your behind."

Pearson laughed, breathed a sigh of resignation, and returned to the field. Only after catching a dozen more passes did he obtain permission from Staubach for a brief respite.

Nobody was required to show up for this voluntary practice session. But, as Pearson looked around, he could see that every player, with the exception of Bob Lilly (contemplating retirement), and Bob Hayes and Pat Toomay (tiff with Cowboys' management), were present. Lee Roy Jordan was there, as he had been since January, his real estate business distractions from a year ago now a thing of the past. Mel Renfro, the Cowboys' aging 33-year old cornerback, looked fit and trim after a near-fatal car accident in April had resulted in his re-commitment to the game. In just a few short weeks, Renfro had shed 25 pounds and was in as fine a physical shape as at any point during his eleven-year career.

Yes, Pearson was certainly pleased by the turnout, yet not surprised. Enthusiastic participation had been a distinguishing feature of this off-season from the very first weight-lifting sessions back in March. On one day in spring, so many Cowboys' players were practicing that equipment manager Buck Buchanan ran out of towels and Gatorade.

"Everybody is more willing to work now than I've seen since I've been here," he said. "I think everybody is happy as opposed to last year when everybody was worked up about the strike. Last year may have been a blessing in a way. It was no fun sitting around and watching the playoffs on television. It gave everybody new incentive to play football."

During the previous season, Pearson was often an unpopular figure within the Cowboys' locker room because several of his offensive teammates felt that Staubach was playing favorites by throwing in Pearson's direction too much. Staubach, who was dealing with the inconsistencies of newcomer Golden Richards on one hand and the unpredictability of Bob Hayes on the other, didn't deny these accusations, which only caused the discord to linger throughout the season. Staubach wanted results, and throwing downfield to Pearson was his best option.

At 5-11 and 180-pounds, the 24-year old Pearson could not be considered large by professional football standards. Nor was he noted for being strong or fast. How then had he come to be regarded as the team's premier wide-out? "I think there are some receivers who have a natural ability to get open and get to the football," said Staubach, "and Drew is one of those. It's not something he's developed since he got here. You could spot it right away. The thing he has developed is the way he runs his patterns. He's always where he's supposed to be. He works hard at that."

Like many of his veteran teammates, Pearson was motivated to get back to the playoffs. To Pearson, a 1974 All-Pro selection at wide receiver, that would require an uptick in personal performance for the upcoming season. It meant doing the small, mundane things, like running precise pass routes, blocking better on running plays, and making the easy catches.

Pearson enjoyed a breakout year in 1974, his second in the NFL, catching 62 passes for 1,087 yards, tops in the NFC. That Pearson also was the recipient of a game-winning touchdown pass on Thanksgiving Day that beat Washington only enhanced his reputation among fans. Yet, Pearson remained hungry for more, both for the team and as an individual.

Still gnawing at his innards was a play from the Cowboys' earlier meeting with Washington in 1974 at RFK Stadium. Dallas was trailing 28-21 and had the ball on the Redskins' 6-yard line with 2:05 remaining. It was fourth-down-and-goal and Staubach found Pearson alone in the end-zone. Pearson dropped the ball. A few weeks later, the Cowboys were eliminated from playoff contention, which had Pearson looking back to that one play, and wondering what might have been.

"I'd have to say that was the lowest point of my short career," said Pearson of his drop against the Redskins, while refusing to acknowledge the slightly behind pass as an excuse. "But something like that is always good for a ballplayer. It's not that he looks for something like that to happen, but it woke me up. It certainly gave me incentive not to drop any more passes."

If his performance during practice on that warm May afternoon was any indication, then Drew Pearson was well on his way to accomplishing just that. He caught every one of more than one-hundred passes that Roger Staubach threw in his direction, making quarterback and wide receiver happy...and their teammates as well.

While Roger Staubach was busy building chemistry with his wide receivers, his backup was out to build camaraderie with some of the older veterans. Entering his second season with the team, Clint Longley was already an established playmaker within the Cowboys' locker room. Such are the benefits of leading a second-half rally over the Redskins on Thanksgiving Day as a rookie. But Clint was out for more than mere professional acceptance. He wanted to be accepted as a person too. But, as Clint was to find out, this was easier said than done.

Clint was like any 22-year old who spent his teenage years out in Colorado: a free-spirit who liked to have fun. It didn't take very long being around Clint to find out that he liked to have more fun than was normal.

Over the course of the off-season, Clint invited numerous players to go on a hunting expedition with him, but none took him up on his offer. Even Walt Garrison, the team's real-life cowboy who liked to rope and brand steers by the dozen, and would ride the backs of the baddest bucking broncs without being asked twice, consciously fought shy of Clint's outdoor adventures.

The more he asked, the more evasive they became, leaving the young quarterback a bit incredulous at the lack of a turnout. Surely, somewhere in a group of fifty good ol' boys, there was one that would take the plunge. After a few months of trying to plan a trip, Longley decided there wasn't. *And a football locker room was supposed to be made up of tough guys? Why, there wasn't a macho man among them!* Why, if Clint didn't know better, he would tend to think they actually disliked rattlesnakes. But that was impossible! Rattlesnake hunting was as much a part of Texas culture as the Cowboys were. What was there to fear about a rattlesnake?

"Generally, when you mention rattlesnake hunting to most people, the first thing they think of is being bitten and dying," said Longley during the spring of '75. "They don't stop to consider that a rattlesnake is one of the most formidable things you can hunt. A big ol' rattler is the meanest looking thing in the world. Once you get to hunting them it's really exciting. And, shoot, I've never been bitten. Fact is, it would embarrass me to get bit."

As a guest with Clint, getting bit could be a bit more than simply embarrassing, though. Clint, you see, was so confident in the success of his hunting missions that he never even packed a snake-bite kit. "They do more damage than good as far as I'm concerned," he said. "There's no reason for someone who has been bitten to start cutting himself all to pieces. You aren't going to fall dead if one bites you. About the worst thing that can happen would be to have one bite you on a small part of your body, like maybe a finger. The poison can destroy tissue pretty quickly in an area like that. I worry a little about that."

In the event that someone was bitten, Longley's plan was simple. Apply ice to the wound to slow the spread of the poison, and then load-up in the pickup truck and rush to the hospital. No sweat! No worries! The plan was foolproof! Especially since Texas hospitals at the time could be spread apart like water holes in a desert.

But when it became apparent that nobody would ever gamble their lives on a snake hunting trip with him, Clint decided that he might as well bring the action to them. So after raiding a den of rattlers with a friend and expertly bagging several of the outspoken reptiles, he drove out to the Cowboys' practice field on one fine spring day to show off his colorful hunting trophies to his football buddies.

Years later, longtime team trainer Don Cochren recalled the scene when Clint singlehandedly cleared the practice field. "One time during the off-season," recounted Cochren, "he brought two sacks of rattlesnakes that he took and threw them out there on the practice field. It was a little cool, but it was a sunny day."

Cochren, along with several Cowboys players, quickly vacated the premises, leaving Clint alone with his find. Such a cold reception failed to discourage Longley, who stuck around and played baby-sitter even while the day was wasting away.

Said Cochren: "After about an hour, he said he wanted to show me something. I went out there and there were about six rattlesnakes out on that field, with their rattles going, and I told him I had seen all that I wanted to see. He had another guy with him. After they left, (locker room attendant Otis Jackson) got the old lawn mower and mowed across where they had been. He said he wasn't going to take any chances if they forgot one."

Clint never accomplished his goal of finding a hunting partner among his Cowboys' teammates, leaving him as the only player in franchise history to ever stalk a rattler for pure entertainment. And by emptying two sacks of rattlesnakes on the practice field, he also earned an additional distinction by becoming the lone person who brought work to a standstill during a 1975 off-season defined by it.

CHAPTER 7

CALIFORNIA COWBOYS

"I don't think I've ever seen morale better at this time. Usually at this time, guys are saying they wished camp started later. Now, they seem anxious to go there."
- **Gil Brandt, just prior to training camp in 1975**

"When they have scrimmage or contact drills, you can hear the pads popping all the way to the other end of the practice field."
- **Tom Landry**

A noise buzzed loudly in the darkened room. Buck Buchanan awoke with a start. The clock showed 5:30 on a July morning on the campus of California Lutheran College in Thousand Oaks. To the majority of locals whose schedule was highlighted by parties and late-night gatherings, arising at such an unearthly hour was a thought most unfathomable. To a former military man like Buchanan, a day that began before dawn could only be categorized as commonplace.

What could not be described as commonplace was the anticipation that warmed his blood while dressing. The 43-year old equipment manager of the Dallas Cowboys had been to hundreds of athletic functions during his adult life, but none that garnered the excitement of a new season of professional football. Today, in less than four hours, the Cowboys would begin their training camp grind, a six-week period that would leave players, coaches and, yes, even trainers, on the brink of exhaustion. Days would be long, nights noticeably short, and nerves frazzled, more often than not. Nevertheless, Buchanan looked forward to it all with an unquestionable relish that helped to lighten the burden of redundancy ingrained in his work.

Upon donning his clothes, Buchanan downed a hurried breakfast, before making his way to the dressing rooms, which were divided for veterans, rookies, and coaches. Buchanan inspected each room, making sure that every jersey, pair of pants, and helmet was in its proper place. Before exiting the dressing area, he checked to ensure the security of the room. Thieves had proven themselves adept in recent years, making off with several jerseys and helmets. Upon checking, Buchanan was relieved to find that all was as he had left it the night before.

After that, it was down to the practice fields – which were comprised of a baseball field and a football field - where he made a lap or two making sure that they had been properly watered. One practice session for every field for every day. Buchanan's expertise in grooming and maintaining a healthy playing surface, which he developed while tending to and supervising more than 120 acres of Air Force intramural athletic fields during an eight-year period, would be tested over the next six weeks as cleats, sleds, and sliding bodies would cut, scratch and dig up the practice field with daily routine.

The sky in the Conejo Valley was lightening in typical beautiful fashion. Though the sun would not peak above the surrounding bluffs for some time, Buchanan felt confident in anticipating another picture-perfect afternoon. This was Buchanan's second trip with the Cowboys to Thousand Oaks, and he was beginning to understand why General Manager Tex

Schramm had insisted on the team training there every summer since 1963. Temperatures in Thousand Oaks were consistently ten degrees cooler than in most cities in southern California. It was weather like this that made the long stay away from home and family well worth it, and, not to mention, aided him in keeping the practice fields in tip-top shape.

At around 7am, Buchanan made his way back to the dressing rooms, where he attended to the needs of the incoming players, who were there to get taped-up for practice. Experience had taught Buchanan to be prepared for virtually any desire the fickle athlete may have, from different colored shoelaces, varied cleat selections, different-styled shoulder pads, helmet pads, and so forth. This was often a long, tedious process, since Buchanan had to take care of both the early-comers and the stragglers.

At 9:15, a group of five workers from the College took to the baseball field and begin setting flags, yard-line markers, rope-runs and blocking dummies in the pre-determined order Buchanan had previously instructed them. A few minutes later, Buchanan walked onto the practice field to make a last-minute inspection and make certain that the arrangements were satisfactory.

By the time Buchanan finished mentally checking off every item on the list, Tom Landry had made his way onto the practice field, clinging to a piece of notepaper in his hand. Wearing a pair of peculiarly short shorts and a jacket emblazoned with team colors, Landry walked toward a group of assembled players and broke the respectful silence that greeted his presence by blowing a whistle that hung around his neck.

After a brief speech from the head coach, players were formed in several groups before another shriek pierced the air, signaling the beginning of a light jogging period. This was it. Training camp had begun. The 1975 Dallas Cowboys were off and running to a time characterized by the miraculous, and a place beloved for dreams come true.

With his roster set for a quick overhaul in 1975, Tom Landry made a few alterations to the Cowboys' training camp schedule. Rather than have the entire team show up in customary fashion in the middle of the month, Landry decided to make sure the rookies got off to a fast start by bringing them to Southern California nearly two weeks before the veterans were set to report on July 20. This would, in turn, give the head coach a chance to work with certain of his rookies in one-on-one teaching sessions.

Spirits were high on the morning of Tuesday, July 8 as Landry and his staff boarded an airliner with 85 rookies and seven selected veterans bound for suburban Los Angeles. Not only was a new season just around the corner for the Cowboys, but it appeared that every vital piece to the puzzle would be there to participate. Less than 48 hours before, Gil Brandt had finally come to terms with Howard Slusher and Randy White on a contract believed to be in the neighborhood of $300,000. The team also agreed to terms with No. 5 draft pick Kyle Davis, the center out of Oklahoma. Both White and Davis, along with Burton Lawless, would arrive in camp at the same time as the veterans, having obligations to participate in the annual College All-Star Game before putting on a Cowboys' uniform for the first time.

The pair of agreements left Bob Breunig as the only rookie still unsigned. Before heading out to training camp, Gil Brandt took one last parting shot at Breunig's agent (Howard Slusher) when he said of the rookie linebacker: "He'll either be signed or traded in the next day or so." Brandt never sounded more serious in his life.

Another serious item of business was that which awaited the rookies on their first full day at camp. According to the team's official daily schedule, Wednesday's lone workout was comprised of a "light jogging" session. What was deemed light by trainers was regarded as infamous by Cowboys' veterans, who warned the youngsters before their trip out west of the devilishly brutal demands that the Landry Mile could place upon even the youngest of legs.

Tom Landry, that brilliant football scientist who fell asleep each night to the symphonic tune of the perfectly-executed play, had a foundational premise that he tested each summer. Unlike the majority of head coaches at the time, Landry was of the belief that each player should report to camp in optimum playing condition. His measure to test each player's stamina was the Landry Mile, a one-mile off-road sprint over hills and through gullies that was further intensified by a strict six-minute time limit. To fail the test as a rookie would be to enter Landry's doghouse, a dark sanctum dedicated to the rehabilitation of the over-weight, under-motivated athlete, and a time-honored step toward the pitfalls of unemployment.

Not only was the Landry Mile a conditioning test, it also helped to trim the fat off the bottom of the roster. Back in the early 1960's, when times were lean, a prospective lineman reported to run the Landry Mile. After huffing through the first quarter, the guy abruptly turned, cut across the field and disappeared over the horizon, never to be seen again.

But, outside of seventeenth-round draft choice Jim Testerman, a basketball player from Dayton who packed his bags and took out after only a few hours in camp, there were no quitters in this bunch of rookies. The Landry Mile was completed with promptitude on Wednesday, and practices began in earnest on the following morning.

Due to the very nature of training camp, when work and sweat often intermixed with blood and tears, lasting memories of practices often consist of outlandish happenings that break up the monotony of two-a-days, while providing a good laugh or two. Having made their summer home in a community of hippies and free spirits, the Cowboys were often blessed with more than their fair share of the unexpected.

One time at a rookies practice, a brightly-colored van materialized out of a cloud of dust. With music blaring from his tape deck, a young man drove the vehicle down the mountain and onto the football field. Upon parking, he opened up the back of his van, produced a lawn chair and sat down. Upon inquiry, he informed a team staff member that Tom Landry was welcome to come into his van at anytime in order to get out of the sun. Landry could also feel free to change the tape and play anything, just so long as he was careful and didn't damage the equipment.

The man was there, so he said, to help Dallas win the Super Bowl, though he seemed crestfallen when he learned that he couldn't drive the van out for any passes. Just when the story was starting to get interesting, the police showed up and played the spoiler, claiming him for an escapee from a local mental institution.

Once, kicking coach Ben Agajanian was working with the kickers, when a conspicuously dressed guy walked out of the stands and onto the field in middle of the work area. He wore green cut-offs, brightly-colored plaid socks, a YMCA tee-shirt and army boots. He announced that he was prepared to leave wife and family and kick for the Dallas Cowboys... just so long as the price was right, of course. Coaches were not impressed by his offer. It took only a few moments for club officials to run him off.

But there was no need for outside sources to make a lasting impression concerning the Cowboys' 1975 training camp. An eager bunch of rookies was there to accomplish all of that. Starting with the very first practice on a sun-drenched Thursday morning, Cowboys' players made each session a lively one by showing a willingness and a dedication to hitting. And hitting hard. Whether it was tackling a ball-carrier, flattening a receiver over the middle, or taking on a blocker at the line of scrimmage, defenders drew a chorus of oohs and ahhhs from teammates, on-looking fans, and even a few coaches. The offense had little choice but to start dealing out some punishment of their own, making for some of the most intense practice sessions that Landry and his staff had ever witnessed.

One of the most impressive hitters early in camp was rookie guard Herbert Scott, who kept Buck Buchanan busy almost daily in repairing his helmet before practice. Scott head-butted so many defenders and crashed into so many piles that Buchanan was constantly seen back in the dressing room putting a new logo on the side of Scott's helmet. "I had never changed so many stars before for any one player," recalled Buchanan.

The only thing, it turned out, that could sap the team's enthusiasm was an unexpected heat wave that settled over the valley, bringing Saturday's practice to a sudden halt. Consistent temperatures in the upper 80s led to several players being taken to the hospital, and resulted in Landry calling for the first water break in the thirteen years the team had been practicing at Thousand Oaks.

Another rookie to make some early-July headlines was Percy Howard, a rookie wide receiver from Austin Peay, a tiny college in Clarksville, Tennessee. The Dallas coaching staff was quietly confident of Howard's ability, and for obvious reasons. In a controlled scrimmage with the San Diego Chargers, the 6-4, 207-pound former basketball player caught four passes for 79 yards and two touchdowns. Howard's only football experience before joining the Cowboys was as a senior in high school, when he was an All-State honoree, catching 13 touchdowns as a wide receiver and notching nine interceptions as a safety.

Said assistant coach Dan Reeves of Howard: "He's such a big target. He can make any quarterback look good. He can catch it anywhere and I don't think he knows fear." An impressive athlete who boasted excellent speed and a 40-inch vertical jump in college, Howard fielded offers from four professional basketball teams and a trio of NFL teams. But when Cowboys' player/scout Cornell Green, a former basketball player himself, turned up at Howard's front door, Percy knew he had found the right club.

"I wanted to play football as a child," Howard related. "And in adolescence I idolized Bob Hayes. I saw him play a few times at Florida A&M and then he became the World's Fastest Human. When Dallas signed him, right away I started liking the Cowboys. When they made me an offer I jumped at it."

"Bird," as Howard was referred to by teammates due to his excellent jumping ability, was the talk of the town at the wide receiver position during that first week of practice. But that all changed a few days later when the Cowboys said goodbye to a world-class legend, and Howard waved a distant farewell to his childhood hero.

CHAPTER 8

THE FAREWELL TOUR

"Bob Lilly invented defensive tackle."
- **Bob St. John, Dallas Morning News Columnist**

The first full week of practices now behind them, Cowboys' players began thinking ahead toward the weekend, and a controlled team scrimmage. Weary of blocking and tackling the same people day in and day out, an afternoon of keeping score would be a welcome reprieve for every player in camp, while also giving the coaching staff a chance to grade the team in numerous in-game situations.

But before this anticipated meeting on the field could take place, a meeting of the minds between respective front-offices culminated in a trade that sent Cowboys' legendary wide receiver Bob Hayes to San Francisco for an undisclosed draft-pick. All of the millions of people who had watched Hayes' career over the past decade realized that this was one of those stop-the-presses kind of announcements, a farewell worth pondering. For in Bob Hayes, there had always been something of the superhuman that held his audience captivated in awe.

Hayes' distinctive attribute as an athlete was a speed so revolutionary as to transcend the age of stopwatches, making numbers and times unwarranted, often unnecessary. Whether in a cow pasture or on a world-class stage, Hayes was faster than the rest of the participants, a fact easily evident to, and appreciated by, the naked eye. A runner whose fluidity remained in stark contrast to the ethereal nature that his speed implicated, Hayes rode the wings of the wind to stardom in two distinct athletic arenas, using a pigeon-toed, elbows-out style to become an unquestioned world phenomenon.

Hayes set a world-record as a 20-year old amateur, covering 100 yards in 9.1 seconds, a mark that stood for eleven years. He outran the world's fastest at the 1964 Tokyo Olympics, earning the United States a gold medal in the 4-x-100 meters by turning a two-meter deficit into a runaway victory in the final leg. As icing on the cake for time well spent in Japan, it was later revealed that his margin of victory (seven-feet) in the 100 meters set a new Olympic record.

The former college fullback at Florida A&M joined the Dallas Cowboys in 1965 as a wide receiver and became a nightmare for every defensive back in the league, using his top-range speed to run past them and into the end-zone. Hayes averaged 46 receptions and 9 touchdowns over his first seven seasons with the Cowboys, and was a starter on their Super Bowl championship team of 1971. Along the way, his game-changing speed forced an alteration in the defensive secondary, as opposing coaches started using zone coverages instead of the traditional man-to-man that Hayes regularly shredded. This change in strategy ultimately led to Hayes' demise in Dallas, as defenses started taking away the deep passes. "The zones took away the greatest asset he had, his speed," noted Tom Landry. "When he was having his greatest years, he was going against a man-to-man. When the zones came in and we went more to a running attack he just didn't do as well as somebody else, and so he was on the second team."

Departures during the early summer months were not uncommon for a club, especially for a team in transition like the Cowboys in 1975. It had been only a few days since a trio of linemen (Scott Hewitt, George Thomasek, and Craig Shuette) voluntarily quit the team. Before that, there was news that the

Cowboys allowed Pat Toomay to sign with the Buffalo Bills in exchange for a 2nd-round pick in the 1977 college draft.

But something of this magnitude was sobering for veterans and rookies alike, though certainly not altogether unexpected. A certified legend among local fans and well respected by many of the veterans in the locker room, it was no secret that Bob Hayes had been wanting out of Dallas for some time. He had openly balked at the notion that either Lance Alworth or Drew Pearson was more qualified than he to anchor the Cowboys' No. 1 receiver position, and became embittered when the rise of young Golden Richards forced him to ride the bench for the 1974 season.

Hayes then followed up the worst season of his career by joining the Players' Association's collaboration against the Rozelle Rule and testifying against the Cowboys before a grand jury the following winter. Even after his testimony was reduced to shreds under cross-examination, Hayes still pointed fingers at Landry, the offensive coaching staff, and certain teammates as the cause for his downfall.

The word that he sent through his agent, Henry Margulls, at the beginning of camp stating that Hayes had no intentions of ever suiting up for the Cowboys again was of little or no consequence to the front-office. Tex Schramm had been seeking out a trade partner for Hayes for several months, all the while knowing that "Bullet" Bob had played his last game in a Dallas uniform. As in the case of Toomay, Hayes' value as a player had become far outweighed by an outspoken nature that poisoned and divided the locker room. The time had come for Hayes to ship out.

One of the first selections that Gil Brandt's famous Draft Computer ever made in 1964, Hayes departed from the club owning the franchise record in touchdowns (71), yards receiving (7,295), average yards per catch (20.0), and average yards per punt return (11.1). While Landry displayed genuine disappointment, and even a tinge of sadness, at the turn of events, Hayes' most pertinent rival in the clubhouse expressed something akin to relief that Hayes' shadow had left for good.

"I simply beat out Bobby Hayes and he could never accept this," said Golden Richards. "Had he stayed this season with the club, I don't think the battle for split end would have been that close.

"I worked hard during the off-season. For a long time, I worked out twice a day. I only saw Bobby twice at the practice field during off-season. This seems to me to be unusual for a guy at this stage of his career.

"I heard and read some of the things that were said. He said I was too little to last a season, things like that. But he never said any of those things directly to me. Some of what was said bothered me. But I think last season here his presence was a definite motivation for me. I thought coming here last year I had a chance to beat him out because he was mostly a deep pattern runner. The football field is more than that."

The rivalry between Hayes and Richards actually started back in the spring of 1974, when the two squared off at a meet sanctioned by the short-lived International Track Association. Richards, at the time, was gearing up for that summer's training camp, where he aimed to dethrone Hayes from his long-standing position as a starter. These "King of The Hill" races would provide Richards with his first chance to serve notice to Hayes that his job was in jeopardy.

The duo ran a pair of closely contested heats, with speeds being regularly timed in the 4.4 range. During one particular race, Golden said he actually won, and that a judge had told him he had won. That's where Golden's luck ran out and into the legend of the World's Fastest Man. "They said they'd go ahead and pay me first place money but wanted Hayes to be the winner," recounted Richards. "He had the big name, the drawing card. That's the last time I ever ran for the ITA."

With Hayes now in San Francisco, the duties for split-end with the Cowboys fell squarely on the shoulders of Richards, while also creating an opening at the No. 3 receiver position that was there for the taking. Would Percy Howard continue his strong play early in camp and claim it? Could tiny free agent Lee McGriff climb the depth chart and make the final roster? Or would it be some other little-known name out of left field to shock the football world?

With these thoughts in mind, the Cowboys looked to an exciting few weeks ahead when the final pieces of their 1975 roster would be selected, while also taking time to pause and reflect upon an honorable career that will be forever unique. Bob Hayes had run his last route and scored his last touchdown with the Dallas Cowboys, making for the first of a pair of monumental farewells over the weekend that would sadden the franchise and signal the end of an era, and the turning of a page.

Said Richards: "Bobby's gone. I wish him well. We all do. But the Bobby Hayes Era is over here."

On Saturday night, just hours after the news of Hayes hit the presses, Bob Lilly dialed Tex Schramm's phone number. Three months had passed since Lilly's letter of retirement had been returned to him by Tom Landry, with the encouragement to give his decision some more thought. Now, with the veterans set to report to training camp in California, Lilly was calling from his home in Texas to let Schramm know that he was officially calling it quits after 14 years along the Dallas defensive line.

There was no talking him out of it this time. As part of his re-thinking process during the off-season, Lilly had sought a second opinion on his surgically-repaired neck and been informed that further injury could result in paralysis, making the choice of whether or not to retire an easy one.

And though both Schramm and Landry expressed understanding at the decision, it was apparent that the loss was felt to be far more than just a name on the roster. The Cowboys, in fact, were saying goodbye to a franchise fixture that was every bit of a Texas-sized monument. "I don't know if you can compare anybody to Lilly," Landry had said earlier in the off-season, when a reporter asked him to make a comparison between Lilly and new No. 1 draft pick Randy White. "Lilly is unique in his time."

Lilly was a coach's dream, the uber-talented athlete driven to win on the field, no matter the cost. The franchise's first ever draft pick back in 1961, Lilly transformed himself from a solid defensive end in the standard 4-3 defense to a perennial All-Pro tackle in Landry's Flex scheme, overpowering opponents with an uncommon amount of strength and quickness. It didn't take long for fans at the old Cotton Bowl to take notice of Lilly's work as both an expert pass-rusher and a willing run-stopper, dubbing him the one and only "Mr. Cowboy."

On a line stacked with standouts, Lilly was the humble luminary, doing the dirty work against constant double- and-triple-team blocks that helped others around him to clean up the play with a tackle, or even a sack. During a nine-year stretch from 1964-72, when either George Andrie or Jethro Pugh led the team in sacks, it was Lilly who received the lion's share of the credit at season's end, being named first-team All-NFL eight times. His lone "lapse" in performance came during the 1970 season, when he was named to the All-NFL second-team, while leading a defensive charge that propelled the Cowboys to their first world championship appearance in Super Bowl V.

The uptick in performance that followed his move from end to tackle also gave his voice credibility amongst teammates when trying to explain the complicated concepts of Landry's Flex defense. When Landry first installed the Flex defense in 1963, it became a source of contention for many Cowboys' players, who found its mysterious code of "keys" and "pre-snap reads" to be a stumbling block in a game that required split-second reactions. But with Lilly promoting its benefits both on the field and in the locker room, the young Cowboys thought it prudent to try their luck at this thinking man's version of football, and were not sorry they did. With Lilly anchoring the line and everyone buying into the system around him, the Dallas' defense soon rose to prominence, earning the nickname of "Doomsday."

When not teaching how to make the most of film study during the week, Lilly was busy making the most of every opportunity on the field, fighting through pain and injury on numerous occasions to start all 196 regular season games over fourteen seasons. The only game he missed during his career was the 1973 NFC Championship Game, when the Vikings rolled over the middle of the Dallas defense to a convincing 27-10 victory.

Landry had been hopeful that Lilly, an eleven-time Pro Bowler, would play one more season in 1975, if only to add some depth and experience to the defensive line rotation. At age 36, Lilly no longer had the stamina to be a full-time player, but Landry still would have liked to use him on obvious passing downs. But there was no sense in Lilly playing through pain and injury any longer. Not where paralysis was concerned.

With a simple phone call and a heartfelt wish for future blessings, Lilly joined Hayes on a fast-growing list of the dear departed. Another member of the old guard had kissed the Cowboys goodbye. Not that a retirement was anything akin to a funeral, because it wasn't. The sun would rise in the east yet again on the morrow, bringing with it another unique set of challenges for coaches, for players... for humanity.

With Lilly now gone from the fold the spotlight in the middle fell on Jethro Pugh, a 10-year veteran whose exemplary play had long been overshadowed by Lilly's presence alongside of him. The No. 2 defensive tackle slot would be decided in preseason between Bill Gregory and longtime mainstay Larry Cole, who was set to slide over from his normal position at defensive end.

There would be some naïve person out there, possibly in the media or maybe in the bleachers, who would expect one of this threesome to emerge as Lilly's replacement. But you wouldn't find Tom Landry harboring these expectations. Perhaps more than any other person in football, Landry knew that Bob Lilly was an irreplaceable part of the Dallas Cowboys, and would be loved by fans for as long as he would be missed on the playing field.

Bob Lilly was unique in his time.
Bob Lilly was unique forever.

CHAPTER 9

THE SHOTGUN

"It was a much more instructional camp than we ever had. We went over things so many times." - **Tom Landry speaking of the Cowboys' 1975 training camp**

"Throughout preseason it was a real mental thing with me. I was worrying more about whether the snap had reached Roger all right than I was about blocking the man in front of me." - **Cowboys center John Fitzgerald discussing the adjustment process of snapping the ball in the Shotgun formation**

With the arrival of the veterans to training camp came an entirely different wrinkle at Cowboys' practices. The tenacity remained the same, but the duties of the players were significantly altered. Whereas Tom Landry and his coaching staff had spent the first several days making sure the rookies were accustomed to the more basic concepts of the playbook, he now broke out some bells and whistles that were sure to confuse both the bright-eyes and the grizzle-haired.

Having fiddled with it over the off-season, Landry announced to his team that the time had come to install the fabled Shotgun formation into the Cowboys' offensive playbook. Class was now in session.

It had been over a decade since Cowboys' scout Red Hickey invented the Shotgun as the Head Coach of the San Francisco 49ers. During the days leading up to a meeting with mighty Baltimore, Hickey's brain was smoking while trying to come up with a game-plan that would give his team a chance to outlast Johnny U. and the Colts. That plan became the Shotgun.

In the Shotgun, rather than lining up in the traditional fashion under center, the quarterback backs up about five yards and receives the snap from there. To Hickey's way of thinking, it was a perfect formation to run an assortment of gadget plays from. Reverses. Double reverses. Halfback passes. Throwback passes. The college option. The read-option. He liked them all.

Starting that week in an upset of Baltimore, Hickey's cutting-edge philosophy worked wonders, transforming an under-manned roster into an above-average club. Hickey's offense overwhelmed opposing defenses on multiple fronts. Not only was the varied attack hard to prepare for, but so was their pace. The 49ers rotated quarterbacks on each play, often operating in hurry-up mode.

If Hickey could have kept his quarterbacks healthy, there's no telling how high the 49ers might have risen in the 1960s. But when injuries depleted the depth chart at quarterback early in the 1962 season, Hickey and his baby were finished. The Shotgun was shelved.

A few years later Hickey, riding the unemployment line, signed up as a scout with the Cowboys.

At the time, the Shotgun's demise was viewed as a blessing of sorts, even in a league that liked to think of itself as innovational. Not that anybody in the league office actually hated the Shotgun. They just didn't have the time or the platform to promote its genius and upside. In addition to his luck, Hickey's timing was abominably poor. The NFL was then embroiled in a fierce brand battle with their rivals over in the American Football League. The NFL viewed themselves as a tough league, founded on defense, the Power I, and the dust-inducing three-yard run. The AFL prided themselves on their aerial finesse, which promoted higher scoring, fireworks and a boatload of manufactured excitement.

To NFL owners, style of play was a sacred line in the sand that needed to be revered, if not by all, by the competitive teams at the very least. They were okay with Tom Landry toying with his wide-open passing offense down in Dallas, just so long as the Cowboys only won three or four games every season. And, to be fair, Landry's case was a bit different than the rest. In addition to trying to trade scores with far superior opponents, the Cowboys were trying to win the hearts of locals while sharing the same stadium with the AFL's Texans. So owners could turn a deaf ear on that front.

Nevertheless, to see Hickey's West Coast innovation crumble into the dust of misfortune was especially satisfying to some in power. Tradition and solidarity were best served that way.

More than 12 years later, Landry dusted off the old Shotgun in the hope of providing a powerful Cowboys' offense with a little extra kick.

Back in March at the start of spring practices, Landry asked John Fitzgerald if the sixth-year center could learn how to snap in the Shotgun. Like a good soldier, Fitzgerald readily assured his head coach that he could. To do anything less would have been to invite demotion, or worse. Fitzgerald knew that Landry would install the Shotgun with or without him. With inflation being what it was, holding onto his job seemed to be the best route to take. Especially now that he was a family man.

So, at Landry's suggestion, Fitzgerald spent hours during the off-season hiking the ball back to Roger Staubach and Clint Longley, or any other willing teammate who happened to be available. Coming off elbow and knee operations, it was all that Fitzgerald could do in his rehabilitative state to bend over and push a football through his legs. The process was more painful than it might normally have been, but still Fitzgerald persisted in his newest task.

The snap was the first and most important part of any successful play. In the Shotgun, it might also have been the riskiest. During a game, the center had to keep his head up in order to bark out the blocking signals to his line-mates and fend off the nearest defender, so he had no choice but to hike the ball blindly. This factor was one reason why coaches of that era had yet to develop a taste for the Shotgun. Simply put, it was too risky. A forward-pass from a proven quarterback did enough to raise blood pressure levels on the sidelines. But for a clumsy center to be shoveling the ball backwards...and *blindly*? That was asking too much, and seemed to be every bit of an open-handed invitation to offensive chaos.

Tom Landry took any worry out of the exercise by boiling it down to a simple case of muscle memory. If Arnold Palmer and Jack Nicklaus could bend a 145-yard approach shot around a series of tall pines within ten-feet of an invisible cup, then surely there was hope that a corn-fed lineman could hit a relatively wide target five yards directly behind him. Should the center, in this case Fitzgerald, work long and hard enough at it, he could master the art and perform his duties with confidence in the heat of battle on Sundays. Practice could still make perfect.

While Fitzgerald toiled on the Cowboys' practice field during the spring months, his head coach was busy taking notes. With first-hand advice from the inventor himself, Landry went about assembling the pieces and the philosophy that would make him the father of the modern-day Shotgun. As opposed to Hickey's 49ers that made a living by tricking opponents from it, Landry needed the Shotgun to increase the efficiency rate of his most basic plays.

More ironic, though, was his most foundational reason for approaching Hickey on the matter. No NFL quarterback had been sacked more over the past two seasons than had Roger Staubach. According to Landry, the Shotgun – the very same formation that left multiple 49ers quarterback on the injured list – would be the key ingredient in protecting Roger "The Dodger" in 1975. In bypassing the traditional drop-back from under center, Staubach would be able to see the field better over the mass of heads at the line of scrimmage. With pass-rushers having to run farther to reach the quarterback, Staubach would have up to an extra full second to determine his course of action, whether that would involve a pass or a scramble. The more

Landry thought about it, the more advantages he found for his quarterback.

What Landry needed from Hickey was the lowdown on blocking schemes and different protection-sets with running backs. How did Hickey handle the different pass-rush angles that the new formation invoked? What kind of ordinary running plays worked best from that set? The questions went on and on.

What he had gleaned over an off-season of picking Hickey's brain on the subject, Landry began sharing with his team under a bright California sun. Since Fitzgerald had yet to be cleared by team doctors for full-contact activities, and since Kyle Davis was still practicing with the College All-Stars, Landry started out by spoon-feeding his offense on the formation's basics. Even that took a bit of patient persuading for it to go down.

Staubach's timing with his wide receivers was thrown off by the new formation. Staubach's "landing spot" where he threw from in the backfield was moved back from earlier seasons, necessitating a quicker release…or did it? Should Roger still drop-back so many steps after receiving the snap like in former years, or just sit pat and fire rockets downfield from there? It took some work on the parts of the players and a bit of discussion amongst the coaching staff to arrive at a compromise. Staubach would be allowed to do both, depending on the particular play-call and his own personal comfort.

On a screen pass out of the Shotgun, it was better that Staubach avoid dropping back seven steps before throwing. If, on third-and-9, he had two fifteen-yard out-patterns being run from his outside wide receivers, then falling back on tradition was left up to him. This adjustment seemed to suit both parties, as Staubach was able to work on his chemistry with his wide receivers without having to think too much in the process.

Later, when the Shotgun was finally put to the test against the Cowboys' defense, the offensive line got a strong taste of the different techniques that were required. Now that the quarterback was often farther behind the line of scrimmage than before, the edge pass-rushers were given a more direct path to the quarterback. This seemed to suit speed-rusher Harvey Martin, who made life difficult in the early going for right tackle

Rodney Wallace. Wallace was filling in while longtime veteran Rayfield Wright worked his way back into playing shape after off-season surgery. It took him a while, but Wallace finally developed a quicker first-move to block Martin's path to the quarterback. The learning curve was just as steep for rookie Pat Donovan, who was just acclimating himself to his position after switching over from the defensive line.

All in all, the Shotgun's first days on the practice field went well. Which is a lot more than can be said for its debut in live game-action. The Cowboys opened up a lengthy preseason schedule with a Saturday night bout in Los Angeles, and by falling flat on their faces provided the Dallas coaching staff with a perfect reason to whip out the drawing board and start all over again.

The difference between practice and authentic game action was on full display from start to finish of the Cowboys' preseason opener against the Los Angeles Rams at Memorial Coliseum. The Cowboys, a tough team on the practice field, were whipped around like ragdolls by the Super Bowl-favorite Rams in a 35-7 blowout.

A moment that perfectly capsulated what the entire evening felt like for the Cowboys came in the third period, after the starters had been pulled for both clubs. Upon returning a kickoff, rookie wide receiver Percy Howard ran over to the sideline, his helmet cockeyed on his head, where he approached equipment manager Buck Buchanan.

"Man," Howard said, "it's rough out there, Buck." To which Buchanan replied, "Those are just the rookies."

Howard wasn't the only Cowboy who felt overmatched on that night. The Dallas defense allowed 445 total yards, while the offense fared little better, accumulating just 156. Penalties helped to stall each of the Cowboys' first three possessions. On their fourth drive, rookie Scott Laidlaw juggled a third-and-1 handoff from Roger Staubach that led to a one-yard loss and another punt. Later in the half, with the ball sitting on the Los

Angeles 10-yard line, Staubach's pass for Ron Howard deflected off the hands of Scott Laidlaw and was intercepted. Other than a 35-yard interception return for a touchdown by David Shaw and strong punting by rookie Mitch Hoopes (three punts for a 48-yard average) there were no bright spots for the Cowboys.

"We've got a long way to go" said Tom Landry afterwards. "We could not offense two plays in a row without a mistake. We just had no confidence we could run an offense.

"Actually, we didn't have that much trouble running the ball on the few plays we executed…when everyone went the right direction. But then something would happen. We are just going to have to cut down and get more concentration. Even the young players aren't getting enough repetition because we have so many people.

"…I didn't see any of that hitting and popping we've had in camp. It's going to take us all summer to work this out. But if we keep working hard enough, we'll be a pretty good team by September."

The practice fields at Thousand Oaks were deserted the following day, as players were given a chance to rest their bruised bodies. The meeting rooms, however, remained busy throughout the afternoon, while Landry went back to the blackboard to re-instill to his young team the fundamentals that would help to avoid disasters like the day before.

CHAPTER 10

MAKING THE CUT

"I disliked Landry's football system because it is for disciplined players, and I was not a disciplined player." - **Thomas Henderson**

"Hitting somebody hard is a matter of confidence. Confidence has improved for me." - **Cowboys rookie Randy Hughes during the latter stages of training camp**

The preseason rolled on, and so did the losing. After packing up and folding their tents in Thousand Oaks, the Cowboys took a charter flight to Kansas City for a nationally-televised tilt with the Chiefs, where a late touchdown bomb delivered them back to family and friends in Dallas as 26-20 short-comers. Five days later at Texas Stadium, a poor tackling exhibition by the defense led to another defeat, this time a 16-13 affair to Minnesota.

A clubhouse filled with young faces had watched its confidence get shaken, frustration mounting from the lack of returns on their laborious mid-week investments. Back on the practice field in Dallas, the situation remained very much the same as it had been in California. In the midst of emphasizing and re-emphasizing the fundamentals and maddeningly tiny details, Tom Landry was still experimenting with his players at different positions.

At linebacker, Landry remained intrigued by a logjam of potential toward the bottom of the depth chart. His three starters (D.D. Lewis, Lee Roy Jordan, and Dave Edwards) had been penciled in since the start of training camp. Behind them was a cast of blue-chip youngsters that Landry had yet to find the perfect spot for.

Randy White arrived at camp in early August with expectations riding his 250-pound frame like an Army backpack. Perhaps it weighed him down just a bit. Before White's first practice with the rest of the team, he was tested in the Landry Mile. He flunked. Landry frowned.

The team's No. 1 draft pick, White was supposed to make the transition from college lineman to All-Pro middle linebacker look like a cakewalk. White's physical attributes certainly made him an ideal fit for the position. But somewhere above his shoulders there could be sensed a disconnect. Though certainly not a half-stepper in the traditional sense of the term, White could constantly be found a half-step behind the play in practice, providing Landry with food for thought at night.

Additional uncertainty surrounding the positioning of fellow rookies Bob Breunig and Thomas Henderson compelled Landry to start an experimental game of musical chairs, where every linebacker would be exposed to all three spots at different times in practice. In the event that the head coach saw what he liked, his horn would blow, the music would stop, and everyone be frozen in position.

So the fun began. Henderson, who dubbed himself "Hollywood" shortly after arriving at Thousand Oaks, showcased his athletic skills when working in the middle, his track-star speed allowing him to chase-down runners on stretch plays and sweeps to the outside. But he struggled with some of the complicated keys of the Flex defense, and was often unsure of his assignments.

Henderson looked more of a natural fit as a weak-side linebacker, which was to be expected after having played his senior season at Langston as one. But Landry wondered if leaving him there wouldn't be doing a long-term disservice to the rookie. Henderson was one of those impressionable specially-talented rookies who had familiarized himself with a collegiate product that could offer no one better than himself. Henderson was used to being the best player on the football field, and didn't always accept the advice of his coaches. He claimed the Flex was too complicated, and far too inclined to thought than action. His idea of football was hauling off and sacking the quarterback, like he did to Roger Staubach on the veterans' first day in camp, much to the chagrin of his coaching staff.

"At Langston I had no pass coverage techniques to remember," Henderson said in late July. "Here I have pass coverages and different defenses and techniques. Like I might have to remember four or five different things to do on a certain running play, and at Langston it was just go…go get him."

Early in camp, Dave Edwards struck up a friendship with the impetuous linebacker. Edwards had impressed Henderson by sharing a few tidbits from his vault of knowledge accumulated over more than a decade of playing the strong-side linebacker position. Though never having attained the status of a perennial All-Pro, Edwards was revered by many players around the league for his flawless technique around the line of scrimmage, even though the joke at training camp was that he was too old to remember where to line up. It seems that on one occasion Edwards and D.D. Lewis accidentally switched jerseys at practice, causing some confusion among coaches and players.

Even while playing in a funky defensive alignment that cluttered the television screen with its array of staggered and off-set linemen, Edwards and his No. 52 jersey were hard to miss on the field. Often when covering a tight end, Edwards would line-up directly across from the offensive player, almost hovering over him, with hands raised chest-high ready to do battle with his foe as soon as the play began. Edwards' strength enabled him to maintain leverage on running plays, and proper footwork and uncanny anticipation helped the 36-year old crackerjack linebacker keep up in pass-coverage.

Seeing that Edwards had the respect of Henderson made it easier for Landry to leave his rookie at the strong-side position early in camp. The daily tutoring, Landry felt, would do

Henderson far more good than an abundance of playing time on the other side. Edwards had the wisdom to make Henderson into far more than just an athletically-gifted linebacker. He could make him into a football player.

"He still has the great physical ability, but he's right in the middle of some super competition at linebacker," said Landry of Henderson in the middle of training camp. "We knew he was somewhat of a gamble, but if we drafted again right now I'd take him in the same place."

Randy White's experiment at weak-side linebacker went about as well as his stint in the middle. Too often, he just looked misplaced. He did show some promise in certain defensive alignments as a strong-side linebacker. But even then, Landry remained uncertain as to what role White would play when the regular season began in late September.

Bob Breunig's tryout in the middle of the Flex was the most impressive of all, convincing the coaching staff to pencil him in as the No. 2 middle linebacker behind Lee Roy Jordan. For the first time since he arrived with the team in early spring, Breunig played with the same confidence that he had shown at Arizona State, with an especial knack for stopping inside runs.

Landry's mid-August game of tryouts proved beneficial to the team. He found a middle linebacker in Breunig that he could hang his hat on. As for the future of White and Henderson? Well, time would tell.

The mood around the locker room lightened in wake of a nip-and-tuck victory over the Houston Oilers. At last, the Cowboys had won a game in 1975!

Amidst a general feeling of relief, Tom Landry remained as dissatisfied as ever. There were only two preseason games remaining, and Landry had yet to see a No. 1 running back emerge from the pack. Evidently, the head coach wasn't the only one who had noticed.

While alarm was the signature emotion among Dallas fans, others found the Cowboys' shaky running back situation to be a yellow brick road of opportunity and good fortune. The lack of proven depth in the Dallas backfield had some players mailing their resume into the Cowboys' office. Even those whom you would least expect.

This letter from a Purdue Boilermaker running back to Tex Schramm appeared in an August edition of the *Dallas Cowboys Weekly*:

Dear Tex,

The reason I am writing is because I am a college player who one day hopes to play for the highly prestigious and well-balanced Dallas Cowboys.

First of all, I think I come well qualified. I am a running back for Purdue Boilermakers. I stand 6'1" weigh 212 pounds and can turn 40 yards in 4.4 seconds. I am a good receiver as well as blocker, but most of all I am a winner. I never view myself as a loser and I never settle for second-best at anything.

Well, Tex, these are my views. Tell Tom Landry I wish him well for the coming season.

Sincerely yours, Mike Pruitt

Long before the law book for player tampering became a tedious novel, it was deemed fit, proper, and courteous for Schramm to pen this response:

Dear Mike,

We hear you loud and clear, and would like nothing better than to see you pull on a Cowboy jersey next season. We'll be watching and waiting.

Regards, Tex

Finding a productive running back via trade - without over-paying for him - was nearly impossible in those days. And it wasn't as if Landry had a lot of familiar faces to turn to at this juncture.

Thirty-four-year-old Walt Garrison announced his retirement from professional football in mid-August. Landry had already anticipated starting the season while his longtime veteran healed from off-season surgery. Now he wouldn't be getting Garrison back at all.

And those praying for a return flight to Dallas for Calvin Hill, in the event that the World Football League should finally run out of cash, were victims of misplaced hopes. During an early-season game with the Hawaiians, the former Cowboys' runner was cut down and fallen on by a host of Southern California Sun defensemen, leaving him with a complete tear of his medial collateral ligament and a tear of the posterior capsule in his knee joint. In layman's terms, Hill blew his knee out. Doctors were positive that Calvin would be able to play football again, but not any time before the following summer.

Were the Cowboys desperate enough to reach out to Duane Thomas? It had been three years since Thomas' defiant insubordination had led to his release from the Cowboys. Surely he had turned over a new leaf by now!

Thomas had recently found his way onto the free-agent market when the Washington Redskins severed all ties with the sixth-year tailback, effectively washing their hands of the pair of high draft picks they had used to acquire Thomas. After two years of being a backup to Larry Brown with the Redskins, Thomas had demanded a salary befitting a starter. Redskins' management balked. And when Thomas then tried to play hardball, George Allen grabbed a bat and swatted the former West Texas State star out onto the streets.

Not to be outdone by any misinterpretation of his exit by a prejudiced media contingent, Thomas called a press conference of his own where he announced that all of his troubles were behind him. Furthermore, he was adamant of his desire to get back into pro football, preferably with Washington, but most certainly with any team that wanted him.

"People out of work say and do the darndest things," observed Frank Luksa of the *Dallas Times-Herald*.

The Cowboys' silence on this topic was deafening.

The rumors that persisted throughout the better part of the exhibition schedule, linking Dallas as possible trade-partners with Miami for Mercury Morris, were finally put to rest when Landry signed off on a deal that brought Denver's veteran running back Bob Anderson to the Cowboys. With his bags barely unpacked, Anderson then jumped in a Dallas uniform and injured his knee during the final preseason contest versus Pittsburgh. Landry did the only thing he could have done. He cut him, and headed toward the regular season with the determination to make the most out of the cards he was holding.

The farewell tour continued into the month of September, where Cornell Green announced his retirement with his blessing to incumbent strong safety Charlie Waters. Green had seen his share of football suns over a 14-year career, but didn't want to be the cause for a good player being sent packing during final cutdowns. It was as classy a gesture as you will find in professional sports, and one well appreciated by the Cowboys' front-office.

In an attempt to keep costs to a minimum, owners had voted for a reduction in roster sizes for the 1975 season, going from 47 players the year before all the way down to 43. The Cowboys, like many other teams, found themselves in a bind as the cutoff date neared. Who to keep? Who to show the door?

Green's retirement paved the way for the aforementioned Waters to ascend into a starting role. It also cleared a reserve safety spot for rookie Randy Hughes. Having fought through a wave of homesickness and "dead legs" early in camp, Hughes turned a corner in August and became known as one of the team's hardest hitters. Hughes wasn't shabby in coverage either, as his pair of preseason interceptions against Minnesota and Oakland attest to.

Another opening came about for the team's second-round draft pick out of Florida. In what many deemed to be the surprise of the summer, the Cowboys traded veteran John Niland to Philadelphia for a high draft choice, and awarded the starting left guard job to Burton Lawless. Even in limited action during the exhibition campaign, Lawless managed to stand out from the pack with his athleticism, being often seen lumbering downfield with the ball-carrier seeking to make an extra block.

The surprises didn't end there. When the smoke cleared from final cuts after a 17-16 preseason-ending victory over Pittsburgh, twelve rookies in all had made the team, a franchise record. They all grew beards, and began to call themselves the "Dirty Dozen." It wasn't long before these twelve enthusiastic, unproven young men began to procure recognition from an awe-inspired public, as they helped the Cowboys navigate their way through a long, winding, and dramatic season whose rainbow was ever bright with promise.

The Dallas Cowboys 1975 Rookie Class

Player	Position	Rd - Pick	College
Randy White	LB/DL	1 - 2	Maryland
Thomas Henderson	LB	1 - 18	Langston
Burton Lawless	G	2 - 44	Florida
Bob Breunig	LB	3 - 70	Arizona St.
Pat Donovan	T	4 - 90	Stanford
Randy Hughes	S	4 - 96	Oklahoma
Kyle Davis	C/LS	5 - 113	Oklahoma
Roland Woolsey	CB	6 - 148	Boise State
Mitch Hoopes	P	8 - 200	Arizona St.
Herbert Scott	G	13 - 330	Virginia Union
Scott Laidlaw	RB	14 - 356	Stanford
Percy Howard	WR	FA	Austin Peay

CHAPTER 11

A SPARKLING BEGINNING

"The Doomsday defense is alive and well!" - **Safety Charlie Waters in the postgame locker room after the Cowboys' season-opening thrashing of Los Angeles**

"We had a great pass rush and coverage but Roger ran and reacted well. It makes me think they respect our defense a lot to use that rinky-dink Shotgun so much."
- **Rams linebacker Isiah Robertson bemoaning a long afternoon against the newest wrinkle in the Dallas offense**

When the NFL regular season schedules were released prior to training camps, it would have been understandable had Tex Schramm afforded himself a grin behind closed doors. Yes, the Cowboys were in midst of a "rebuilding" operation and, yes, the schedule was an inordinately tough one, but the shrewd mind of Schramm would have been quick to perceive a slight advantage from the lineup of the games.

Thanks to the NFL's revered scheduling rulebook, Schramm could accurately project the substance of their 1975 campaign as soon as the previous season had concluded. In addition to the Cowboys' home-and-away battles with division rivals, Schramm could look forward to a rare road trip to New England for a tussle with the Patriots, a battle in Irving against the Kansas City Chiefs, a trip to the Motor City to face the Lions, and several others as well. What he could not foresee was the order in which the games would be scheduled, a summer revelation that likely left the Cowboys' General Manager slightly more optimistic about getting off to a fast start to the season.

Like any other club, the Cowboys preferred to play their toughest opponents in the confines of their own stadium. But to take full advantage of the late-summer Texas heat, they needed a high-stakes showdown with a top team on opening day.

And that's exactly what they received from the office of NFL Commissioner Pete Rozelle, when it was announced that the Cowboys would host the mighty Los Angeles Rams at Texas Stadium on September 21 to open the season. It was a small, unheralded victory for Dallas, but one that could prove to be crucial.

Since their move from the Cotton Bowl to suburban Irving in the fall of '71, Dallas had hosted only one season-opening game, an afternoon spent with the Philadelphia Eagles the following summer that provided the Cowboys all the information they needed as to how strong a home-field advantage they possessed during the season's first leg. Philadelphia started fast that day, parlaying two Tom Dempsey field goals into a 6-0 second quarter advantage. That's when the Eagles hit a wall that only a combination of mental preparation and proper physical conditioning could break through, of which the Eagles had none.

With temperatures in the low-80's, and the relative humidity at eighty-percent, the sleek and stylish Texas Stadium – complete with a quaint hole in the roof that only amplified the temperature down on the field - quickly turned into a Texas-sized dutch oven that sapped the strength and willpower from the visiting team. Standing on a sideline drenched in hot sunlight and going full throttle on every play to try and upset the defending world champions, while starters were trying to play a full game for the first time in nine months, meant it was only a matter of time before the Eagles succumbed to the conditions. And succumb they surely did.

With a defense suffering from fatigue and exhaustion by the early stages of the third period, the Eagles were unable to stop a strong Dallas running attack that used four different backs to pile up 154 rushing yards and two touchdowns, as the Cowboys turned an early deficit into a 28-6 victory.

What a little sun, sweat and humidity did to the Eagles then could also happen to an equally un-acclimated Rams' squad. Dallas weather was not Los Angeles weather. And Texas Stadium was certainly not to be confused with the Coliseum. This much the Cowboys knew. Not that anybody outside of Dallas gave it too much thought. If their tussle in Los Angeles during early August was any indicator, the Cowboys had little chance of pulling off the upset against an NFC powerhouse such as the Rams. No matter which way you looked at the matchup, and no matter Dallas' streak of ten consecutive victories in NFL openers, the Rams were the far superior team. Such was the harsh reality of the moment.

Cowboys' executives could only hope that six weeks of progression and a heavy dose of Texas heat would level the playing field and allow Dallas a chance at accomplishing what many deemed to be impossible.

The moment Mitch Hoopes took off running with the football, he was scared. Scared of getting tackled, scared of failing, and scared of the look Tom Landry would give him after the play.

This was not the dull life of an NFL punter that the rookie had expected when he graduated from Arizona State. Instead of kicking a ball from a pre-determined spot behind the line of scrimmage and watching it sail off into the sky, Hoopes found himself putting all the strength he could muster into his gangly legs which were lumbering across the Texas Stadium turf with a host of Rams' defenders closing in for the kill. An All-State halfback in high school, Hoopes had no concerns about holding onto the football in this situation. This wasn't to be the first time he had ever been tackled. He just didn't know if his 4.8 speed could get him to the line to gain before he was slammed down to the artificial surface. But get there he must, for the preservation of life, limb, and employment.

Coming in the second quarter of a scoreless tie on opening day, this wasn't a do-or-die moment for the Dallas Cowboys, though it might have served as one on a personal front for the ball-carrier. Mistakes were not tolerated on Tom Landry's football team, especially from rookies making their NFL debut. The pressure of wearing a starred helmet was a tangible thing that even Hoopes had felt during the few months he had been with the team. "It doesn't take much to get cut around here," he admitted.

Hoopes had avoided being cut thus far by turning in a fine preseason of work with his kicking foot that convinced Landry to release veteran Duane Carrell at the conclusion of the exhibition schedule. Carrell, as it turned out, was promptly scooped up by the Rams, so was on the sidelines watching while his former teammate seemed to be doing his best to draw the ire of the Dallas head coach.

Upon receiving the snap from center, Hoopes had seen a Los Angeles defender break through the middle of the line, and quickly decided to forego the kick and run for yardage. In such a quick manner had the play developed that ample time was not afforded him to question the soundness of his judgment. All he knew now was that his feet were running, and probably much faster than anyone on the Dallas sideline thought they could.

Needing thirteen yards, Hoopes raced down the left sideline, thanking his lucky stars that the yardstick was on the same side of the field, till a Rams' player started dragging him to the ground. With one final effort, he then lunged forward while reaching the ball out in front of his body. The result was a Cowboys' first-down by inches and one relieved punter lying on his backside. Whether he had made a mistake in pulling the punt down and running with it would be decided the next day by the coaching staff. For now, though, Hoopes was elated that he was able to turn a potentially disastrous play into a good one.

Hoopes even received a "way to go" from Landry when he got back to the sideline. "He usually isn't that way," Hoopes noted afterwards. Landry's was an unusual response to an unusual happening. The first of many unforeseen events which would come to define this late September afternoon in Irving, Texas.

Thanks to the efforts of their wide-eyed rookie punter, the Cowboys were able to post their first score of the new season a few plays later, when Toni Fritsch booted a 25-yard field goal through the uprights for a 3-0 lead. The successful kick was especially satisfying for Fritsch, the unfortunate author of a 32-yard shank earlier in the opening quarter.

Obtaining an early lead also proved to be a calming influence on Roger Staubach, who spent a very busy afternoon in the Cowboys' backfield. The Dallas offense was moving the ball well in the early going, but that didn't mean everything was functioning as planned.

Though Landry was staying persistent with handoffs to Robert Newhouse and Doug Dennison, it still wasn't enough to assuage the pass-rush of the Rams' mighty front four, all of whom took turns running laps around Burton Lawless. Lawless' chief adversary for much of the game was All-Pro defensive tackle Larry Brooks, a pass-rush artist who got the better of the rookie guard on more than one occasion. "I didn't play very well at all," Lawless willingly admitted in the postgame locker room.

As a result of Lawless' struggles, Staubach experienced an active existence in the pocket on this day, even if the defense couldn't always get their arms around him. Their inability to pin him down consistently may have been due to two factors which they were helpless against. By lining up in the Shotgun formation instead of under center, Staubach created a different set of angles for the pass-rushers to defend, while also allowing the quarterback extra time to see and react to the pass-rush before it reached him. For a scrambler extraordinaire such as Staubach, this was all the advantage he needed to wear-out a feisty Rams' defense.

Aided by a lead, though slim as it was, Staubach settled his nerves and his teammates, taking satisfaction in protecting the ball above all else. Rather than force the issue with an ill-advised pass downfield as he had at times during the previous two seasons, Staubach either tucked the ball and ran, or simply dumped it off to a runner out of the backfield.

Staubach's newfound conservatism was in stark contrast to his quarterbacking counterpart on the Rams' sideline, who interpreted Staubach's efficiency as a sign that he needed to step-up his own performance if his team was going to maintain pace with the Cowboys. Lacking the same athleticism that Staubach possessed, James Harris was in no way prepared to run from trouble when the play broke down. But he did have an arm, and a strong one at that.

Not that it had done him or his team any good in the early going. On this afternoon, the Los Angeles backfield was a tiny square of turf littered with ill-tempered Cowboys' defenders bent on inflicting punishment to whomever the ball-carrier happened to be. Since running back Lawrence McCutcheon was going nowhere fast on early downs, that wound up being Harris more often than he cared for.

But now with his team trailing on the scoreboard, Harris, who had yet to complete a single pass in the game, felt required to pull the Rams' offense out of a rut and match wits and scores with Staubach. That's when he made his first mistake of the game, forcing a sideline pass that was intercepted by Mel Renfro and returned to the Los Angeles 24-yard line.

To compensate for his own team's poor pass protection, Tom Landry called for a quick screen pass to Drew Pearson. After watching the pass from Staubach into his hands, Pearson was able to escape from an off-balance defense for an 18-yard gain that set-up a first-and-goal situation for Dallas.

Three plays later witnessed the Cowboys on the cusp of taking control of the game, with the ball sitting on the threshold of the end-zone. Only six inches from a touchdown and a two-score advantage for Dallas, Landry was faced with the season's first critical decision. Should he take the easy points, or have his offense try to stuff it in on fourth down? Landry didn't have to look very hard to find a reason to leave his offense on the field. Attempting a point-blank field goal was no certain undertaking on this day, as Fritsch's earlier miss attested to. The fact that the Dallas offensive line was holding their own on running plays, allowing Cowboys' tailbacks to average roughly three yards per attempt, also gave him confidence. Another such effort on fourth-down would be more than enough to give the Cowboys their first touchdown of the new season.

And even should the Ram defense rise up and make a stop, Landry perceived that the brilliant play from his defensive unit was anything but an aberration, and was likely to continue as the game progressed into its later stages. More than most head coaches, Landry was especially sensitive to the "feel" of each particular game. Landry could sense that the Los Angeles offense was dead in the water on this day, so why not try to put the nail in the coffin immediately? Jumping ahead by two scores just might be too much for the Rams to overcome.

So Landry motioned for Staubach and the offense to remain on the field, and duly sent the play in. With the Los Angeles defense likely prepared for either a sneak from Staubach under center, or a handoff to Dallas' backfield bowling ball Newhouse, Landry decided instead to give the ball to the smaller Doug Dennison. The result was a beautiful exhibition of cunningly conceived power football, as the 6-1, 202-pound Dennison squeezed through for a touchdown.

Foregoing the field goal was the right choice, as evidenced also by Fritsch's errant point-after kick a few moments later. The score was now 9-0 in favor of the Cowboys, thanks to Landry, and small thanks to Fritsch.

Dallas maintained that advantage into the halftime break, as the 49,091 in attendance marveled at the one-sided nature the game was taking on. The Dallas offense, though certainly not dominant in any sense of the word, had at least held serve against one of the league's top defensive units, twice moving the length of the field for scoring opportunities.

Staubach's limited success was far more than James Harris could console himself with after 30 minutes of play. With first-half drives starting at the Ram 18, 19, and three times at the 20-yard line, the sixth-year quarterback had struggled to the point of having failed to move the Los Angeles offense past its own 36-yard line.

The timing for such a disastrous half could not have been less fortuitous for Harris, who was already feeling pressure from team Owner Carroll Rosenbloom and fans to prove himself a franchise-caliber quarterback, despite the fact that he was making just his twelfth start in a Rams' uniform. After being named the full-time starter when the Rams sent veteran gunslinger John Hadl to the Packers in a trade during the 1974 season, Harris broke the color barrier for starting quarterbacks in the playoffs, then broke the hearts of thousands of California football freaks with a sub-par outing that, many felt, cost his team a chance at the Super Bowl in a playoff game against Minnesota.

In the 1974 NFC Championship Game in Minnesota, the Rams were trailing 14-10 and had the ball on the Vikings six-inch line. It was second-down, so Los Angeles' Head Coach Knox called for his big quarterback to lean ahead and try to sneak it into the end zone. Vikings' defensive tackle Alan Page then jumped off-sides resulting in a penalty flag. But after conferring, the officials ruled that Page was drawn offside by future Hall of Fame left guard Tom Mack.

Now backed up just outside the 5-yard line, the Rams ran John Cappalleti for two yards, before trying to catch the Purple People Eaters defense off their guard with a pass play. The surprise play fooled no one, as the pass from Harris was tipped and intercepted, thus ending the game.

In a 2014 interview with ESPN The Magazine, Mack recalled the scene vividly.

"We came off the field," said Mack, "and Chuck is yelling at me for jumping off-sides, and I scream back, 'I didn't do anything!' I bet him the game-check I didn't do anything, and you know what? The game film backed me up. But I never did get the money."

Wrote Knox in his autobiography: "Instead of blaming the ref, or even Mack, the fans and some media had the audacity to blame [Harris] for that call. Blamed it on what they thought was his sometimes off-beat signal cadence. Can you imagine that? Maybe by then fans had realized that James Harris really was our starting quarterback, and was going to be our starting quarterback until he lost his job. Since they didn't like him, they had to find something against him. And that's when it started."

According to the skeptics, Harris was less than the ideal fixture for a push to the Super Bowl, a sentiment that surely grew in strength back home in the Napa Valley after such a lackluster performance during the first half in Dallas. Harris did little, if anything, to sway public opinion in the second half, as his day straight from the depths of football hades continued into the third period, much to the chagrin of Knox, who could only watch as his quarterback continued to struggle under the relentless pressure from the Cowboys' defense.

Harris' luck went from bad to worse in the third period when he coughed up the ball after being hit while looking to pass, and Jethro Pugh recovered for Dallas. It was one of five Rams' fumbles on the day, and led to another Dallas score, Fritsch connecting from 39 yards away moments later.

When Renfro robbed Harris for a second time later in the quarter, Knox figured he had seen enough, opting instead to send backup Ron Jaworski out onto the field for the Rams' next series. Knox would say in his postgame briefing that the decision was only to spare his starter from additional punishment, and was not in any way an indication of discontent or impatience with Harris on the part of the Los Angeles coaching staff.

Knox's words, though well-meant, did nothing to nullify what had been a simply horrid outing for the Rams quarterback. Harris retired from the game having completed only one-of-ten pass attempts for a grand total of five yards. His three interceptions and one lost fumble only added depth to what was already a very insulting statistical line for him.

A fourth-quarter touchdown drive led by Jaworski helped to intensify the pressure building up around Harris. A quarterback who only eight months before was voted the MVP of the Pro Bowl had officially fallen out of grace with the Rams' faithful.

While Harris' body and career were getting bludgeoned by a ferocious Cowboys' defense, Staubach was busy turning in a mistake-free performance that allowed Dallas to coast home for the 18-7 victory. Though he passed for only 106 yards on 10-of-23 passing, it was Roger's legs, more often than not, that kept the chains moving for the Dallas offense.

"We had a great pass rush and coverage, but Roger ran and reacted well," lamented Los Angeles' linebacker Isiah Robertson. "It makes me think they respect our defense a lot to use that rinky-dink Shotgun so much."

His 56 rushing yards (many of which came out of the Shotgun formation) was Staubach's highest total in a regular season contest since Week 9 of Dallas' 1971 championship season when Roger was very much "The Dodger," running circles around a hapless and helpless Eagles' defense for 90 yards. That just happened to be the second game after Landry had finally ended a maddening system of rotating quarterbacks with Staubach and Craig Morton, settling on the former Navy standout as the Cowboys' full-time starter.

While Los Angeles' defenders were marveling among themselves at Staubach's freedom of movement in what was now a very spacious pocket, the fact of the matter was that Roger was merely in the early stages of acclimating himself to Landry's new offensive wrinkle. Little did everyone know that his second game operating from the Shotgun would be even more impressive than the first. But Staubach wouldn't be wowing anyone with his feet this time. Rather, the following weekend's early-season showdown between Dallas and St. Louis was to be one Sunday when Staubach's arm would steal the show, and put the NFC on high alert that the Cowboys and the Shotgun were a duo both dynamic and deadly.

CHAPTER 12

THE FORTUNES OF OVERTIME

"It was the most exciting game I've ever been in." - **Roger Staubach**

"It was a long afternoon. It's enough to turn a man gray." - **Tom Landry**

While Dallas' season-opening upset of Los Angeles had served to inject even more confidence into an already enthusiastic Cowboys' locker room, it did little to arouse any excitement among the local fan base. As of Tuesday afternoon, 29,000 tickets – more than one-third of the total allotment – remained unsold for Sunday's looming showcase versus division-rival St. Louis at Texas Stadium. The week went by, and Tex Schramm was hopeful for a big turnout. A note in the Sunday edition of the Dallas Morning News said "a crowd of

55,000" was expected, "though it could be larger." Yet by the time the ball was teed-up for the 1 p.m. kickoff, church services were finished and only 52, 417 had been admitted through the stadium turnstiles. The attendance number was slightly larger than the previous week, but still left more than 10,000 empty seats that Schramm, from his suite high above the playing field, couldn't help but notice.

Schramm took it as a personal affront to his abilities as a promoter that so many fans would choose to stay home and watch the game on the tube from the comfort of their couch rather than witness these exciting Cowboys in person. Mentally, Schramm cursed himself for a lack of foresight. He should have been more vigilant during the off-season months to promote the health and well-being of the franchise as it related to the immediate future. The publication of the *Dallas Cowboys Weekly* magazine, which was under Schramm's personal supervision, had certainly helped in that regard, but based on the number of unused seats staring back at him, didn't have the necessary impact.

Schramm cursed the lack of humanity inside the stadium. He cursed the struggling economy which led to it. He cursed the preseason prognostications from those know-it-all sports magazines which had dragged the Cowboys' brand through the mud. *The Cowboys...a .500 team? Of all the gall!!*

He cursed the ever unpredictable institution that was Texas weather patterns. Fans didn't want to pay their hard-earned money to watch what they anticipated was a mediocre team. And they certainly didn't want to do so while broiling in the sun. According to the thermometer at field level, the temperature was already in the 80s, and climbing steadily.

Pestered by a combination of frustrations over persistent low attendance numbers and anticipation for the imminent kickoff, Schramm had worked himself up into an emotional frenzy by the time both teams took to the field. He squirmed in his chair. He scowled at the field. He drank a liberal amount of Scotch. After pausing to pay homage to the unique flavor, Schramm would then drink more. Not that it affected him. It never did.

Only when the game actually started did Schramm sit up and begin audibly voicing his anxiety. Among low mutterings to himself, Schramm yelled out of frustration, he exhorted his players, while taking additional time in liberally cursing the efforts of the opposition. Tex Schramm wanted the Cowboys to win, oh, so badly. Even if once-loyal fans didn't care enough to show up, and even if Cowboys' players themselves seemed disinclined to pluck and bury a most dangerous of divisional foes.

As a byproduct of having used his football genius as the impetus to win championships in two major market cities – Dallas and New York – Tom Landry's was a recognized name up and down the east coast and throughout much of the continental southwest. With that one-of-a-kind iron chin and sleek fedora to match, Landry cut just as unmistakable a figure as well. Landry's head coaching counterpart in Week 2 could not lay claim to the same status, though his name was quickly becoming known by his NFC Eastern Division rivals.

Don Coryell was in his third year on the St. Louis Cardinals sideline, and was well on his way to becoming an unquestioned offensive genius. Coryell's was a philosophy taken right out of the school-yard. Good weather or bad, his teams were going to throw the ball all over the yard.

After using this philosophy to help the Cardinals win the Eastern Division crown in 1974, it had become official that Coryell's was more than simply a passing fancy. Certain too was the fact that Coryell's sharp football mind was enhanced by equally impressive talent on the playing field.

He had taken Jim Hart, an undrafted, unproven talent out of small school Southern Illinois, and made him into an All-Pro at quarterback. Mel Gray and Earl Thomas were already recognized as one of the top wide receiving duos in the league. And Terry Metcalf, all 5-foot-10-inch, 185-pounds of him, had been molded into a defensive coordinator's worst nightmare.

Despite being the shortest player on the field, Metcalf owned the distinction of being the most dangerous with the ball in his hands. Metcalf was listed as a running back, but in St. Louis that didn't restrict him to merely taking handoffs from the quarterback. With Coryell's influence, Metcalf was morphed into a dual-threat receiver, using his exceptional speed and precise route-running to get open from numerous starting positions; tailback, H-back, and wide receiver.

With an offensive line defined by mean-streaked guards Conrad Dobler and Dan Dierdorf, the Cardinals had a well-rounded unit that was more than capable of scoring points in a hurry. Hence, Coryell's confusion over his team's inability to do just that in the first half against the Cowboys at Texas Stadium.

Coryell knew the Dallas defensive personnel like a glove, and had piled up points against them in the past. In the previous two games against the Cowboys, St. Louis had averaged 22 points per contest. But now, with the second quarter well under way, the scoreboard boldly indicated a 0-0 deadlock between two teams touting a pair of the league's best offenses.

Coryell was beside himself on the Cardinals' sideline. Hart was misfiring. Metcalf was blanketed. Gray was going nowhere. And the offensive line was getting manhandled. Coryell's well-oiled machine was out of sorts, lacking aggression and looking flustered against a confident Dallas defense.

It wasn't until he was running off the field and toward the tunnel at halftime that Coryell figured out what exactly was ailing his team. The Cardinals' bench was positioned in bright sunlight, leaving his players fully exposed to the infamous Texas sun through the half-finished roof at Texas Stadium. At the postgame news conference, Coryell would cry foul over this competitive disadvantage, claiming that both teams should have stayed on the same side of the field, such as was the habit at Minnesota's old Metropolitan Stadium. But it would take more than complaints to help his team get out of their funk after intermission. The temperature was in the low 90s, and the high-flying Cardinals - slowly but surely - were wilting in the sun, as their first loss of the young season grew imminent.

The Cowboys, on the other hand, were experiencing their own set of woes. While the Cardinals had the sun to blame for their early inefficiencies, Cowboys' players simply had themselves to blame. A passing attack that had been expected to shred what was billed as an average St. Louis secondary did nothing of the sort for the better part of the first half. Roger Staubach couldn't seem to get on the same page with Drew Pearson. Running backs Robert Newhouse and Doug Dennison struggled to produce yards on the ground. If not for a last-minute march just before halftime that concluded with Staubach's 1-yard scoring pass to Jean Fugett, the first two quarters would have likely been considered a waste altogether.

As it was, a sleepy first-half of play concluded with the Cowboys owning a 7-3 lead. The polite applause that followed the home team to their locker room was nothing to be compared with the loud cheers that filled the stadium in the second-half, when a pair of Dallas' linebackers teamed-up to author one of the more stunning and unlikely victories that Cowboys' fans had ever seen.

The game that everyone was expecting came to fruition in the third quarter. Drew Pearson put the Cowboys ahead 14-3 with his 12-yard scoring grab from Staubach early in the period. Then Hart answered back for the Cardinals with a touchdown toss of 23 yards to Mel Gray. And before the Dallas bench had finished celebrating Charles Young's scoring dive from one-yard away, the Cardinals had struck again, this time with an 80-yard Hart-to-Earl Thomas scoring bomb.

With the pressure to score being keenly felt by everyone in the building, Tom Landry figured the time had come to pull a rabbit out of the hat on the ensuing kickoff return.

Against Los Angeles the week before, it was a play from rookie punter Mitch Hoopes that turned the tide in Dallas' favor. Now, that honor fell on the confident shoulders of rookie linebacker Thomas Henderson, who was told by special teams' coach Mike Ditka that the Cowboys were going to run a double-reverse on the kickoff.

For possibly the first and only time in his professional career, Henderson sensed his own limitations. "I don't know if I can," replied the 220-pound linebacker, drawing attention to a hip-pointer that he had suffered late in the first half.

But when his position coach Jerry Tubbs asked him if he was good to go a few moments later, the old Henderson had reemerged. "Yeah," said Hollywood, "I think I can run that sucker."

Jim Baaken kicked the ball deep to Rollie Woolsey, while Henderson ran up-field as if intending to block. Before the Cardinals coverage team reached him, Henderson doubled back toward the ball-carrier. What he saw upon turning was anything but what he expected. Woolsey had dropped the ball, and was stooping to pick it up at the three-yard line, thoroughly scrambling the play's timing. "I was afraid he wouldn't give it to me then, but I went around and took it anyway," said Henderson.

Woolsey relinquished the ball, and turned to the right. Henderson, curling to the left, started sprinting down the near sideline. In front of the runner was a convoy of well-placed blockers, including rookie Randy Hughes, that paved the way with one smashing block after another. Randy White supplied the final block, giving Henderson a clear path to conclude his 97-yard scoring return with a thunderous dunk over the goal-post that sent the Texas Stadium crowd into a frenzy.

On the St. Louis sideline, an awe-struck player remarked of Henderson, "Who is that guy? Wasn't he a lineman?"

"We practiced that play one day last month," said Henderson of his touchdown return. "We saw the Rams do it and decided to try it. Woolsey wasn't supposed to drop the ball but it worked out well anyhow. I was supposed to drop back like I was blocking, and take the ball. Randy White drove a guy down into the ground with a good block and helped me get loose. The fumble really set it up a little better... You know, 97 yards ain't bad for a linebacker."

The Dallas lead swelled to 31-17 on a 40-yard field goal from Fritsch early in the fourth quarter. And when the Cowboys' defense held on the following Cardinals' possession, it appeared as if the Texas Stadium crowd would be gifted with a fourth-quarter sleeper for the second consecutive week. But then

Woolsey's ongoing bout with the dropsies came back to bite the Cowboys.

Woolsey, as he had earlier, fumbled while running up-field on a return, and watched helplessly as Steve Neils recovered for St. Louis at the Dallas 31-yard line. That's when Hart, who had used a play-fake in the backfield on an earlier touchdown pass to Earl Thomas, again used a fake to his halfback and this time went downfield to an open Jackie Smith for a 35-yard scoring play with 8:38 remaining.

Later, with time winding down, the Cardinals' offense crossed over into Dallas' territory again. Tom Landry, seeking to put an emphatic end to St. Louis' comeback bid, dialed up a blitz for his defense. The aggressive call left cornerback Benny Barnes in man-to-man coverage on Cardinals wide receiver Mel Gray. Barnes, a reserve defensive back, was filling in for Mel Renfro, who was riding the bench while dealing with muscle spasms.

Hart realized the mismatch and quickly fired a pass in Gray's direction. Gray came back for the ball before turning up-field, side-stepping Barnes, and outraced the rest of the Cowboys' defense into the end-zone. Baaken's point-after kick knotted the score 31-31 with 46 seconds left.

Staubach nearly pulled off a miracle in regulation by quickly moving the Dallas offense into scoring range. But when Fritsch's 39-yard attempt at the gun was blocked, a sudden-death overtime period had officially become an improbable reality. When St. Louis won the coin-toss and elected to receive, it appeared as if this reality was quickly turning into a nightmare. The Cowboys, once leading by two touchdowns in the fourth quarter, appeared destined to cough the game up as a tired, weary, thunderstruck defensive unit took to the field once again.

After the kickoff return, the Cardinals assumed possession at the 31-yard line. Forty yards later, the ball rested on the Dallas 29, while frustration mounted on the Cowboys' sideline, now drenched in full sun.

An on-looking Roger Staubach had already conceded the inevitable. "I'll be honest... I thought it was over," Staubach said later.

The Dirty Dozen

In the Cowboys' huddle, emotions were equally as stark before the approaching second-down play. "Frankly, I just prayed a bit in the huddle," recalled Lee Roy Jordan. "I knew we had to get a turnover... that was the only way." Jordan's prayer of desperation proved to be a prelude to an extended moment of confusion that promised to be discussed by both teams for a long time.

Only a week before, Don Coryell had watched Baaken boot the Cardinals to victory over Atlanta with a 25-yard kick in the closing seconds of regulation. Evidently, Coryell saw no comparison between that and a potential 45-yard game-winner against the Cowboys. So, rather than play conservative and call for a handoff, Coryell asked his quarterback, who had already accumulated over 300 yards through the air, to throw one more time.

The play-call was a simple one, relying on the same play-fake to the tailback out of the same I-formation that had worked for a pair of long touchdowns earlier in the game. This time, however, the Cardinals were going to dump it off short to speedy halfback Terry Metcalf.

By the time the play started, the Dallas defense was thoroughly out of sorts. Metcalf acted out the fake, darted into the line and then cut sharply to the outside. D.D. Lewis was supposed to be covering Metcalf, but didn't. Dave Edwards thought chasing Metcalf was his responsibility, but he was turned around by the play-fake. When Hart realized that neither of the Dallas linebackers were in the vicinity, he threw an off-balance pass toward an awaiting Metcalf.

What Hart didn't account for was the instinctive nature of Dallas' cagey middle linebacker. Lee Roy Jordan had lined up on the strong side of the play, away from where Metcalf was going. His responsibility was to cover the fullback who had curled out of the backfield toward him. But when he noticed Metcalf hurrying faster than usual through the line, Jordan followed a hunch that led him across the field and straight to a shocking interception.

Upon gathering the ball in his hands, Jordan gathered his feet, managed a quick pirouette, before rumbling and bouncing his way downfield on a 38-yard return that set the Dallas offense up with prime field position.

"It was just a dumb call," Coryell said of the decision to throw. "...Jordan is a fine linebacker, and I guess he sensed it. He couldn't have guessed it, because he'd never seen it before. He jumped on it."

Upon reaching the Dallas sideline, Jordan was congratulated enthusiastically by a host of teammates, many of whom had no idea that the Dallas defense had blown a coverage on the play. Those who did know were just as confused on the bench as they had been on the field. "Dave and D.D. were both thanking me for covering for them," Jordan told the press after the game. "Don't tell them any different."

Taking over at the St. Louis 37-yard line, Staubach completed passes of 12 and 11 yards to advance the ball to the 14. Three running plays moved the ball inside the 5, where the Dallas quarterback iced the game with a short scoring toss to Billy Joe Dupree, who spiked the ball in the end-zone with emphasis after receiving a bear hug from Burton Lawless.

Dupree's mere presence on the field was indicative of the never-say-die attitude which embodied the Cowboys' efforts for the day. On two separate occasions, the Dallas tight end had been knocked from the action. Early in the game, he had to be helped from the field after jamming his back. Then, with 34 seconds remaining in regulation, Dupree collided head-on with cornerback Roger Wehrli, leaving each participant lying prostrate for a moment on the unforgiving Tartan turf. Dupree finished the game with 6 receptions for an even 100 yards, giving the third-year pro out of Michigan State his first career 100-yard receiving day.

The unthinkable had now become official. In the first two games of the season, the Dallas Cowboys had knocked off a pair of NFC favorites.

Somewhere, Tex Schramm was smiling.

CHAPTER 13

DOME WRECKERS

"That run was a super run."
- **Linebacker Lee Roy Jordan commenting on Charles Young's 29-yard burst that set up another second-half Dallas touchdown**

Since the day it opened in October of 1971, the prime source of conversation about Texas Stadium had been that can't-miss half-finished roof above the playing surface. Some said it looked odd. Others thought it quaint. Former Cowboys' quarterback Don Meredith once said that Texas Stadium was "typically Texan. They built it but they didn't finish it. They left a hole in it." In 1973, linebacker D.D. Lewis even gave the roof a spiritual connotation, saying that "God looks through the hole in the roof to watch His favorite team play," a quotation that local football-loving evangelicals quickly latched onto.

Over the years, Tex Schramm tried to save face on more than one occasion by acting as if a half-finished roof had been part of the construction blueprint all along, claiming that he wanted the fans covered, but the players exposed to the elements. Nobody in the media dared to question Schramm too closely over this. *If that's the way Schramm wants the story told, then why not?* Next to Tom Landry and Roger Staubach, Schramm posed as the most important sports figure in the state, which practically meant he was the third-most important person in the region.

If Texas Stadium was supposed to be the hallowed home of God and a balding Front-Office Genius, then who was the press to say otherwise? After all, those newspapermen had their own reputation to overcome, and would stand little chance of surviving public wrath by contradicting what Schramm had already minted as gospel truth.

So without pausing to discuss the merits of the varied theories that pertained to the perplexing roof atop Texas Stadium, it's certain that Schramm's unfinished castle in suburban Irving was food for some architectural thought around many NFL camps in the early 1970's. *Why not build on what ol' Tex has given the Cowboys in a home stadium? Why not, say, build a roof, and this time see the job through to the end? A few lights, a little air-conditioning... Hey, if it worked for hockey in Canada, then it could work for football in America too. But wouldn't it be cool to see football come indoors!*

The Detroit Lions surely thought so, and in 1973 started building their very own domed stadium 30 miles north in the suburb of Pontiac, Michigan that would open in the fall of 1975. After years of playing second fiddle to the baseball team at old Tiger Stadium in downtown Detroit, the Ford family was finally giving the diehard Lions' fans a place all their own to be proud of. Filled to the brim with the latest advancements in engineering, this dome was capped by a Teflon-coated fiberglass roof, which was supported by 29 blowers rimming the stadium. At long last, the game of football was coming to the arena.

Such a ground-breaking event it was that NFL bigwigs placed Detroit's first game in their climate-controlled playground on the national airwaves of ABC's *Monday Night Football* against professional football's darling franchise. To help the buildup for this ribbon-cutting ceremony, the league scheduled two softies (Green Bay & Atlanta) to start the Lions' 1975 season, a pair of teams that Detroit easily disposed of. Thus it happened that the 2-0 Detroit Lions squared off against the 2-0 Dallas Cowboys for a high-profile NFC showdown that was as memorable for the hot air inflating the multi-million dollar roof as for the hot air emanating from the well-oiled mouth of Howard Cosell.

Tom Landry found himself faced with a familiar dilemma as the third game approached. Hope as he might, the issues in the Cowboys' backfield would just not subside with time. Every week, it was something new to address.

In a perfect world, Landry would have watched Doug Dennison implant himself as the unquestioned starting running back coming out of the gates. But the second-year runner had accomplished anything but that. Dennison had been afforded his fair share of opportunities. He had carried the ball 17 times in each of the first two games, yet was averaging less than 2.5 yards-per-carry. His longest run of the young season was a 9-yard scamper versus St. Louis.

Landry was caught in the middle and forced to make adjustments on the fly. With Dennison ineffective in the extreme, Landry looked in the direction of Robert Newhouse for production. Newhouse gave his coach a much healthier 3.9 yards-per-attempt, resulting in a shift in roles. As the only effective runner in the Dallas backfield, Newhouse couldn't be a full-time fullback as was anticipated during training camp. Dennison, consequently, found himself switching positions with Newhouse at strategic moments throughout a game.

While Landry was certainly relieved to find a reliable runner in Newhouse, the resulting role reversal was a little disconcerting to him. Newhouse was the only pure fullback on the roster. His stumpy build and low center of gravity made him an ideal blocker, and nobody could rightly question his running ability from that position. Though not gifted with blazing speed or startling agility, Newhouse was nothing less than a natural with the ball in his hands.

But the circumstances that demanded Landry give Newhouse the bulk of the carries was creating additional challenges for the head coach. For the first time in sixteen seasons with the Cowboys, Landry couldn't fit a Cowboys' runner in the position that best suited their individual skill sets. To maintain offensive balance, Landry had to split Newhouse between fullback and tailback. Doug Dennison seemed more comfortable as a runner when lined-up closer to the ball, though he was no better than an average blocker from that position. Charles Young's speed made him a no-brainer at tailback, but his per-carry average as a fullback had increased over the summer months.

Landry had yet to find enough trust in Scott Laidlaw as a runner, using him occasionally as an underneath option for Roger Staubach on passing downs. Laidlaw, the Head Coach diplomatically pointed out, had made the most of limited action during the first two games, hauling in six receptions for a total of 61 yards, with a long gain of 24 yards against the Rams. What Laidlaw had in God-given ability, he lacked in seasoning. That would come in time.

This positional shuffleboard taxed Landry's ingenuity, requiring him to design multiple plays for specific players from different positions and incorporate them in the weekly game-plan. Landry, now more than ever, would be calling plays with particular individuals in mind. The advantage for the Cowboys was that the opposing defense could often be left guessing on running downs as to who would take the hand-off from Staubach. The drawback was that it was hard for Dallas' runners to get in a groove while trying to master multiple positions.

Having come up with a more productive formula with Newhouse and Dennison in the backfield, Landry hoped to get his two runners more comfortable in their new roles. Then the news came down from the medical staff that Dennison had suffered a foot injury against St. Louis and would be unable to go for the Cowboys' next game against Detroit.

That meant the return of Young to the lineup where he, like Dennison before him, would be indoctrinated as to the rudiments of his hybrid role in the Cowboys' backfield. Having watched Young limp through the summer months with a whole host of ailments, Landry wasn't at all sure how this next experiment would work out, if at all. If it had been solely up to the Head Coach, veteran Preston Pearson would have replaced Dennison, but Pearson was still struggling with certain parts of the playbook. Pearson was set to see an increase in playing time while replacing Dennison on kick returns, but would only see limited action on offense. Landry would have to be satisfied with that for the time being.

The revolving door at running back had turned again, causing Tom Landry more than one moment of disquiet during the week, and providing a perfect opportunity for Charles Young to prove that he belonged.

When the NFL's exhibition schedule got under way in early August, news agencies across the nation were flooded with material urging them to call the Detroit Lions' new arena "PonMet Stadium." The media wasn't overly-thrilled with the moniker, but were fairly cooperative toward this request during a long and tedious preseason slate.

About an hour before the Lions were set to kickoff against the Cowboys in their regular season home opener, another handout circulated through the press-box stating that the official name had now been changed to "Pontiac Stadium" and that the seating capacity had risen from 80,338 to 80,638. It seems that 300 seats magically appeared behind the players' tunnel. The only question remaining now was when the next handout was scheduled for release.

While the media was being given the run-around on the inside of the stadium, motorists had come to a standstill on the outside. A traffic jam that one observer from the Automobile Club of Michigan reported to have been the worst jam he had seen in five years had cars backed up for several miles along Opdyke and Featherstone roads as much as 90 minutes before kickoff. The congestion was reported to have centered around a 9,900 space pre-paid parking lot around the stadium.

Attendants, it seemed, were duty-bound to collect a $3 pre-paid parking ticket from each motorist. Those that couldn't hand over a ticket were kindly asked to turn around. And when the motorist tried to oblige, well, then... you get the picture.

Sometimes delays are relative. At other times they are not. The traffic jam that caused many a Lions' fan an anxious moment in trying to get to their seats on time was nothing compared to what Saints' fans had to complain of at the newly-opened Superdome, where roosting pigeons had been leaving tell-tale signs of their presence on the seats.

Just before game time, attendants in the parking lot were told to forget about collecting tickets and let everybody pass through. And why not? ABC was in town. The Cowboys were in town. And climate-controlled football was here to stay!

Blitz. It was a word that the Dallas offense had become quite familiar with during the days leading up to their matchup with Detroit. The Lions were a team that used this tactic on defense to an extreme that few had ever seen. In victories over Green Bay and Atlanta, the Lions sent at least one linebacker on a blitz seventy-percent of the time, and two or more defenders fifty-percent of the time.

Its effectiveness was obvious to all. Detroit had intercepted three passes, recovered two fumbles, and sacked opposing quarterbacks seven times for combined losses of 53 yards, while allowing an average of 234 total yards per game. "Sometimes," said Cowboys' assistant Ermal Allen, "it looks like they're rushing all 11 men."

When Tom Landry turned on the tape of Detroit, he saw more than just a unit crashing into the line of scrimmage with additional man-power. More than simply being aggressive, the Lions were taking calculated risks, disguising their defenses by using various stunts and pre-snap shifts. They confused opposing offensive lines, leading to breakdowns in blocking assignments and resulting in free rushers coming at the quarterback.

Landry spent extra time during the week going over pass-protection with his offense, taking especial care to ensure that rookie guard Burton Lawless was keeping up. Lawless would have the toughest job of any of his line mates, going up against Lions' defensive tackle Larry Hand. In the early going on Monday night, though, it looked as if Landry's teaching sessions were for naught, as the Lions blitzed the Cowboys' offense to a first-half standstill.

Preston Pearson squelched the boos that had greeted the Cowboys when taking the field by returning the opening kickoff to the Detroit 45-yard line. A pass-interference penalty against Detroit's Levi Johnson while covering Golden Richards led to the initial points in the Lions' new domed stadium, a 21-yard chip-shot field goal off the foot of Fritsch.

Superior special teams' play continued to bail out a Dallas offense that looked stunned in the face of a crashing Lions' defense. Despite having first-half drives that started at the Dallas 42 yard line or better, the Cowboys went into halftime having scored just nine points, as the duo of Robert Newhouse and Charles Young were joined in their struggles by Roger Staubach, who tossed an early interception.

For the third consecutive game, the Dallas defense pitched a near-perfect game through the first two quarters, staking the six-point favorite Cowboys to a six-point lead going into the dressing room. Ends Harvey Martin and Ed "Too Tall" Jones did a good job staying in their gaps, a necessity against a diverse Lions' rushing attack that had incorporated the college-style option into their playbook. Outside of a slow second-quarter march that used eleven minutes and resulted in a field goal, the Dallas defense had allowed virtually nothing.

The game changed early in the third quarter on a special teams' play, only this time it wasn't the Cowboys making it, but their opponent. As the culmination of yet another failed drive from the Dallas offense, Mitch Hoopes had his punt blocked by the outstretched hand of Levi Johnson, giving Detroit possession at the Cowboys' 29-yard line. It was Johnson's third blocked punt of the 1975 season, and left special teams coach Mike Ditka fuming on the Dallas sideline.

Back on the playing surface, events were picking up. A Lions' team whose early-season successes had been due to their opportunistic nature went quickly to work against the Dallas defense, using an end-around to wide receiver Jon Staggers to gain 14 yards and move the ball within safe striking distance for their struggling quarterback, Greg Landry. A conservative first-half approach had called for Landry to execute an array of handoffs to runners Altie Taylor and Dexter Bussey. Now that Detroit was on the doorstep of surging in front for the first time, the Lions opted to let Landry throw it on fourth-down-and-2. The timing for this change-up in philosophy was exquisite, as the pass to Bussey out of the backfield caught the Dallas defense napping, the 7-yard scoring play giving Detroit a 10-9 lead.

With their team now in front on the scoreboard, the crowd of 79,784 ecstatic Lions' fans began taunting and booing those sleek, stylish, and heavily-favored Cowboys. The anticipation of an upset victory volubly increased when the ensuing Dallas possession ended in another Hoopes punt, a renewed wave of sarcastic cheers reverberating off the Teflon-coated fiberglass roof.

And just when this battle of unbeatens was starting to take on a compelling nature, just when it appeared that the home team was about to rise from their long-standing habitat in the NFC cellar, the bottom dropped out and revealed the fallacious expectations that went along with the Lions' unblemished record. The same fans that had come out of their seats upon Dallas' earlier special teams miscue were glued to those same seats when a similar turn of events bit the hometown team.

Late in the third quarter with the score still 10-9, Detroit punter Herman Weaver mishandled a low snap from center Richard Hicks. His first thought upon gathering the ball was to get off a hurried kick, but that plan was scratched by the looming presence of Cliff Harris. So Weaver exercised his only remaining option. He ran...away from Harris and straight into the arms of Rollie Woolsey at the Detroit 33-yard line. The crowd grew hushed as Weaver removed himself slowly from the playing area, perhaps sensing that the old, familiar, inept Lions were about to emerge. What happened next confirmed their fears.

Staubach jump-started the Dallas passing game with a 30-yard completion to the always reliable Drew Pearson. Pearson's big-gainer was immediately followed by a bruising three-yard touchdown run from Charles Young. After Fritsch shanked the extra-point, the Cowboys' lead was 15-10.

Young, seeing his first extended action of the season, took it squarely upon his own shoulders to increase the Dallas advantage. On the final play of the third quarter, with Dallas needing first-down yardage, Young veered outside on a draw-play from the Shotgun formation, and broke a tackle before flashing his speed down the sideline all the way to the Lions' 42-yard line. The 29-yard play could have gone the distance had Jean Fugett known the location of the runner and provided Young with a block. "That run was a super run," said Lee Roy Jordan. "We're backed up, in trouble, and suddenly we're setting up for business in Detroit territory."

After the teams switched ends, Young removed any culpability from Fugett's name by outrunning the coverage of linebacker Charlie Weaver and making a juggling 42-yard touchdown catch from Staubach in front of Johnson. After that, it was simply a matter of piling on for the Cowboys, literally and figuratively.

Provided with a sizable second-half lead, the Cowboys' pass-rushers came out in full force to thoroughly squash any comeback hopes that the Lions may have been entertaining. Led by the quartet of Harvey Martin, Jethro Pugh, D.D. Lewis and Randy White, the Cowboys sacked Greg Landry eight times over the final eighteen minutes, giving them a total of 11 for the game, an NFL-record. By the time Landry was relieved by backup Bill Munson late in the fourth quarter, his net passing total had fallen to one-yard.

When Cowboys' defenders weren't running circles around Detroit's offensive line, the Dallas offense was putting an emphatic exclamation point on the victory. Earlier in the game, Tom Landry had noticed how quickly the Lions' secondary stepped up to defend a pitch to Newhouse, especially cornerback Lem Barney, who was locked in one-on-one coverage with Drew Pearson. Landry filed the information away, and planned on trying a halfback pass later in the game, if the opportunity presented itself. "I wanted to try it at about midfield because I felt we'd score if we hit it," Landry said.

Landry, as he so often was in 1975, was correct in his assumption. With the ball resting on the Detroit 46-yard line, Newhouse took another pitch while heading toward the outside of the defense, stopped, turned, and made a soft pitch to a wide-open Pearson in the end-zone. Pearson finished the scoring on the next Dallas possession with his third touchdown of the game, catching a 37-yard pass from Staubach that deflected off the hands of Johnson.

"I was impressed with the Lions," Tom Landry said diplomatically during postgame interviews. "They played us real close in the first half and, except for hitting a couple big plays, the game could have been much closer... "It's amazing we're still unbeaten, considering we're in a transitional phase with so many new fellows. The veterans are keeping us going."

One of those veterans was linebacker D.D. Lewis, who finished the game with two quarterback takedowns. Lewis was pleased, no doubt, with the Cowboys' 3-0 start, but steadfastly refused to place too much emphasis on it.

"I just wish everybody wouldn't start talking and writing about a championship for us now," he said in the postgame locker room. "Just let us do our thing from week to week and see what happens."

CHAPTER 14

ELEMENTS OF VICTORY

"I was overthrowing almost every ball...I've never seen a wind like that." - **Roger Staubach, after a challenging afternoon at windy Shea Stadium**

"It was a guessing game out there because Craig knows us so well. On that play, I guessed right."
- **Cornerback Mark Washington on his game-changing interception of former teammate Craig Morton**

Gauging the status of the Dallas Cowboys during the 1970's was not a very difficult chore. To locate the direction of the wind one needed to only take a head count at Tom Landry's weekly press conference on Tuesday afternoon. If Dallas had won a big game over the weekend, the banquet dining hall would be packed. If not, then there was sure to be more chairs than faces staring back at the Cowboys' Head Coach.

Less than eighteen hours after Landry's team finished their second-half drubbing of Detroit, the Cowboys' Head Coach gazed out upon a gathering of less than full capacity. The Cowboys were 3-0, and still, there were certain members of the media who were not impressed. Rather than catch a few thoughts from Landry about the Cowboys' win over an overhyped Lions' squad, they found it much more expedient to catch up on some much-needed rest after landing back in north Texas in the wee hours of the morning.

Despite sleeping for only two hours himself, Landry was in a noticeably good mood at the familiar function, and even chided the writers who chose not to attend. "I can't say much for their staying power," Landry laughed.

Those who were in attendance proved to be somewhat preoccupied over the latest mini-drama that had enveloped the organization. Apparently, while Landry's Cowboys were carving up the Lions on the field on Monday night, Howard Cosell was occupying himself in the ABC television booth by taking pokes and jabs at Cowboys' players. Needless to say, Cosell's comments didn't go over well with sympathizers of the silver and blue, particularly those that centered around the ability – or lack thereof, according to Cosell – of Robert Newhouse. Cosell, it seemed, could not fathom the local perception that depicted Newhouse as the heir apparent to the departed Calvin Hill. In Cosell's mind, Hill was a certified All-Pro talent. Newhouse was anything but that. "Newhouse," said Cosell over the national airwaves, "is not a good running back."

Watching the game at home on TV was Robert's wife Nancy, who recalled the anger she felt when Cosell's words spilled over the airwaves. "I shook the TV," she said. "I said, 'What are you saying about my Robert?' I doubled up my fist and shook it at him and thought, 'If I could get to that man…'"

Nancy wasn't the only one feeling outraged. So put out were fans over this unwarranted attack on the Cowboys' leading rusher that they bombarded the Cowboys' club office with telephone calls the following morning. One woman even came in person to complain.

Landry was asked for his take on the matter, though reporters were dutiful in noting that Cosell's outspoken nature during the broadcast was balanced out by the conservative tones coming from booth partner Frank Gifford, who termed the Dallas pass-rush as "awesome." Said a grinning Landry: "Oh, Frank is an old friend of mine, but I'm not so sure about that other guy. I used to think he was my friend, but lately he has been turning."

Landry's comments were hardly the final chapter in this story. In fact, while Landry was talking, Bob St. John was penning an article about Cosell that appeared in the next day's editions of the Dallas Morning News. Below is an excerpt from St. John's well-written piece entitled "The Picture Of Idle Talk:

"*My favorite Howard Cosell story happened one Monday night when the ABC team was doing a St. Louis Cardinal game. Howard was saying he'd had lunch or dinner or somesuch with Jim Hart and, as I recall, the talk was about how Hart was his own man because he called his own plays. My mind is not completely clear on what followed but I believe Howard even said Hart had talked to him about calling his own plays.*

"*This struck me as odd because, in fact, Jim Hart does not call his own plays. Since Don Coryell became head coach of the Cardinals, he's shuttled wide receivers to call Hart's plays.*

"*Anyway, as one colleague remarked, if Cosell actually had dinner and lunch with as many players as he said he had, the guy would weigh 300 pounds.*

"*I was having lunch or dinner or somesuch with Alex Karras the other day and we were talking about Cosell. Karras remarked the thing which most impressed him about Howard was his "quickness of mind." Karras said he'd seen Howard do a 15-minute monologue off the top of his head during a dead period. "He didn't say a thing but it sounded very interesting. The guy has a very, very quick mind."*

"*I remember saying if Cosell could sound interesting that long without saying anything he was a natural for politics. Some feel he will enter that area. Some wish he would.*"

Over the next few days, letters poured in by the bushel to Tex Schramm's office from irate fans. A few epistles were even published in that week's edition of the *Dallas Cowboys Weekly* magazine. Mike Jackson of Sherman wrote: "Who do we contact to button up Howard Cosell's lip? He has no respect for the Dallas Cowboys. He continues to run down the team. Please tell the man he will not be welcomed to the Dallas area."

An Amarillo fan sounded ready to turn Cosell out onto a nearby plantation, writing, "Is there any way to stop Howard from talking so much? He makes me so mad I would like to stuff about five pounds of fresh packed cotton in his mouth."

Perhaps the most descriptive letter (that was published) came from a Mrs. Lester Rogers of Jacksonville, Texas, who wrote, "The degrading character attack on the Cowboys by Howard Cosell was disgusting. I hope a bird nests in his toupee, then maybe he will wash the egg off his face."

The soap opera having been dissected to the satisfaction of every one present, the conversation at the luncheon was allowed then to drift back to more relevant football matters. One reporter asked Landry to compare his current squad with others that he had coached in Dallas from the previous fifteen seasons.

"As far as the pure joy of coaching, it's one of the best I've had," said Landry. "We have great morale. Our young players still don't execute – not the way you would associate execution with Cowboy teams of the past." He quickly added, "They make up for a lack of execution with attitude and enthusiasm. Maybe the great execution will come later this year or next year. We've been doing some things well by accident. But we are making the plays necessary to win."

Landry's team would be especially challenged to continue those trends for a fourth consecutive week. The veteran-laden Cowboys had struggled in recent years to bounce back from a Monday night contest, having dropped the last two. The fact that Dallas was in the midst of back-to-back road games made it even tougher from a logistical standpoint.

After beating the Lions on Monday night, the Cowboys had to catch a red-eye flight from Detroit, land in Dallas at 4 a.m. Tuesday morning, and then fly to New York on Saturday afternoon. Even with a rotation on defense, and a revolving door at the running back position, the enthusiasm and energy for Landry's team would be put to the test.

In addition to the inherent concerns of a quick turnaround, Landry would also have to prepare his team for an unusual indoctrination into outdoors football. After three weeks of playing in the cozy confines of Texas Stadium and PonMet Stadium (or Pontiac Stadium, or whatever the Lions wanted to call it), the clean-cut Cowboys were in for an extreme awakening as to the assortment of factors that could make football along the east coast a rough-and-tumble game of wits. They were not only going to New York, the Cowboys were going to Shea Stadium, a venue whose spirit was marked by a hallowed baseball diamond and a whistling wind whose effect was as unpredictable as a spitball.

New York, a city long accustomed to the grating tones of dissatisfaction, witnessed a landmark event in the spring of 1964. The strong band of provincially-challenged protestors, weary from the emotional trauma that only years of oppression under the weight of stringent local customs could give, were finally given standing – and sitting – room to cheer on their very own sports franchises. Move over Yankees. Move over Giants. Shea Stadium, with all the splendor that 54 public restrooms, four restaurants, and a 60-ton scoreboard could provide, welcomed the outsiders of the city into its gates to cheer on New York's "other" teams, the Metropolitans of baseball, and football's Jets. Set in the heart of Queens, this brilliant venue gave its city and its fans a newfound sense of social elevation, and a brief respite from the pervasive conflicts in the outer world.

In 1969, these professional upstarts shocked a skeptical sports world by bringing home multiple unlikely championships. First in January, Broadway Joe Namath backed up his guarantee of an upset victory of Baltimore by orchestrating a 16-7 upset of the heavily-favored Colts in Super Bowl III. Then, later that October, the "Miracle Mets" concluded a sensational season with a World Series' triumph over another favored Baltimore franchise, the Orioles.

Five years later their fans' jubilation was turned to stone-faced horror, as grand and majestic Shea Stadium was invaded by the same neighbors it was alleged to have forever shutout. Perhaps emboldened by a sense of jealousy at the $30 million structure from the neighboring province, funding was provided for a renovation of Yankee Stadium, which necessitated the

Bronx Bombers inking a two-year contract to share the Mets' stadium, starting in the spring of 1974.

The football Giants played their home games for the 1974 season at the Yale Bowl, but when negotiations for a one-year extension broke down, they were essentially forced into calling Shea Stadium their home for the duration of the 1975 campaign. Thus, on the afternoon of Columbus Day, the New York Giants became the fourth professional sports franchise to host a game at Shea Stadium in 1975, welcoming the Dallas Cowboys for a divisional matchup that would go down in the NFL annals as the one, the only, and the forgettable "Dust Bowl."

Craig Morton insisted that there were no hard feelings. But in the eleven months since Tex Schramm traded him to the New York Giants for a No. 1 draft pick, sticking it to the Dallas Cowboys had been at the very top of Morton's to-do list.

Morton was a good quarterback that considered himself under-appreciated while in Dallas. He had won big games with a star on his helmet and had even led the Cowboys to their first Super Bowl. Yet all of that wasn't enough to prevent the magic of Roger Staubach from supplanting him from what he considered to be his rightful place under center for the Cowboys. Now, as the established starter with the Giants, Morton sought to use this first encounter against his old team to prove to Tom Landry – and the rest of a Staubach-worshiping world - that he had indeed made a mistake in making Staubach the franchise quarterback in Dallas.

This meeting of one-time teammates was the main storyline that the press harped on in the days leading up to the clash of longtime division foes. *Craig vs. Roger. Roger vs. Craig. Friends or rivals? Who's the better quarterback?*

Based upon the events of that Sunday, it was hard to determine who was the better quarterback. As Cowboys' players went through their pre-game stretching routine on the over-used surface inside Shea Stadium just prior to kickoff, it became apparent that the elements would far succeed the quarterback battle in overall significance. A spirited, relentless wind off the Atlantic coast was whistling throughout the stadium, moving in cyclone-like swirls, hearty gusts, and powerful jet streams. In the end-zone near the open end facing the east, flags that stood only ten yards apart blew in opposite directions. Hot-dog wrappers that had blown down from the bleachers were caught up in numerous tiny whirlwinds that danced across the field. Plastic cups rolled heedlessly along the walls, collecting in corners as if by common accord. And toward the closed end of the stadium was a dusty haze from the windswept dirt on the infield.

What Tom Landry was to later term as "the worst swirling wind I've ever seen" resulted in a noticeable alteration in offensive philosophy. From the aggressive passing attack that the Cowboys had employed in victories over St. Louis and Detroit, Landry now called an audible opting for the conservative formula formerly used in the Calvin Hill days. The Cowboys were going to grind it out on the ground-up, chewed-up, wind-blown surface of Shea Stadium.

What the Giants had in mind wasn't so evident at the outset, due to a fumbled exchange on the very first play from scrimmage between Morton and center Bob Hyland. D.D. Lewis pounced on the loose ball for Dallas, a recovery which led to a field goal and a 3-0 Cowboys lead.

The game then settled down into a series of short runs, errant passes, and poor punts from both sides. The Cowboys, as seemed to be their custom so far through four games, owned the advantage in field position, thanks in large part to a stifling defensive effort. But the wind and an inconsistent running game prevented them from extending their slim lead.

A special teams play in the second quarter by New York broke the monotony and injected a renewed spirit into a lifeless crowd of over 56,000. After a fine 50-yard punt off the foot of Mitch Hoopes, the Giants set up a 34-yard run-back for Danny Buggs by cutting down wide man Benny Barnes and shoving Thomas Henderson to the inside. By the time Buggs was taken down, he had reached the Dallas 34-yard line.

Two plays later, Morton dumped the ball off to fullback Joe Dawkins on a screen pass that moved the ball 24 yards to the

Dallas 7-yard line. "That play belonged to Dave Edwards and me," said Lee Roy Jordan. "Two guys blocked me out and Dave ran into an official." Said Edwards: "I could have made the play. Next time I'll run right over the guy [official]."

Giants' fullback Larry Watkins sealed the scoring drive moments later with his block of Mel Renfro that allowed Doug Kotar to go around left end untouched for a five-yard touchdown run.

Another inadvertent Morton fumble in the backfield when he bumped into a pulling guard gave the Cowboys three more points, drawing them within one-point on the scoreboard.

When the Giants, via an errant Morton pass, gave the ball back to Dallas just before the halftime whistle, it appeared that Dallas would re-take the lead. But on second-and-2 from the 15-yard line, Roger Staubach threw into the wind toward Billy Joe Dupree in the end-zone. Dupree was open on the play, but stumbled while the ball was in flight, allowing the defender to rally and make an easy interception. Intermission came with the Cowboys trailing 7-6.

The third quarter belonged to both defenses. Without the threat of a downfield passing game, the Cowboys came after Morton relentlessly, using an assortment of blitzes. Cliff Harris broke through to take down the Giants' quarterback once. So too did Ed "Too Tall" Jones.

But the player that seemed to benefit the most was Bill Gregory, the forgotten defensive tackle who spent his first few years in the league buried behind Bob Lilly, Jethro Pugh, and Larry Cole. In his first extended playing time of the season, Gregory was inspired by the adverse conditions, filling up the defensive stat sheet on his way to a career day.

Having been tagged by Tom Landry as the starter against the Giants after Cole was sidelined with an injury, Gregory tallied an interception and a fumble recovery. And when not taking the ball away from the opponent, he was simply making life miserable for them. Overshadowing his numerous quarterback pressures was when Gregory bulled over two New York blockers on his way to nailing Morton for a 9-yard loss.

As the third quarter wound down, it appeared that Gregory's efforts might be undermined by an ineffective Dallas offense. When not being chased in the backfield by defensive end Jack Gregory, Staubach watched his receivers lose one battle after another with the tricky, swirling wind. Cowboys' receivers finished the game with three drops.

Even when the Cowboys did something right, it turned out to be wrong. With the ball at midfield, Mitch Hoopes pulled another rabbit out of his magic bag of fourth-down tricks when he faked a punt and started to run. Upon seeing several Giants converging, Hoopes quickly got off a kick while on the run and watched the ball come to rest on the New York 4-yard line. Hoopes' extraordinary play was erased, though, by a Dallas penalty, only adding to the angst on the Dallas sideline. "It was getting a little discouraging there for a while," Gregory said of the offense's struggles. "But we've been off and the offense has helped us. We knew if we hung in there the offense would get going."

There to give the offense a push in the right direction was Dallas' defensive back Mark Washington. During a pause in the action while the medical staff attended to a fallen Cowboys' player, Washington conferred with fellow cornerback Mel Renfro about the Giants strategy. Renfro had already nabbed one Morton pass, one of four turnovers forced by Dallas, and it was becoming evident that, for the Cowboys to get the upper hand, someone on their defense would have to come up with another one. Considering the opponent, that was easier said than done. Said Washington: "It was a guessing game out there because Craig knows us so well."

On the very next play after the stoppage, Washington took a calculated guess and hit the proverbial jackpot, jumping in front of an underthrown pass for New York wide receiver Walker Gillette, and regained his balance before shaking off multiple would-be-tacklers on a disjointed 21-yard runback that gave Dallas possession at the New York 17. In the postgame locker room, Washington was more than articulate in providing details about the interception, and the events leading up to it. But, as a byproduct of a jarring takedown, he had no recollection whatever of his return.

The Dallas offense responded by moving to the four-yard line where, on third-down, the Cowboys lined up in the Power I formation, with three running backs, and tight ends Billy Joe Dupree and Jean Fugett. No wide receivers were on the field.

Based on the formation, Giants players figured Dallas was going to play it safe and try to pound it over the goal-line. If that didn't work, they would still be left with a chip-shot from Fritsch that would give them the lead.

But Tom Landry wanted more than just a field goal. So on third-down, Staubach faked a play off-tackle. The Giants' safeties stepped up, playing the run all the way. Fugett blocked inside on defensive end Jack Gregory, then slipped outside into the end-zone and caught Staubach's throw for the touchdown.

"Mark made the big play for us," said Tom Landry. "It seems like offensively or defensively or someway we've just been able to make the big play. This had not been a good week for us. We came home after that Monday night game in Detroit, stayed up all night on the return flight and were sluggish all week. Fortunately, our defense was exceptional, made the key turnovers and kept us in the game."

There were more big plays from the Cowboys as the game progressed, this time from the offensive side. As the Giants punt team came onto the field for the seventh time a few moments later, boos began to descend from a restless crowd who sensed a familiar ending for the hometown team. What they did not anticipate was the fashion in which that ending was authored.

Roger Staubach, rendered ineffective for three quarters by a restless breeze and persistent pass-rush, put the entire Dallas offense on his shoulders for a dramatic culminating drive that ran the clock dry and sapped the will from a game New York defense.

On a march that began at the Dallas 13-yard line with 10:26 remaining, Roger turned into every bit "The Dodger" on multiple occasions, as the offense inched its way downfield. On a second-and-7 play, Staubach ran for seven yards. On a third-and-2, he passed to Fugett for eight. On third-and-9, he scrambled for eight more yards, setting up what looked to be a Dallas punt from the New York 38-yard line.

But while the troops followed Hoopes onto the field, the ball coach on the sideline was quickly scanning his play sheet. Upon finding the play he wanted, Landry signaled for a timeout and prompted a round of murmurs throughout the crowd by sending his offense back onto the field. In the minds of the paying public and the consumers on television, this was an unwarranted gamble on the part of the Cowboys' aging, graying head coach. Surely, without a doubt, he was playing with fire in windy conditions that begged him to punt the ball deep into the Giants own end.

According to Landry though, going for it on fourth-and-1 was the logical decision to make. It would have been "unusual," in the words of Landry, for the Giants' defense to dig in and stop them in this particular situation. And this coming from the same man who, before this last drive, watched his offense fail to put together a march of longer than 29 yards.

Ah, but such is the confidence derived from having a magical play up your sleeve. Landry had one, old and timeless as it was. The Giants, so Landry divined, didn't have the manpower to stop a dive to Charles Young out of the power formation.

Landry, as he so often was in 1975, was completely right in this regard. Young bulled his way ahead for 3 yards, extending the drive and giving Giants' players -and fans - reason to start watching the clock.

On the ensuing third-down play, it was Staubach that put the final nail in the Giants' coffin. Needing nine yards from the New York 35, Staubach eluded the pursuit of Gregory again and picked up ten yards. The clock ran out. The game was over. The Cowboys, by a 13-7 final, emerged from dusty Shea Stadium a sparklingly clean 4-0.

Landry spoke for every person in the Dallas locker room when he summed up the day's work. "At this point it's difficult to say what's a big game and what isn't," said Landry. "But if we'd lost this one it would have neutralized our win over the Rams. We're just happy to get out of New York with a win."

Asked if he said "lucky" or "happy" Landry quickly responded: "Happy."

Chapter 15

SHADES OF IMPERFECTION

"Nothing happened to us that we didn't deserve." - **Tom Landry, after his unbeaten Cowboys were upset by Green Bay**

"There was no way they could beat us, but they did." - **Rayfield Wright, trying to make sense of Dallas' first loss of the season**

    Were Tom Landry to have put it to a computer test, he would have discovered that 29 percent of the 1975 NFL regular season was now complete. Based on his team's unblemished won-loss record through four weeks, he would have also had to admit a one-hundred percent success rate. This was odd so far into October, if not altogether unexpected.
    As a general rule, youth on a Landry-coached team was better served holding a clipboard on the sideline and learning from the veterans. The Flex defense was supposed to take anywhere from two-to-four years to get comfortable with. And Landry's 600-page offensive playbook was as thick as it was complicated for the inexperienced mind.

But prudence had taken a back seat early in the 1975 season, as circumstances required the Cowboys to play rookies at numerous stations throughout the lineup. Burton Lawless was manning the left guard position, having beaten out veteran John Niland in training camp.

Randy White was seeing time at strong-side linebacker and defensive end. Thomas Henderson had a limited role at linebacker in the Cowboys' nickel defense. Randy Hughes played in certain third-down situations in the defensive secondary. And the special teams, unless one looked closely, might be assumed to have been comprised exclusively of rookies.

Still, the Cowboys played with the cunning of a cagey veteran-laden team throughout the season's first month, conquering two NFC favorites at home to start before going on the road and taking care of business against lesser opponents. One of the themes throughout this four-game winning streak had been a flair for making the necessary play, something that Landry considered to be anything but an accident.

"A positive attitude is responsible for this," explained Landry. "Attitude and good morale. When you have this going for you good things just seem to happen. I don't know why, but they do. If you don't think something will happen for you, then it generally doesn't. This team believes it will."

However, emotion and a positive outlook would only sustain a football team for so long. If the Cowboys wanted to extend their stay on top of the conference, Landry was insistent that they needed to clean up some things on the field. The record may have indicated perfection on their part, but the tape showed something entirely different.

Landry's team, it might be argued, were undisciplined at times. In each of their four victories, the Cowboys drew more penalty flags than did their opponent, including an astounding 12 infractions in Detroit. Five fumbles thus far posed as another telltale sign of carelessness. Still, Landry remained encouraged by the weekly progression the Cowboys had shown. "If we don't play better this week than we did in New York, we're in trouble," Landry said. "We were certainly in jeopardy of losing that one.....We're a bit surprised to have our first four games. It would have been asking quite a lot for us to beat Los Angeles and St. Louis in our first two games. But progress is about on schedule. It takes experience and time to make a good executing team. This might come for us in two, three games or it might not come until next season......Still, this club has a flair for making the right play at the right time, and this is something you can't put into a computer and predict."

Perhaps the only predictable factor heading into the season's fifth weekend centered around the Cowboys' next opponent. The Green Bay Packers were winless so far in 1975 and fourteen-point underdogs going into their game at Texas Stadium. But whenever the Packers and Cowboys collided on the field, strange things usually happened in such an unexplainable way as to leave the Cowboys shaking their heads, and grasping for answers.

Of the more than 65,000 fans who gathered on a glorious October afternoon inside Texas Stadium, there likely wasn't more than a handful who gave the visitors much more than a fighter's chance to pull off the upset. The storyline for both teams through the season's first months had been well documented. The hometown Cowboys were unbeaten, and the Green Bay Packers nearly unwatchable.

Once a team with a beloved head coach and a star-studded roster, the Packers had fallen upon hard times in recent years, missing the postseason in six of the last seven seasons. The state of the franchise going into their early-season meeting with Dallas was somewhere between decay and ruin.

Fans in Wisconsin were still grinding their teeth over injustices done by former Packers' Head Coach Dan Devine. Devine scurried off to Notre Dame after the 1974 season, leaving a 6-8-2 team behind which had already traded away six of their first nine draft picks and bequeathed the club a 35-year old quarterback named John Hadl who was suffering from "dead arm." On the way out the door, Devine's parting blast shook the souls of faithful Packers' fans. "There's no way you couldn't win with this team," said Devine.

Devine didn't stop there, even dragging the townspeople through the mud a few weeks later. When *Time Magazine* came down to South Bend to interview him about his new coaching gig, Devine claimed that the people of Green Bay had shot and killed his dog, referenced his daughter with an objectionable term, and a host of other things.

The published article was later said by Devine to have been blown way out of proportion. It seems the dog had rushed a neighboring chicken house and was trying to escape with the prey in his mouth when the protective owner took exception. Fans tried their very best to forgive him for that injustice, but couldn't forgive him for what he had done to their team.

Devine, by all accounts, had taken his best swing at ruining the franchise while in Green Bay. Consider the following: In midst of his final season with the team, instead of accepting the Cowboys' proposal of sending a No. 1 pick in 1975 and a No. 2 pick in 1976 to Dallas in exchange for Craig Morton, Devine sent much, much more to Los Angeles for an older, less talented quarterback in John Hadl. Dallas had originally wanted to make a deal with Green Bay that would have brought cornerback Ken Ellis to the Cowboys. Rather than accept that, Devine cut off negotiations with Dallas and instead sent two No. 1 picks, a pair of No. 2 picks, and a No. 3 selection for John Hadl.

What the Packers got in return was an aging veteran signal-caller in Hadl with diminishing arm strength. With a depleted supply of draft-choices to fill in the gaping holes around him, the Packers were a franchise dead in the water to begin the 1975 season, as evidenced by their first four games when they were outscored 104-55.

The team that first-year head coach Bart Starr brought to Irving for a showdown with the 4-0 Cowboys was also depleted by injuries. All-Pro cornerback Willie Buchanon was out for the season with a broken leg. Starting middle linebacker Jim Carter, who had been in and out of the lineup in recent weeks while hobbling on a bad leg, lost his backup on Wednesday when Larry Hefner underwent knee surgery.

Also missing was All-Pro linebacker Ted Hendricks, who had joined the World Football League during the summer. With so many holes on the defensive side, the Packers were having trouble stopping even the worst of teams. Against New Orleans the previous Sunday, the Saints ran 86 offensive plays to the Packers 47.

There were some who thought the disparity in plays would be even greater against a potent offense such as the Cowboys. Whether it was the Packers' unimpressive won-loss record or lingering effects from jet-lag that plagued them during a short week in New York, the Cowboys offense began the game listless and apathetic. New backfield starter Preston Pearson had nowhere to run. Neither did Robert Newhouse. And it didn't seem to matter whether Roger Staubach started the play under center or in the Shotgun. Nothing was working for Dallas. "We were running into brick walls that first half," said Blaine Nye.

Tom Landry thought the problem more troubling than mere brick walls. Instead of playing harder to make up for the absence of Charles Young (sprained big toe) and Burton Lawless (bruised thigh), the Dallas offense seemed content with stargazing against a starless Packers team. "Our overall effort was not good," said Landry of that first-half of play.

For their part, Green Bay's output was just as dismal, as both teams entertained a dreadful scoreless tie deep into the opening frame. If not for a mistake on the part of Drew Pearson, the first-half would likely have been a complete wash.

After making a short pass reception in Dallas' territory, Pearson had the ball knocked loose by big defensive tackle Dave Pureifory, leading to a Johnnie Gray recovery at the 25-yard line. Moments later, little Joe Danelo made his debut in a Packers' uniform a successful one. Filling in for the injured Chester Marcol, Danelo booted a 24-yard chip-shot field goal through the uprights to break the stalemate. With Danelo's departure to the bench, a familiar battle of punts and offensive inefficiencies broke out again.

With less than a minute to go in the second quarter, the Dallas offense was showing signs of waking up from their doldrums, having driven deep into Green Bay territory. That's when third-year cornerback Perry Smith added to an already long day for Pearson, by stepping in front of the Cowboys' receiver and authoring his first interception of the season. As the offense jogged off after another failed drive, a mixture of boos and grumbling began to filter throughout the sellout crowd.

Landry could hardly blame them for their displeasure. He might have done the same in their position. The Head Coach trudged toward the halftime tunnel a stolid picture of concern, his team having been blanked in an opening half for the first time in five games.

But with Preston Pearson's 48-yard second-half kickoff return, the Cowboys came to life in a marked way. Through gaping holes in the Green Bay defense, Pearson and Newhouse carried Dallas down the field on their most impressive drive of the game. Foregoing the pass, Landry's reenergized team pushed and bowled over the Packers front-seven, fire in their eyes and pay-dirt in their sights. At last, Newhouse walked over from a yard out to give the Cowboys a 7-3 lead.

Surprisingly, the Packers responded well to this surge. In the middle of the week, feisty 5-foot-8-inch running back Willard Harrel had promised to respect Texas Stadium's Tartan turf. "Sometimes during a game I have to spit," Harrel said, "but I can't do it on artificial turf. I feel like I'm spitting on carpet."

The rookie runner from Pacific made no such promises of respect for the Dallas defense. Harrel shocked everyone in the stadium by taking a third-quarter sweep around the right end and streaking past the entire Cowboys' defense for a 26-yard touchdown run. Danelo's failed point-after try meant Green Bay owned a perilous 9-7 advantage.

Using the same strategy as before, Dallas came out and let their big offensive line fire off the ball and smash the Packer front. The Cowboys made it look easy on another run-oriented march that was capped by Doug Dennison's flying leap over the pile from 3 yards out. At the end of the third quarter, the Cowboys held a 14-9 lead and looked bent on pulling away.

With Dallas now in front of an inferior foe, fans inside Texas Stadium began to diversify their interests. With about eight minutes remaining in the fourth quarter, a roar erupted from the crowd during a lull in the action. The outburst had nothing whatever to do with the game in front of them. It was merely the reaction to an announcement that the Houston Oilers were leading the Washington Redskins at the Astrodome early in the fourth quarter.

The Dallas advantage swelled to eight-points after Mark Washington's kamikaze tackle of Harrel forced a fumble deep in Green Bay's end of the field. Stepping up to defend the run from his outside cornerback spot, Washington threw himself, a rolling block, into Harrel's knees, jarring the ball loose and somersaulting the runner over Ed "Too Tall" Jones. The good news was that Lee Roy Jordan recovered for Dallas. The bad news was that Washington left the game with a cracked rib. "I was supposed to make the tackle," Washington observed while grimacing from his locker, where he was barely able to take his socks off, "but not that way."

An ill-timed lapse on the Cowboys' kick-coverage unit allowed Green Bay to make up the three points they had given Dallas on the fumble. Steve Odom's 73-yard return of the ensuing kickoff led to a 29-yard Danelo trey, making the score 17-12 with less than five minutes remaining.

With three minutes left, Green Bay was set to punt the ball back to the Cowboys on fourth-and-18 from their own 29-yard line. The crowd, anticipating a 5-0 start from their Cowboys, began to file out in droves as Dave Beverly boomed a soaring 47-yard punt downfield to where Golden Richards waited.

What the remaining fans saw down on the field was the blonde-haired specter of Richards fielding the punt, making the move, and then coughing up the ball after a prodding hit from Larry McCarren. Before he could find the ball, Steve Luke found it first at the 31-yard line, setting Green Bay in perfect position to steal a game in Texas.

After a short gain on first down, the Packers lined up both wide receivers on the right side, leaving Rick McGeorge as Hadl's only option from the left. During the halftime break, McGeorge had informed his quarterback that he had been getting open underneath the deeper routes of the wide receivers. Hadl had responded in the second-half by finding McGeorge on a 30-yard catch-and-run that kept the Packers close. Now, they were going to dial up the same play with hopes of surging ahead in the final minutes.

The Dirty Dozen

When McGeorge started across the field on the second-and-five play he was picked up in coverage by Lee Roy Jordan, who was in good position initially. But Jordan's aged legs were no match against those of the 27-year Packers tight end. Having separated slightly from his defender after a few steps, McGeorge made a fine reaching catch and ran into the end-zone with 1:52 to play. "It was a good throw," said Jordan, who had an interception and a fumble recovery during the game. 'I thought it was going over his head. He just outran me."

McGeorge concurred, giving all of the credit to his quarterback. "It was just an excellent throw," he said. "John put it right where he had to."

Dallas still had one more chance to make right a day filled with wrongs. With 1:28 left, the Cowboys had a first-down at their own 42-yard line. From the Shotgun, Roger Staubach threw a perfect strike to Billy Joe Dupree along the sideline at the Packers 36. Dupree, struggling with a broken finger suffered a week before at Shea Stadium, had already let one pass go off his hands. This time he tried to corral the ball with his body, while taking a downward glance to make sure he got both feet down in bounds. But his timing was poor, and the ball bounced off his shoulder pads. "It was there and I missed, that's all," said a matter-of-fact Dupree.

Dupree's drop was followed by consecutive sacks of Staubach, ending the comeback threat. For the first time in 1975, the Dallas Cowboys walked off the field as losers. With a 4-1 record, their stranglehold on the NFC East had been loosened. They, in fact, were mortal.

"Nothing happened to us that we didn't deserve," Landry assured a group of reporters in the postgame locker room. We had too many turnovers. Of course Richards' fumble was critical. I don't think we'd have given them the ball back in the final two minutes."

Players echoed the head coach's sentiments, though some allowed a little more emotion to leak through with their statements. "They didn't deserve to win," said a calm Robert Newhouse, who finished the day with 92 yards on 17 rushing attempts. "We gave it to them. But we came in 4-0 and were a little flat the first half... Maybe we need this now."

On the following Wednesday, the World Football League officially folded its tents and departed from the professional football landscape. Those cashless deposits had finally caught up with them like a blood-seeking creditor. Without money, and just as deprived of constituents in the bleachers, the league could not hope to function at all, much less at a level that would compete for the NFL's dollar. They waved goodbye with all the fanfare of a traitor.

There was a hope residing in more than one NFL camp that, of the 380 players now newly unemployed, a few might come back to their former teams. But Pete Rozelle was having none of it, declaring that anyone who had played for the WFL in 1975 was ineligible for NFL competition until the following season.

Rozelle's edict was quickly challenged by a group of lawyers, and Congress threatened to come in and intervene on the matter. It seemed nothing where the World Football League was concerned could be solved in a simple manner. Would its ripple effect never subside?

CHAPTER 16

THE WILL TO WIN

"Man, I'm beat. I don't think I've ever done so much running in my life. I don't think I have ever made two such important catches so late in one game."
- **A sweat-streaked Drew Pearson after his late-game efforts ignited a fourth-quarter rally**

"It was one of the most important field goals I ever made." -
Toni Fritsch, describing the impact of his game-winning kick

It had been a rough seven days in the life and career of Golden Richards. Once an acknowledged up-and-comer at his position, Richards now found himself existing in the role of an outcast after his costly fourth-quarter fumble versus Green Bay. At a team function early in the week, local fans mercilessly heckled the Cowboys' wide receiver, anxious not to let the 24-year old forget the mistake that directly led to the team's initial loss of the season.

Even his wife joined in the criticism. At a players' wives' luncheon, she introduced herself to the audience as "Barbara

Richards, ex-punt returner of the Dallas Cowboys." Everyone laughed.

An opportunity for a bounce-back awaited Richards the following Sunday at Veterans Stadium, where patrons were sure to be screaming about more than just fumbles to Cowboys' players. Richards received reassurance heading into this crucial divisional matchup against Philadelphia from a wide range of Cowboys' officers, including Tex Schramm, Gil Brandt, Tom Landry, and special teams coach Mike Ditka. Schramm even went so far as to guarantee that Richards would score a touchdown against the Eagles.

Much to the delight of Schramm, who loved to call his own shot and then crow about it, Richards did just that, silencing his critics with an electrifying first-quarter run-back. With his first touch of the football since gift-wrapping a Packers' victory the Sunday before, Golden corralled a punt at the Philadelphia 43-yard line, anticipating a hole to open up in the middle of the field. The only crease he saw upon fielding the kick was on the right side however, prompting Richards to sprint in that direction.

What began as a crease turned into an opening as Richards reached the corner. And when he received a block from Randy Hughes, the speedy Richards found himself running all alone down the sideline and all the way into the end-zone for a touchdown. With the scoring play, Richards was able to distance himself from his misfortune of the previous game, while the Cowboys were able to draw even on the scoreboard in a game that featured everything under the heading of the unexpected.

If there were any efforts on the part of Dallas patrons in trying to conjure up reasons why the slow-starting Eagles would roll over and play dead against a hot Cowboys' team, there needn't have been. Even had Eagles' players wanted to take a day off versus Dallas, beleaguered Head Coach Mike McCormack wouldn't have allowed them to. McCormack was on edge from the season's outset, as his team found out in the wake of listless defeats to the Bears and Giants to open the season. Before Philadelphia's Week 3 matchup with Washington, McCormack charged his players with lacking a killer instinct, and even referred to several players as curs and mutts. McCormack's public comments got the ear of his team, and led to a surprising upset of the Redskins.

Another two-game skid thereafter provoked another public declaration from the Eagles' camp, this time from Philadelphia's strong-armed quarterback who was taking direct aim at their next opponent. Roman Gabriel put the Dallas locker room on notice during the early part of the week when he called the Cowboys "arrogant" and a team with "no class." Furthermore, he said the only guy along the Dallas front four that anybody had heard of was Jethro Pugh and that the others were "nobodies."

"I don't like the Cowboys," divulged Gabriel. After three hours of pushing, shoving, punching and gouging on Sunday afternoon at Veterans Stadium, it was safe to say that nobody else on the Eagles roster did either. Provoked by a transparent injection of mutual disfavor, an inherently physical game took on the flavor of a heavyweight boxing match in this Week 6 showdown destined to be decided on the final play.

Thomas Henderson was standing just out of bounds with Po James as both teams prepared to exit the field at halftime with Philadelphia leading 14-10, when the Dallas linebacker received a blatant shove. Henderson responded with a left hook up high to James, which resulted in Henderson's prompt ejection from the game.

Later, another rookie, Bob Breunig, was discussing matters with an Eagles' player, who abruptly clubbed Breunig with a right. Breunig reacted as every good defenseman should – by delivering a right cross of his own. The scrum was broken up quickly by game officials, who considered it prudent to avoid flashing the disqualification card on this occasion. Play on!

Once, Randy White, running full speed, blasted Roman Gabriel well after the pass had been delivered, drawing a roughing-the-passer penalty. It appeared that White had hit Gabriel with his right hand, though he recalled the incident quite differently. "I never touched him," said Randy, who then took a moment to think, before adding, "I hit him with my head."

Dallas Morning News columnist and Cowboys' beat writer Bob St. John then did his best Pinocchio imitation, telling White in the postgame locker room of a fallacious remark that was supposed to have come from Gabriel's mouth. "Randy, did you know that Gabriel just referred to you as a 'cheap shot?'"
"He said that!" Randy responded. "Listen, he said that! Boy, wait. Just wait!"

While White was boiling over Gabriel's alleged remarks, Cliff Harris was basking in the glow of a divisional conquest that was more than just about the final score, but settling a personal score. In a 1974 meeting with Philadelphia at Veterans Stadium, Eagles wide receiver Harold Carmichael came out for the first play and yelled at him, "Harris, we know your weakness, and we're going to run every play at you." It shook Cliff up, causing him to struggle in a 13-10 Cowboys' loss.

A year later, Cliff's confidence proved to be unshakeable, as Harris' strong play from his weak safety position was one of the leading factors in a defensive turnaround that kept the Cowboys close in the second-half.

Oh, but even Harris had his tales about the Eagles and their cheap shots. "One guy reached up and slugged me," said Cliff. "This other guy grabbed my finger and tried to twist it off." Bob St. John lied again, telling Cliff that Roman said he was a "cheap-shot artist" too. Cliff's face turned red, before pointing out that Bill Bradley was "one of the worst ever." Then Harris grinned, before adding, "Anyway, if I am, I'm a thoughtful one. Bradley isn't."

This tour of the locker room continued for St. John, who then went over to Harvey Martin with the same fairy tale about Roman Gabriel. Martin's eyes got wide, before saying, "Listen, I don't believe all this high school [stuff] he's coming out with."

And when St. John went over to Thomas Henderson and informed him he was one of many young trouble-makers on the team, Henderson sounded proud of the fearless exuberance which the Cowboys exhibited. "Just call us the dirty dozen," Henderson said.

These aggressive post-play tendencies that received a lot of attention from the press in postgame coverage merely underscored the physical nature of the game itself. Beginning in the middle of the field where the mass of humanity generally congregates was a fearsome struggle between the heavy hitters and pile-movers, as each side pushed, shoved, and gouged for position. Provoked into a desperate emotional frenzy by the lusty encouragement from the bleachers, the underdog Eagles overwhelmed the Dallas offensive line, crashing in on early downs and punishing the ball carrier.

A week after stampeding the Packers for over 200 yards on the ground, an unusual alignment from the Eagles that had all three of its linebackers aligned on the inside of the formation completely stumped the Dallas running game. Outside of individual runs from Doug Dennison of 14 yards and Robert Newhouse of 9 yards, Cowboys' running backs were averaging less than one-yard per attempt.

A non-existent running attack contributed to an inconsistent passing day from Staubach, who found it increasingly difficult to advance the ball through the air on the Eagles' side of the field. Four different times Staubach moved the Cowboys inside the Philadelphia 35-yard line. Not only did the Cowboys fail to cross the goal-line on each occasion, but struggled to put any significant dent on the scoreboard as well, accumulating all of three points in the process. "I was very discouraged," admitted Landry. "We kept moving down there and couldn't put the ball across. The reason was we never established a running game."

On the other side of the ball, the Dallas defense had troubles of their own. Pass-rushers like Harvey Martin and Randy White had a hard time getting a grip on the wet, artificial surface. Trainers tried four different types of shoe surfaces, but nothing seemed to work. Lack of a pass-rush led to some big plays in the passing game for the Eagles.

Harold Carmichael, the lanky Philadelphia wide-out, was reported to have been "benched" by the Eagles' coaching staff during the week. But Carmichael ran wild through the Dallas secondary in the first half, catching touchdown passes of one-yard and eighteen-yards to stake Philadelphia to a 14-7 halftime advantage.

The deficit could have been even greater for the Cowboys, thanks to an impromptu appearance of Mitch Hoopes. As fans learned in the opener versus Los Angeles, Hoopes was a master at extending drives with his legs. What the football world didn't know was that Hoopes fancied himself somewhat as a quarterback as well. His surprise pass deep in Dallas territory during the second quarter was the source of much consternation among the Cowboys' coaching staff, who envisioned the Eagles extending their lead even more.

On fourth-and-13 from the Dallas 24-yard line, Hoopes audibled to a fake-punt pass, calling for Thomas Henderson to sneak out to the left. If not for the heady play of safety Bill Bradley, the trick play might have worked. Bradley broke up the pass attempt, nearly jumping in front of Henderson and intercepting it.

"I couldn't believe what I was seeing," a grimacing Landry said after the game. "It was a mistake on Hoopes' part. He did it on his own." Special teams coach Mike Ditka, who chewed on his punter's ear after the play, concurred wholeheartedly with the head coach's assessment. "You don't do those things down on your own end of the field when you are behind," said Iron Mike.

Not everyone in the Dallas locker room was against the call. Henderson, in fact, went so far as to blame himself for the incompletion. "I raised my hands up too soon and Bradley saw it," said Henderson. "We knew if the outside man rushes, I'm gonna be free. But Bradley read it. If Mitch puts a bit more steam on it, I still think we have a first down."

The Dallas defense banded together in the wake of Hoopes' mistake, pushing the Eagles all the way back to the 36 and forcing a punt. Disaster had been avoided, the flawed instinct of a rookie punter rendered moot.

The Cowboys trailed Philadelphia by a score of 17-10 with 3:50 remaining when Dallas took over at its own 38-yard line. Using another array of Staubach passes, the Cowboys crossed the midfield stripe once again, seeking to break through the frenetic wall of defense that the Eagles had constructed on their side of the field.

Taking advantage of soft zone coverage downfield, Staubach bypassed his wide receiver options and instead sought Newhouse coming out of the backfield. Having caught the Eagles' defense out of position, Newhouse was able to turn the short pass reception into an 18-yard catch-and-run that gave the Cowboys a first down at the Philadelphia 30-yard line.

It was in the aftermath of this particular play that Philadelphia's roughhouse style finally got the better of them. Having baited Thomas Henderson into an ejection, frustrated Randy White to the point of committing an unnecessary infraction while taking Gabriel to the turf, and thrown dozens of punches in between, the Eagles had grown confident in their bullying of the Cowboys as the game progressed. But, as Dallas looked to be mounting an attempt at stealing a game they had trailed throughout, one Eagles' defender overreached himself.

Bill Bradley, a hard-nosed safety with an affection for mixing it up with opponents during and after plays, made the biggest gaffe of the afternoon as players separated following the 18-yard gain, punching Newhouse in front of God, man, and referee. The flag flew, and Bradley flew into a rage, knowing full well that his mistake had given the Cowboys an extra 15 yards in field position. The line of scrimmage, once situated at the 30-yard line, was now at the 15, prompting a chorus of murmurs from the Philly faithful.

Bradley's unwanted moment in the spotlight set the stage for another member of the Philadelphia secondary to join him in infamy. Reserve cornerback Cliff Brooks was in the game only because of a second-quarter ankle injury to regular starter Joe Lavender. Up to that point, Brooks had enjoyed a fine outing off the bench, knocking away several Staubach passes. But in the final 64 seconds, with Drew Pearson lined-up across from him, that all changed.

The Cowboys gave back a few of the yards they had gained in the assault on Newhouse and were desperate for a big play. The game-clock was fast approaching one-minute to play. Philadelphia's defense was prepared to stop anything directly downfield, with two safeties lingering deep in the secondary. Landry's only alternative as the play-caller was to look for yardage in the middle of the field. That's why he dialed the well-known number of the team's premier wide-out.

Though only 6-feet tall and a frail 180-pounds, No. 88, Drew Pearson, had a special knack for finding openings on the football field for his quarterback to throw to. Pearson didn't have blazing speed, but was an established deep threat. He didn't have amazing quickness, yet always seemed to beat his defender to the ball on short, underneath patterns. Pearson, more than anyone else on the Dallas roster, knew how to play the game of football. If anybody could penetrate the zones inside the Philadelphia defense, it would be him.

Blanketed all afternoon when running in close proximity to the goal-line, Pearson was able to beat Brooks to the inside on a slant route this time. Staubach, correctly anticipating the spacing in the defense, waited just for a moment before letting go of a brown leather dart that sailed between the outreached arms of two defenders and into the mitts of Pearson for the game-tying touchdown with 1:04 showing on the clock.

Pearson's jubilation on the Dallas sideline was cut short by the need to catch his breath. His fourth touchdown catch of the season had tied the ballgame, but it looked like the Cowboys were going to get the ball back with a chance to win in regulation. For Drew Pearson, there was still more running to do.

The Eagles, now in full meltdown mode, butchered their final chance on offense, with Gabriel twice throwing incomplete in addition to fumbling a handoff. Rather than run out the clock and play for overtime, the Eagles found themselves punting the ball away to Dallas with less than a minute on the clock.

The Cowboys regained possession on its own 40 yard-line with 30 seconds remaining, yet still managed to run seven plays. The last in the series came on second-and-10 at the Philadelphia 45, with Dallas needing to gain about 15 yards to give Toni Fritsch a chance. Landry called a pass to the strong side to one of the running backs, but as the huddle broke Staubach told Drew Pearson to run a deep sideline route. "He was supposed to be a nothing receiver on the play," Staubach explained later. "I just thought he'd be open."

The play began with 11 seconds remaining. Pearson ran down the sideline, slowed down, and came back with Brooks and strong safety Randy Loga closely defending. As the ball sailed toward the sideline, the gloomy overcast skies seemed to spell doom for the comeback Cowboys. Logan, coming up quickly behind the intended target, seemed destined for an interception.

If Logan could grab onto the ball and break away from the grasping Pearson, there was a chance he could author a most memorable runback. The crowd, hoarse from cursing the Cowboys for three hours, came out of its seat in unified anticipation. Revenge was imminent, if not palpable. Surely, this was the straw that would finally break the Cowboys' back.

But the only broken product in Veterans Stadium were the hearts that bled Eagle green. There was to be no interception, no waltz into the history book for Randy Logan, and no warm postgame fuzzies for the City of Brotherly Love. The ball that hung against the sky and teased the crowd into believing in the impossible wound up in the hands of Pearson himself, who had stepped inside of Logan at the last instant. After making the catch, Pearson turned up-field and gained several more yards before running out of bounds to the tune of an ingratiable silence at the 25-yard line. All that remained was three seconds, and a host of doubts encircling the foot of one particular member of the Cowboys.

It had not been the best of days for Toni Fritsch. In three earlier attempts, Fritsch had missed from 48 and 41 yards. His one successful kick, a 30-yarder, had bounced through off the side of the left upright. After one of Fritsch's misses, viewers on television were greeted with the picture of Landry talking rather strongly to his kicker. When asked about it later, Landry said, "We were just going over some of the fundamentals of kicking."

Before going out for his pressure-packed 42-yard kick, Landry offered some more advice. "Keep your head down, Toni, and kick it through." Fritsch nodded, and then trotted toward the huddle. Landry watched him go, before turning his back to the field. With a victory and a spot atop the division riding on the execution of a wobbly-footed kicker, Landry could not bring himself to watch this final momentous play in regulation. "Usually, when you're missing like that the chances aren't good," admitted Landry afterwards.

With Landry's stomach in knots and a crowd of 64,203 watching with bated breath, Fritsch backed up a few steps from where Charlie Waters had marked for the hold, and with his arms resting by his side waited for the snap from rookie Kyle Davis. After a brief pause, Davis hiked the ball back to Waters, who executed a perfect hold for the oncoming foot of Fritsch. As befitted the style of Austrian soccer players, Fritsch approached the ball at an angle, before setting his plant foot on the hard artificial turf and booting the ball up and over the defense and into the sky. And against what seemed to be monumental odds, the ball wobbled straight and true, sailing through the uprights.

With the final gun sounding throughout a hushed stadium, Cowboys' players mobbed Fritsch in celebration. Gone were the frustrations from the pair of previous misses, as America's favorite football team found sweet solace in the administrations of a foreign-born soccer player. By a 20-17 score, the Cowboys had discovered victory and an unlikely hero.

"Today, Toni smile," Fritsch said. "I knew my chance was coming... It was our only chance to win. I tell you truly I wasn't nervous. I don't think about it, except to tell myself it's now or never. But it was yes or no kick. This time it was yes and we are all happy."

Front-office cornerstones Gil Brandt (left), Tom Landry and Tex Schramm (right) turned back the clock in January of 1975 with one of the franchise's deepest draft classes.

No one player personified the Cowboys' bounce-back effort in 1975 more than middle linebacker Lee Roy Jordan. A 13-year veteran, Jordan slimmed down to 205-pounds in the off-season and then cashed in on his hard work later that fall by tallying a career-high six interceptions.

A standout at the University of Florida, rookie Burton Lawless earned a starting job along the Cowboys' offensive line at left guard. Aided by Lawless' strength and athleticism, the Cowboys finished the 1975 season with the top-ranked rushing offense in the NFC.

Charlie Waters' presence around the line of scrimmage was a common theme throughout the 1975 season. In his first year at strong safety, Waters helped the Cowboys finish No. 4 in the NFL in rush defense.

Mitch Hoopes' punting ability won him a starting job over veteran Duane Carrell in training camp. His improvisational skills as a runner earned him more than one stare from Cowboys' coaches on the sideline. In this picture, Hoopes tests the stiff Shea Stadium wind during the "Dust Bowl" in Week 4.

Shown here in Week 4 versus the Giants, Cowboys' center John Fitzgerald snaps the ball to Roger Staubach. To the right, rookie Herbert Scott (68) is filling in at left guard for Burton Lawless, who had dropped out earlier in the game with an injury.

Boise State product Rolly Woolsey showed up in a big way for Dallas in 1975. His speed as "gunner" on the Cowboys' punt teams was a major factor in Dallas having one of the NFL's best coverage units for the season.

After winning a bout with homesickness during training camp, rookie safety Randy Hughes made a place for himself in the defensive backfield working alongside veterans Charlie Waters and Cliff Harris in Dallas' nickel pass defense.

Though he struggled early, Randy White showed everyone down the stretch why the Cowboys made him their No. 1 pick. White's three-sack performance against New England in Week 9 helped Dallas snap a two-game losing skid with a 34-31 victory.

Despite constant criticism from Howard Cosell's corner of the globe, Robert Newhouse enjoyed a career year in 1975 as the starting running back in Dallas, finishing fourth in the NFC with 930 yards rushing.

Before undergoing season-ending knee surgery in late November, rookie running back Scott Laidlaw played well in limited action. Here, Laidlaw carries a defender for a few extra yards during Dallas' Week 4 victory over the Giants.

A full-time contributor to the Cowboys' kick-coverage units, Pat Donovan started the final regular season game of his rookie campaign at right tackle versus the New York Jets. Donovan's involvement in an ill-fated punt against Minnesota in the playoffs is still talked about to this day.

The third linebacker taken by Dallas in the 1975 draft, Bob Breunig shook off a concussion early in training camp to make the final roster and earn himself a place on select nickel defensive packages.

With Ralph Neely (73) and Rayfield Wright (70) offering protection, Roger Staubach looks downfield for an open receiver during the 1975 NFC Divisional Playoff game against the Minnesota Vikings.

Drew Pearson's touchdown catch of a "Hail Mary" pass from Roger Staubach provoked an assortment of reactions from within Metropolitan Stadium. Fans threw oranges onto the field (orange can be discerned just below the knee of Paul Krause (No. 22) in above picture), while defensive back Terry Brown stares in disbelief at the official signaling a touchdown (see picture below). Cowboys' players, meanwhile, high-fived each other all the way to Los Angeles and the NFC Championship Game.

Preston Pearson (shown here carrying the ball against St. Louis in Week 12) gave the Cowboys a big lift as a pass receiver in 1975. His three-touchdown afternoon at Los Angeles in the NFC Championship Game vaulted the Cowboys into the Super Bowl.

One of the most electrifying talents on the Dallas roster, rookie linebacker Thomas Henderson waves to a crowd of fans at Love Field Airport before departing for Miami and the beginning of Super Bowl Week.

A hard-nosed player in his own right, Dallas safety Cliff Harris found himself on the wrong end of the equation after this field-goal attempt in Super Bowl X, as Pittsburgh linebacker Jack Lambert slammed him to the turf.

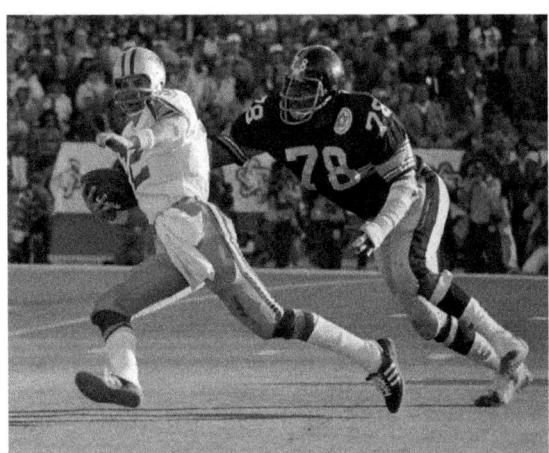

Not even the Shotgun could slow down Pittsburgh's vaunted "Steel Curtain" pass-rush at the Orange Bowl. Here, Roger Staubach is taken down by Dwight White for one of the Steelers' Super Bowl-record 7 sacks.

Decisions, decisions, decisions. Here, Tom Landry strokes his chin while plotting the Cowboys' next move during the second half of Super Bowl X.

Tom Landry's decision at the end of training camp to keep an injured Percy Howard on the Dallas roster paid huge dividends later that January. Howard's fourth-quarter touchdown grab in Super Bowl X brought the Cowboys to the doorstep of yet another comeback victory.

A fine season notwithstanding, defensive tackle Jethro Pugh can't hide the agony of the Cowboys' Super Bowl defeat to Pittsburgh in the post-game locker room.

The Dirty Dozen

CHAPTER 17

BLOOD, BLOWS & BITTERNESS

"It was one of the most stupid things I've ever done."
- **Roger Staubach, after punching a Redskins player in overtime**

"To be a kicker is to be a gambler." - **Toni Fritsch**

A dejected Cliff Harris sat on a stool in the Cowboys' locker room, head in hands, nursing a hurt neck, an aching head, and a broken heart. Now in his sixth year with the Cowboys, Harris had tasted the sweetness of a Super Bowl victory and participated in some brutal defeats, but nothing had ever prepared him for the cloud that now hung over him. "This is heavy,' he said. "Very heavy. I don't believe it happened. We won. I thought we'd won… we'd won twice and still lost……Imagine what this would have done for us… to them, losing here."

Harris was a catalytic performer from his free safety position, a player who could change the course of a game with an interception or a bone-jarring collision. And anyone, be they friend or foe, knew full well that Harris preferred walloping somebody more than anything else.

Delivering physical punishment was a way of life for Harris when on the football field, his first call of duty, so to speak. Over the years, Cowboys' coaches had tried to dissuade Harris from his tendency to look for the big hit, pleading with him to better position himself for an interception. Try though he might, Cliff never could fully adapt to this philosophy, clinging to his middle linebacker's mentality in the Dallas secondary.

Once at a team function, Golden Richards represented the rest of his teammates when he presented Cliff with a red fire helmet, complete with siren. Cliff's teammates wanted him to wear the hat and turn on the siren so they could hear when he was near and get out of the way. His teammates knew that they had better bring the ball-carrier down to the ground quickly, or Cliff would come crashing in for a kill shot and might hurt a Cowboys' player in the process.

Early in the 1975 season, "Captain Crash" practically knocked Mel Renfro senseless while attempting to bring down a runner. There had been several others over the course of the next few weeks.

All of that aggressiveness seemed to backfire on Cliff in Dallas' Week 7 showdown against Washington at RFK Stadium. The punishment that he had been doling out for years seemed to come back to him like bread upon the water during a brutal afternoon of action in the shadow of the nation's capital.

Harris went into the Redskins' game with his left shoulder hurting, so he had determined to use his right shoulder to make a tackle. He injured the right shoulder. Later, somebody also missed a tackle on Moses Denson and collided hard into Harris' head. He suffered a neck injury. His own teammate, Larry Cole, missed a tackle and hit Harris, knocking the 6-foot-1-inch, 190-pound safety over the pile. "I have never felt so bad physically in my life," he said after the game. "I can't shake my head yes. I can't shake my head no. I can't even move my head. I got killed out there."

To be fair, Harris was far more than just a punching bag for the Redskins, finishing the game with eight tackles, one pass defended, two interceptions, and one touchdown. It was his play on a pass for Washington tailback Mike Thomas in the fourth quarter that put Dallas in position to win the game. But on the strength of one ill-advised punch from an improbable figure, Harris' efforts were deemed as wasted, and his body rendered an aching mass of sweat, blood, and bruises.

The NFL annals will never record a rivalry more provocative to unlikely happenings than Dallas versus Washington. Only when the Cowboys and Redskins get together could a big-hitter like Cliff Harris be physically bludgeoned to the threshold of immobility, and only under such circumstances could Roger Staubach lose his cool in the heat of battle, forgetting that a football field was not a boxing ring.

There was to be no hiding from the reality of a loss for the Cowboys on this day, nor the misery of an overtime defeat to the hated Redskins. The Cowboys, as a team, had played hard, but not always smart. Their intent had been pure, but their execution frequently lacking. From start to finish, silver-linings of defeat colored the accounts of a game so overridden with emotion and disdain as to result in three hours of thrilling highs, heart-wrenching lows, and one infamous finish for the ages.

The wheels of social progression had enjoyed quite the ride through the streets of Dallas during the first half of the 1970's. Segregation in public schools had been virtually abolished, stricter policies aimed at preventing discrimination in the workplace were passed into the law-book, and the gospel of tolerance had a shiny new permanent pulpit in the public square.

But what the advancements of equality upon the heartstrings of this prominent city in north Texas could not change was the uninhibited disdain that citizens everywhere harbored for its most oppugnant heckler. On the streets of Dallas, George Allen was regarded as a man suffering from an incurable psychological malady, with an intellectually defective personality from birth. Inside the offices of the Dallas Cowboys, the mention of Allen's name provoked memories of an out-and-out cheater, burdened by a warped sense of humor.

It's no accident that affection for Allen in Washington D.C. was of the opposite vein, tending toward admiration and hero-worship. Since 1971 Allen had been the Head Coach of the Washington Redskins, and certified antagonist of their fiercest rival, the haughty Cowboys from Dallas.

Nobody in America knew how to get under the skin of the Cowboys quite like Allen did. He talked trash before games, often lying through his teeth to make a good story. He sent spies to the enemy camp, issued indirect threats at Cowboys' players, and cursed the team from Dallas with all the fervor of a soul-rotten sailor. Most importantly, Allen backed up all of his off-the-field theatrics by coaching the Redskins to five victories over Dallas in his first nine attempts, including a lopsided win in the 1972 NFC Championship Game that sent Washington on to Super Bowl VII.

Allen's hatred for the football franchise from Dallas reached back into his days as head coach of the Los Angeles Rams during the '60s, and stemmed from a football philosophy that was the polar opposite of that which Tom Landry and Tex Schramm had tried and proven with the Cowboys. During an era in which the league draft was complicated by the presence of the AFL, Allen shelved the notion of waiting for young players to develop, and dedicated himself to improving the Rams by trading away youth and draft picks for established veterans.

It wasn't very long before Allen had his first dust-up with the Cowboys. In 1967, Dallas General Manager Tex Schramm said a suspicious vehicle had been parked near the team's practice field. Alert and inquisitive, he alleged a license plate check traced the car rental to Johnny Sanders, head scout of the Rams.

The incident didn't end there. Allen responded with a hilarious countercharge, claiming that the Rams discovered a man sitting in a eucalyptus tree with binoculars, spying on their practice. A futile chase of the culprit ensued. Allen said the man looked like Cowboys' scout Frank "Bucko" Kilroy.

Schramm laughed out loud at Allen's comical comeback. Kilroy weighed in the vicinity of 300 pounds and did well to climb out of shoes much less up a tree. Allen, it turned out, not only had the first laugh but the last one as well, as the Rams went to Dallas and whipped the Cowboys 35-13.

When Allen transferred his allegiance to Washington a few years later, he brought with him his belief in veterans and his disdain for all things Cowboys, quickly building a team of retreads and rejects that became known as the "Over The Hill Gang." Encouraged by sharing a division with Dallas, Allen's obsession with coming out ahead of them reached heights unseen. For George Allen, beating the Dallas Cowboys had become a year-round chore that gave little room for morals or ethics.

A year after correctly predicting that his defense would knock Roger Staubach from a Thanksgiving Day matchup in Irving, Allen was determined to get an insider's view at the Cowboys' new Shotgun offense for their Week 7 meeting in 1975. On the Friday before Washington was scheduled to play Cleveland, a full nine days in front of their tilt with Dallas, the Redskins came to terms with Jim Arneson, an offensive lineman who was with the Cowboys during training camp before being traded to the Browns.

Arneson's lasting imprint from two-plus seasons with Dallas was a short-lived stint as a long-snapper that ultimately forced Tom Landry to beg Dave Manders to come out of retirement. Once upon a time in August of 1973, Arneson got off the most wayward snap in team history, sending the ball sailing over the punter's head and back into the Texas Stadium wall. Earlier in the same game for a field goal attempt, he had launched one over the holder, past the kicker and far, far downfield. By the time the ball stopped rolling, Dallas had given back 35 yards. Long after he gave up on thoughts of making a go of it at center, the nickname "Hike" followed Arneson wherever he went.

This wasn't the first time that Allen tried to pick the brain of a former Cowboys' player in the days leading up to the game. In 1971 the Redskins signed Steve Goepel, a quarterback, after he'd been cut by Dallas, and grilled him on the Cowboys' offense.

A face-to-face meeting between Allen and Arneson left the Redskins' Head Coach with only one conclusion: Tom Landry had installed the Shotgun formation because Roger Staubach couldn't read defenses, a fact which Allen willingly shared with the media early in the week.

"The Shotgun has helped Staubach," said Allen. "He has trouble reading defenses, picking up keys and it gives him more time to throw… more time than he should have. I hope we see a lot of the Shotgun on Sunday. It's what Dallas uses on long-yardage, which means it's to our advantage."

Washington defensive tackle Diron Talbert, a noted Staubach heckler between the lines, heartily concurred. Said Talbert of Staubach: "He still hasn't learned to read defenses. After seven years, he still don't read them well. They do all they can for him, call his plays, put him back in the Shotgun so he'll have more time." Talbert even dared to add that Landry probably wasn't playing his best quarterback, a long-distance plea for Clint Longley to be inserted into the lineup.

All trash-talk aside, the Redskins insisted that the Shotgun would not affect their approach in defending the Cowboys' athletic quarterback on Sunday. "Our philosophy is that if he scrambles it's all up to him," said Allen of Staubach. "We're not worried about it. But he scrambles at his own risk. That's the way it's always been."

Perhaps taking a cue from Bob St. John, who fanned the flame of the Dallas-Philadelphia rivalry a week before, former Washington quarterback Sonny Jurgenson took it upon himself to continue the needling of Dallas' beloved quarterback from his newfound perch with the media. In his first season covering NFL games for CBS Sports, Jurgenson authored his list of the top-eight active quarterbacks in the league. The list read in this order. Fran Tarkenton. Joe Namath. Billy Kilmer. Ken Stabler. Bob Griese. Dan Pasorini. Jim Plunkett. And, finally, Archie Manning.

According to the author, Roger Staubach failed to make the list because he didn't call his own plays, an alleged mark of manhood in professional football among old-timers. When pressed for comment, Staubach did his best to deflect attention away from himself while not forgetting to question the validity of Jurgenson's selection process. "He didn't pick Ken Anderson and he's the best quarterback going now," said Staubach.

As befitted his good nature, Staubach showed no visible signs during the week of being affected by the noise coming from Redskin country. But simmering deep inside of him was a desperation to prove the Washington naysayers wrong. Nobody could have divined just how or when Staubach's desperation would boil up, over and out onto the field of competition, marring an exemplary effort and sending his team spiraling downward into the clutches of their third defeat in four games.

The term "hostile environment" was still about a quarter-century away from being affectionately driven into the ground by America's verbally-challenged media, but no term categorized so exquisitely the scene which awaited the Dallas Cowboys when they would walk out of the tunnel and onto the RFK Stadium playing surface for their late-afternoon battle with the Washington Redskins. Dave Edwards, 36, was the oldest member of the 1975 Cowboys' team, and well-seasoned in the art of intimidation that the setting provided for the visiting team.

When not listening to curses in his ear, Edwards could watch Redskins' fans re-inventing profane gestures and heckling the Dallas bench with such artful elementary taste as to leave even Dr. Seuss impressed. And the teetering, tottering bleachers, swaying in the wind from the crowd's incessant stomping, was enough to make anyone nauseous with motion sickness. "It sounds like 200,000 people are crowded in there watching," said Edwards of playing at RFK. "And every one seems to hate us."

Edwards and the Cowboys handled the crowd and the noise admirably well in the early going, trailing Washington by a score of 3-0 as the first quarter approached its end. So far, the Dallas defense had executed its game-plan of corralling Redskins' rookie running sensation Mike Thomas, and forcing Washington to rely on the suddenly unreliable arm of Billy Kilmer. Though afforded solid protection from his patched up offensive line, Kilmer was simply having an off-day against Dallas, with one errant throw followed by another. But it wasn't Kilmer who made the first mistake of consequence for the Redskins.

What had been a defensive standoff turned into a game of mishaps for the Redskins in the waning moments of the opening quarter. That's when Mark Washington stuck his nose in on another running play, using a vicious tackle to knock the ball loose from Thomas, which the Dallas cornerback recovered himself at the Washington 18-yard line. Moments after the teams had switched ends of the field, Roger Staubach dropped off a short pass to Preston Pearson out of the Shotgun, and watched as Pearson put his foot in the ground and outraced linebacker Brad Dutek for the 12-yard score.

On the ensuing possession, Kilmer's popularity with local patrons went from sub-par to sub-zero when his pass for Thomas found the mitts of Cliff Harris, who executed a spontaneous return of 27 yards to put Dallas in optimum position to extend their lead at the Washington 32. While the fans continued to boo their off-target quarterback with uncommon fervor, Staubach continued to knife his way through the Redskins' defense, quickly moving the Cowboys into scoring position. On third-and-10 from the 11-yard line, Staubach lined-up in the Shotgun again to set up his second touchdown pass of the game, this one a dart to Drew Pearson in tight coverage to give Dallas a 14-3 lead.

The tone of the game seemed to change later in the quarter when Harvey Martin came up limping on a severely sprained ankle. With Dallas' best pass-rusher now a shell of his former healthy self and relegated to hopping around on one leg, Kilmer was afforded enough time in the pocket to right the ship and mount a furious aerial comeback. His 46-yard touchdown strike to Frank Grant drew the Redskins within four points, restoring enthusiasm to the home crowd and the notoriously evil sideways grin to the face of George Allen.

After spinning their wheels early, the Redskins had found their way and felt confident they would make a game of it yet. The Cowboys carried a 17-10 advantage into halftime, but found cause for frustration in numerous mistakes that prevented them from enlarging it more. While running open in the end-zone, Preston Pearson dropped Staubach's 16-yard pass that ended a 64-yard march, and was an ominous precursor to a missed field goal by Toni Fritsch on the next play. And at the end of the second quarter, Dallas had moved 43 yards against the clock to the Redskins 3-yard line. But on third-down, Staubach faded back to pass and had the ball stolen from him by crashing defensive end Ron McDole, emphatically squelching another scoring threat.

The full-time presence of Randy White at defensive end in relief of the injured Martin failed to spark a listless Dallas pass-rush in the second-half, as the Redskins took up where they had left off in the second quarter by moving the ball up and down the field, almost at will. Kilmer capped a 66-yard third-quarter drive by passing two yards to Charley Taylor to tie the game, prompting chants of "Bil-ly" from the bleachers. "I really had the crowd on a string," laughed the Washington quarterback. "It was 'yes, boo, yea, boo.' But if I let that bother me, I'd have to go back to pressing pants with my old man."

If not for an interception by Lee Roy Jordan and an errant aim by Washington place-kicker Mark Moseley, who missed on two field goal attempts, the Redskins would have surged ahead. Bad luck on another Cowboys' special teams adventure lent additional cause for George Allen to grind his teeth.

Mitch Hoopes, the rookie punter who found delight in auditioning for skill positions in the most impromptu manner, caught the Redskins' off guard with another surprise maneuver that Landry and Mike Ditka could only marvel at. Punting from his own end-zone on fourth-and-19 from the Dallas 9-yard line, Hoopes had no choice but to bail out due to a heavy Redskins' rush. Hoopes took off running to his right, toward the sideline, then stopped and passed to fellow rookie Bob Breunig, who latched onto the ball and fought his way up-field for a gain of 21 yards. So caught up in the moment were the officials that they failed to notice that the Cowboys had too many blockers downfield on the play. What should have been a penalty against them resulted instead in a Dallas first-down.

Hoopes' turn at quarterback was one of the few incidents in the second-half when something went right for the Dallas offense. Plagued by ill-timed penalties and poor pass protection, the Cowboys wasted strong rushing efforts from Robert Newhouse and Doug Dennison, leaving the game in the hands of its defense down the stretch.

As the fourth-quarter clock approached five minutes remaining, the Redskins appeared poised to put an end to a thoroughly entertaining stalemate and complete the comeback in dramatic fashion. Washington had possession of the ball in its own end of the field, with every intention of continuing their second-half butchering of the Dallas defense, and walk off the field as winners, gloaters, and leaders of the NFC East.

Cliff Harris, it turned out, had other ideas. Harris had been shadowing Thomas for much of the afternoon, and had already tallied one interception on a pass intended for Washington's highly-touted running back. With the game on the line in the fourth quarter, it was time for Harris to go for another.

The Dallas free safety, playing perhaps his finest game in a Dallas uniform, took advantage of an off-balance throw from Kilmer, stepping in front of Mike Thomas to record his second theft of the afternoon. The sea of green that lay in front of him could only be an open invitation to a raucous celebration among teammates on the Dallas sideline and another uncensored verbal chastising of Washington's mercurial quarterback. The "worst pass" of Kilmer's season had provided Harris with the first touchdown of his career, the 27-yard return putting Dallas on top 24-17 with 5:03 left.

More misfortune awaited the Redskins' signal-caller just around the corner. Kilmer had guided the Washington offense into Dallas' territory, causing the groans of frustration among fans to be turned into silent, anxious anticipation of a late-game miracle. Yet when Kilmer directed a downfield pass to Roy Jefferson, the miracle seemed to have been extinguished into a vapor of false hope. Jefferson, you see, had slipped to the ground, leaving Mark Washington alone with every intention of making Kilmer's fifth interception the climactic one of the afternoon.

But Mark Washington was not to be a hero on this day. A willing tackler against the run, Washington had also proven himself to be a solid corner through the first half of the 1975 season. What the Dallas coaching staff also saw every day in practice was a tendency to struggle with hand-eye coordination, often leading to missed interceptions. That his momentary spell of uncertainty should crop up in a critical moment of a high-stakes divisional game seemed somehow fitting for a player that some coaches had nearly written off going into the season. Mark Washington was a good player whose profile and scouting report seemed too small and insignificant for the bright lights of the big stage in crunch time. He could run like his Dallas counterpart Mel Renfro, but sometimes forgot how to catch like him. He was a starter, but not a star. He was human, even when the situation called for him to be a hero.

With the skill of a newly-positioned outfielder, Washington lost the ball in the lights...blinked...and dropped it. It was as simple a mistake as it sounds. He dropped it, and marveled at the chance he had so dispassionately flubbed. There was no mistaking the anguish along the Dallas sideline. Tom Landry turned his head away in frustration. Ernie Stautner kicked at an imaginary bench. And teammates jumped up and down, wearing a smile of ironic disbelief.

Their disbelief turned to horror a few moments later when Kilmer completed a lengthy drive with his seven-yard touchdown pass to Jerry Smith. A game that had no end to unlikely twists and turns appeared to have no end at all. With Moseley's successful extra-point try, the Cowboys and Redskins were on the cusp of playing a fifth period.

But with 1:52 showing on the fourth quarter clock, Landry decided to put Roger Staubach in the Shotgun and hope for the best with the few plays remaining. Given time to throw in the pocket against a conservative Redskins' defense, Staubach quickly moved the Cowboys to the Washington 21-yard line, where with 14 seconds remaining Toni Fritsch was called upon to make himself a hero for the second consecutive week.

Given the emotional tenor of the game, Fritsch's earlier miss from 33 yards seemed to be an eternity ago. But Diron Talbert was of the hope that Fritsch's temperamental nature would enable him to recall it, so Talbert jumped up and called timeout just before Kyle Davis snapped the ball to begin the play, figuring that a little extra time to ponder the moment would mess with Fritsch's head.

Who can but say that Talbert's gamble paid off. After the timeout, the ball on the 38-yard attempt came off Fritsch's foot like a low-flying, flailing duck that quacked, fluttered, and finally sailed wide left of the mark.

Fritsch's postgame claim that the ball had been tipped at the line of scrimmage was rebutted by his head coach. "No, I don't think anybody blocked it," Landry said. "But he hit it so low that all anybody would have had to do was stick their hand up to hit it."

Once imminent, overtime had now become an unwelcome certainty for the Cowboys at RFK. Had they taken care of business in the first-half, the Cowboys would have been able to coast home with a victory. Instead, they found themselves embroiled in a sudden-death overtime period, with the first team to score being declared the winner.

The Cowboys correctly called the coin-toss and, as expected, elected to receive the ball first. Staubach wasted no time in calmly moving the Cowboys into Washington territory. The pressure was now on the Redskins' defense to prevent the Cowboys from getting into Fritsch's kicking range. Pressure was also building inside of the head of Staubach, who envisioned this drive as his last opportunity to stick it to the loudmouthed Redskins. These forces of human emotion, pushing and shoving in opposite directions, made for a mystifying and perplexing moment of sports theater in the shadow of the nation's capital, and became the talk of the football world for the next 24 hours.

On second-and-12 from the midfield stripe, Staubach took the snap from John Fitzgerald while standing in the Shotgun. Spotting an open receiver downfield, Staubach let loose a pass just as he was blindsided by blitzing linebacker Chris Hanburger. While Staubach crumpled to the turf, the ball fluttered and came to rest in the arms of safety Ken Houston at the Washington 36-yard line. Houston's subsequent 14-yard return gave Washington the ball at midfield.

With the noise inside RFK Stadium at a deafening pitch, Staubach picked himself up off the chewed-up grass, embittered by his misfortune, and angry at what he perceived to be a cheap shot by defensive back Pat Fischer during the interception return. "I think Fischer ran 40 yards to get Staubach, and that tells you something about Fischer," a visibly upset Lee Roy Jordan detailed in the postgame locker room. What was also evident was that the moment had gotten the better of the Dallas quarterback. Confronting his assailant, Staubach promptly punched Fischer in the head, and then began to dish out even more punishment on Hanburger before being separated by Ralph Neely and others. Staubach's display of temper that would have earned him a medal in the Navy instead earned the Redskins 15 additional yards, moving the ball to the 35-yard line of Dallas. From there, Kilmer needed only ten plays to cover the distance and win the game for Washington on a quarterback sneak with six minutes and thirty-four seconds elapsed in the extra period.

The Redskins' jubilation at outlasting their arch-rival was nearly matched by the enjoyment they got in re-living the meltdown of Dallas' invincible quarterback. Even Hanburger, one of the few good-natured players on a Washington team loaded with trash-talkers, couldn't help but admit surprise – and glee - at what transpired after his hit upon Staubach. "I just left my feet and tried to hit him chest-high," said Hanburger. "Then I flew about three or four yards past and landed on my face......I started to get up and someone was on top of me. It was Staubach. I jumped up and Ralph Neely grabbed me. I don't know why he did it but I'm glad he did. The official was right there. It was beautiful."

Laughing a few lockers away from Hanburger in the Redskins' dressing room was the sweaty, smiling figure of Diron Talbert. After taking a beating all day on running plays at the hands of Cowboys' guards Herbert Scott and Blaine Nye, Talbert was in a reflective mood after the game, even offering up some compliments for his quarterbacking nemesis. "That's the best Staubach has done since he's played against us," admitted a straight-faced Talbert. "I thought he handled the Shotgun pretty good. The Cowboys did a lot with that stuff today. That Shotgun isn't too bad as long as you've got a guy back there who can operate it. Yeah, Staubach showed us something today." Then

Talbert wrinkled his nose and gave a slight smirk. "But the pressure caught up with him in the fifth quarter," he said.

When cornered in the Dallas locker room, Staubach didn't run from his actions, describing the ill-fated late-game sequence as a "stupid" play on his part. "I'm a nice guy, remember?" said the normally even-keeled Staubach, trying to force a smile. "This is the only time I remember losing my temper on the football field... It wasn't necessary for Fischer to block me. The play was over. But it was legal. I just hit him back."

Aside from the drama surrounding Staubach, the remaining Cowboys' players wallowed in depression while dressing for the return flight to Dallas, groping for answers that would somehow rationalize such an inexplicable defeat. Cliff Harris sat with head in hands, staring at the floor. Charlie Waters lay slumped back in his locker, eyes glazed over as if reliving the game frame by frame. And Clint Longley likely wondered what might have turned out differently had he been in the game.

Slowly, one by one, each came out of his reverie and awakened to a strong sense of denial. They had been beaten on the scoreboard, yes, but not beaten physically. The Redskins hadn't shoved and pushed the Cowboys around the field like everyone in Washington had anticipated. That, at least, was a moral victory that the losers could hang their hats on going forward. "Washington was on the brink of losing all day,' said Blaine Nye. "And then we lose. I do know one thing... they're not better than we are. No way."

"This sounds funny after what happened today," said Golden Richards, "but we WILL win the division. We WILL win the division."

As the team prepared to board the plane, it was reported to Tex Schramm that George Allen had toasted the Washington victory by bringing a giant victory cake into the Redskins locker room. Schramm's reaction to this news likely summed up the feelings of everyone on the Cowboys' charter.

Said Schramm of Allen: "I hope he chokes on that cake."

The fallout from the Cowboys' Week 7 loss in Washington reached much farther than just the visitor's locker room. The fans back home had their own emotions to cope with too. Some, as you will discover below, handled their disappointments better than others.

Decades before he became an award-winning sports columnist for the *Charlotte Observer*, Scott Fowler was an average American boy whose big day was ruined by the Cowboys' fourth-quarter collapse. He recounted the unpleasantries of that evening in a April 1996 article that revealed just how much this particular loss affected him.

Writes Fowler:

"I was born in Texas and raised on Cowboys lore. I got a miniature Dallas Cowboys uniform when I was 7. My grandfather once saw Hall of Fame defensive tackle Bob Lilly in a restaurant and snagged his autograph for me. Lilly was nice to my grandfather; that seemed important.

"Quarterback Roger Staubach remains one of my heroes.

"In 1975, on the day of my 11th birthday, I wanted one thing most of all for a present – for Dallas to beat the Washington Redskins that afternoon.

"It didn't.

"Toni Fritsch missed a short field goal that would have clinched it in regulation. The game went into overtime and Washington won 30-24.

"I stormed into my room, angry tears streaming down my cheeks, and ripped out several sheets of notebook paper. I scribbled various mean things about Toni Fritsch upon them and stuck them on my door with tape.

"I couldn't seem to catch my breath.

"A day later, my parents were driving me to the hospital with the worst case of asthma I ever had. To this day, we all blame my devotion to the Cowboys for this bout of wheezing."

CHAPTER 18

TAKING AIM

"I wanted to rush for 200 yards and spike the ball in his face."
- **Robert Newhouse, on Howard Cosell**

Owners of a 5-2 record at the season's midway point, the Dallas Cowboys could afford to take a deep breath and comfort themselves for having exceeded all expectations thus far. Whether it was the high number of outgoing veterans, or the unproven abilities of the rookies that replaced them, the pigskin prognosticators, to a man, had Dallas penciled in as a seven-win club for 1975. Eight wins possibly, if things fell right for them. Nobody in their right mind, with the possible exception of Cowboys' Vice-President Gil Brandt, who was of a positive turn of mind, thought the Cowboys had enough juice left in the tank to reach ten wins. Lo and behold, as of early November that was the pace they were on.

True, Dallas' most recent loss in Washington left them on the outside of the playoffs as things stood, but a pair of early-season victories over quality teams such as Los Angeles and St. Louis suggested that this Cowboys' bunch, though infiltrated with youth, were more than capable of making up ground in the standings down the stretch.

With seven weeks remaining on the regular season slate, Dallas was mired in a three-way tie with St. Louis and Washington. Based upon a set of complicated tie-breakers, the Cowboys were technically in third-place. With head-to-head dates against both clubs looming large toward the end of the calendar year, it became imperative for the Cowboys to take care of business over the next month against a slew of sub.500 teams and stay within shouting distance of the front-runners within the NFC East. Only then would those back-to-back dates in December against the Cardinals and Redskins be of any significance and allow the Cowboys to leapfrog them to the top of the standings.

How Dallas proposed to stay near the front of the playoff pack with so many team members under-performing was a dubious question indeed for head coach Tom Landry. Coming out of preseason, Landry had envisioned the Dallas offense only a pair of complementary runners away from operating like a well-oiled machine. Now in early November, several weeks removed from settling upon the duo of Preston Pearson and Robert Newhouse as his primary regulars in the backfield, while also finding small roles for Doug Dennison and Charles Young, Landry remained at a shortage of solutions when trying to plug the leaks that prevented the Cowboys from upping their scoring average.

Even with the carries being spread out over a quartet of runners, the Dallas offense still performed inconsistently on a week-to-week basis. After failing to show up in the first-half up while hosting the Packers, the Cowboys couldn't run the ball at all against Philadelphia.

A week later, a scintillating first two quarters of action saw the Cowboys' offense post 17 points against the Redskins and was followed up by a second-half in which they failed to score at all. Over the last four weeks, the Dallas offense was averaging

15 points a game, while failing to produce more than 17 points in any game. Those numbers were in stark contrast to the first three weeks of the season, when Dallas beat up on the Rams, Cardinals, and Lions while averaging 30 points per contest.

The longer Landry studied the film of recent games, the more apparent it became that there wasn't just one flaw in the unit's armor. Reliability, in recent weeks, had become a question mark almost across the board.

Preston Pearson, though a solid runner between the tackles and a knowledgeable pass receiver, had dealt with injuries in recent weeks, limiting his effectiveness. His second-quarter drop of a would-be touchdown against Washington was also fresh in the mind of the Cowboys' Head Coach.

Two-hundred and twenty-five-pound tight end Jean Fugett, though certainly a better athlete than Billy Joe Dupree, struggled to hold his own while blocking linebackers and big defensive ends on running plays. Fugett was a valuable asset to have in the lineup, with the ability to play in tight or farther out as a slot receiver, but Landry still longed to have Dupree back in his usual starting role. With Dupree's broken finger being what it was, Landry couldn't anticipate that happening anytime soon.

In four starts at guard, Burton Lawless had shown above-average run-blocking ability, yet had struggled from the outset in pass-protection. Lawless' replacement the past three weeks while out with an injury, Herbert Scott, was more natural at blocking for the pass.

Even Roger Staubach, as evidenced by his guerilla tactics in overtime, had proven unreliable to a point, costing his team 15 precious yards that nearly guaranteed the Redskins of victory.

Further compromising these offensive shortcomings was the temperamental toe of Landry's field-goal kicker. Aside from his heroics against Philadelphia, Fritsch had earned more eye-rolling than accolades from the Dallas sideline. Through seven games, Fritsch had missed four extra-points, made 4-of-7 attempts from 30-39 yards, and was just 2-of-6 from beyond 40 yards.

Landry considered it to be poor execution on the part of his kicker that led to these struggles. Fritsch, on the other hand, thought it merely a product of the odds. Speaking after he kicked the Cowboys to victory over the Eagles, Fritsch said, "I have much confidence. People forget that I am [the team's] leading scorer. Sure I miss many field goals, but I think they forget if you try many you are going to miss more."

Kickers... They were one species of the football race that Landry would never claim to understand.

Based upon his body of work, there was one player Landry recognized as having accomplished everything that had been asked of him through half a season. Standing conspicuous as one of the few dependable members of the Dallas offensive unit was Robert Newhouse, all five-foot ten-inches of him. The heir-apparent to Calvin Hill, as voted on by fans during the summer months, Newhouse had acclimated himself rather nicely to his shared role in the Dallas backfield. And despite not being the featured back like his predecessor, Newhouse was piling up yards at a similar rate.

Through the first-half of the 1974 season, Hill accumulated 466 rushing yards, a total easily comparable to Newhouse's 436 through seven games in 1975. Newhouse had also quieted the skeptics who questioned his abilities as a pass receiver, distancing himself from Hill's mark of twelve receptions for the entire 1974 campaign with 16 catches of his own, including six for 55 yards against Philadelphia.

But, like Staubach a week before, Newhouse viewed the Cowboys' next game against Kansas City as a means to prove a point of personal significance. A tough runner on the field with a quiet, business-like manner off it, Newhouse had been holding a grudge for over a month, and had circled the night of Nov. 10 as his one and only primetime opportunity to unleash a torrent of righteous holy terror upon the conscience of Howard Cosell.

Nobody, not even the thousands of fans who peppered Tex Schramm's office with complaints, were more outraged at Cosell's unflattering description of Newhouse during the Detroit game than was the subject himself. Newhouse had never made himself out to be a premier tailback like Calvin Hill, but he certainly considered himself to be an NFL-worthy player. To awake the morning after a blowout win over the Lions and find out that Cosell had used his far-reaching microphone to put even that into question was too much for Newhouse to contemplate.

It was simple now. Newhouse was not only playing to beat the Chiefs on Monday night, but to make Howard Cosell eat his own words while the mic and the lights were hot. "I wanted to rush for 200 yards and spike the ball in his face," said Newhouse.

Newhouse never came close to fulfilling his mission. Before a packed house at Texas Stadium and a national audience on ABC, the Cowboys' stumpy, bowling-ball of a running back put the crowd on his back and commenced to deliver a wild roller-coaster ride that went up early with shouts of delight, only to come crashing down for all to see, leading to another fourth-quarter collapse for the Cowboys while stripping Newhouse of his badge of dependability.

CHAPTER 19

MONDAY NIGHT MADNESS

"It's been a lot of fun down here, though, it really has, Howard. You have a way of turning on a crowd, or turning on an entire city." -**Frank Gifford**

"The Cowboys not only lost. They humiliated themselves." - **Sam Blair, columnist for the Dallas Morning News**.

    Of the many lessons that Lee Roy Jordan learned during his lengthy career with the Cowboys, there was one that remained at the forefront of his thoughts during the week leading up to Dallas' Week 8 showdown with Kansas City. Jordan cared not that the Chiefs were in a rebuilding phase with first-year head coach Paul Wiggin, nor that they were fast losing touch with Oakland in the AFC's Western division. He also found it hard to acknowledge the fact that the Cowboys could probably beat Kansas City while blindfolded.

None of these factors meant a thing for Jordan when compared with the outcome of the previous Sunday. Dallas had lost to Washington. That in itself spelled trouble for Monday night's up-coming game. "We put so much importance on the Washington game that when we lose it, it takes a long time to recover," said Jordan. "Check on what's happened to us after the Washington game up there the last few years."

Jordan certainly had his facts in order. In 1973, Dallas followed a brutal down-to-the-wire defeat against the Redskins with a discouraging 37-31 loss, in which Rams' wide receiver Harold Jackson scored four receiving touchdowns. A year later, another close loss at Washington left a deflated Dallas squad with just enough energy to squeak past a bad Houston team 10-0.

What Jordan feared was a week of lackadaisical preparation that would turn into half-hearted concentration during the game. He was worried about the uncharacteristic mistakes of a football team dealing with the effects of both physical and mental fatigue.

Jordan hoped that a favorable turn of circumstances would lift the team's energy level early in the game to get them off and rolling. Without it, the veteran linebacker felt certain that the favored Cowboys were primed to be upended for a second consecutive week. No matter the venue. No matter the foe. And no matter what witty words the Irving faithful could conjure up for America's most controversial television commentator.

It has been acknowledged upon more than one occasion that Texans are the friendliest folks on the face of God's good earth. Seemingly nobody within the state's expansive borders is ever too busy for a handshake, a "Howdy!" or a few minutes of healthy conversation.

But, as Howard Cosell would soon find out, these perks are not always evident for the high-profile personality whose manners they find lacking. What awaited Cosell for *Monday Night Football's* only trip to Dallas for the 1975 season promised to be anything but hospitable, and every bit of rude. As a student of cultural history, Cosell was himself prepared for the onslaught of criticism that awaited him and did his best to hide from it, refusing to do a single interview with the press in the days leading up to the game. Rather than diffuse the situation, Cosell's evasive manner only seemed to enhance local anticipation surrounding the game.

On the Tuesday prior to the game between Dallas and Kansas City, more than 24,000 tickets remained unsold. By the time Monday night rolled around and kickoff was imminent, Tex Schramm was pleased to announce a full house in attendance of more than 60,000 fans anxious to get a peek at their struggling football team and a shot at the man named Cosell.

The loyal Texan had little use for Howard Cosell, whose caustic and oft-times snippy criticism of the Cowboys made him a definite outsider. But based upon his disparaging remarks pertaining to the ability of Robert Newhouse during the Detroit game, Cosell had gone from a mere outsider, to a Texas-sized enemy.

The state's uninhibited dislike of the popular commentator would be on full display before a national television audience, as Cowboys' fans came to Texas Stadium armed with their most descriptively witty signs, portraying "Howie" as anything from the hind-end of a donkey to a mealy-mouthed jack-o-lantern with greasy hair. As you may have guessed, some banners were fit for television, while others were not. Not that Cosell was offended in any way. Or was he?

There were rumors that came out after the game suggesting that Howard was not happy when the ABC television cameras showed a particular banner to the nation. It bore a caricature of Cosell, minus his toupee, and declared, "Bald Is Beautiful!" So the story went, Cosell got one of the producers on the phone in the truck and declared that if they showed one more shot like that for the pleasure of the viewing audience he would walk out of the booth. This revelation dispelled the common notion that Cosell was a man without feeling, and officially welcomed him in as a bona-fide member of the human race.

Cosell, to his credit, acknowledged his past remarks about Newhouse during the telecast, and duly refused to rescind them. He also shared a laugh with broadcast booth partners Frank Gifford and Alex Karras when the ABC cameras focused on particular specimens from various artwork displays in the crowd.

But as the evening progressed, Cosell's omnipresent charm and not-so-subtle digs at the men in blue and silver became overshadowed by a startling display of ineptness by the football locals from Dallas. Still reeling from their emotionally-sapping defeat in Washington eight days prior, the Cowboys bumbled and stumbled their way into another fourth-quarter nail-biter with a far inferior Kansas City club, leaving many onlookers to wonder if this odd collection of Cowboys were riding a dramatic wave of destiny, or in fact existing under the tantalizing banner of the doomed.

In the manner of solemn smoke rising toward the heavens, a tangible blanket of electrically-charged anticipation lay over the quaint roofless castle in Irving, sanctifying the evening's events as both memorable and historical. For one night, the epicenter of the Texas religion known as football was inside Texas Stadium, where nearly 65,000 had gathered to cheer on their team in action, poke fun during stoppages at a notorious television quack, and pay tribute to the state's all-time football team at intermission.

An audience oft-noted for a casual demeanor couldn't help but reveal the excitement that carried them to the stadium for this rare weeknight event. Good-natured jokes were shared, the locale of the ABC television booth pointed out, and fans inspected each other's homemade signs with all the relish of schoolchildren. Flash bulbs exploded in rapturous admiration of Cowboys' players as they went through warm-ups. When Tommy Loy finished performing the Star-Spangled Banner with his customary trumpet, the crowd's appreciation was marked by an enthusiastic ovation.

Then the game began.

Eight days had passed since both teams had last stepped onto a playing field. Watching the early events, the casual onlooker might have figured it had been eight years.

Mike Livingston, a one-time standout at South Oak Cliff high school and SMU in Dallas, got off to a shaky beginning in front of his hometown fans by fumbling the snap on Kansas City's first play. Livingston saved face by emerging from the bottom of the scrum with the ball.

The next play held no such luck for the underdog Chiefs. Bursting through a hole off left guard, Ed Podolak had the ball knocked from his arms by a chasing Ed "Too Tall" Jones, a fumble which Cliff Harris recovered at the Kansas City 44-yard line. Dallas returned the favor shortly after. Sparked by a 29-yard zig-zag run from Doug Dennison, the Cowboys had moved to within a foot of the goal-line when, on third-down, Roger Staubach lost control of the ball while reaching out for a handoff. The loose ball bounced off the belly of Dennison and back into the mass of bodies near the line of scrimmage. Emmitt Thomas fell on the ball for Kansas City on the 1-yard line.

A tale of two kickers unfurled itself later in the quarter. Toni Fritsch, still smarting from the verbal flogging that followed him from his critical miss versus Washington, was escorted off the field to a chorus of boos after his 43-yard field-goal attempt was blocked. It was Fritsch's eleventh failed kick in 25 attempts on the season, and the fifth consecutive game in which he had missed a kick.

His counterpart, Jan Stenerud, then demonstrated the proper touch from distance in the closing seconds of the frame, booting a 51-yard line-drive field goal that extended a streak of eight successful kicks, dating back to October 19 against San Diego. In breaking the scoreless tie, Stenerud won himself a few new fans from the audience, who longed for the day when the Cowboys would have a place-kicker of his caliber.

A frantic-paced second quarter began with the spotlight on Robert Newhouse. Taking a pitch from Roger Staubach on a sweep to the right side, Newhouse slipped past two defenders while running horizontally, turned up-field, hurdled another would-be tackler before running back across the field. By the time Emmitt Thomas pushed him out of bounds, Newhouse had traveled about 100 yards for a 19-yard gain.

Upstairs in the ABC booth, Howard Cosell was beside himself with skeptical admiration. "Bobby just had a good run," acknowledged Cosell. "An exceptional run," countered Frank Gifford next to him.

Gifford continued to needle Cosell's prejudice against the Cowboys, using his description of the ensuing first-down handoff to Preston Pearson to provoke his broadcast partner into making even more inflammatory remarks. Cosell proved quick to take the bait. "First-and-10 from the 15," Gifford announced, "as the awesome Cowboys move inside."

"That's what started it all," Cosell declared. "Frank Gifford characterized the Cowboys as awesome [during the Detroit game] and they went on to lose two of their next four games, including giving Green Bay its only victory of the year. And a win tonight, and they'll be tied for the division lead in the National Football Conference Eastern Division. Which doesn't speak well for the strength of the league," responded Cosell.

Alex Karras cut short this dialogue by proposing a compromise on Cosell's part that promised to benefit the entire television crew. Said Karras: "Well, since we're in Dallas, let's call 'em awesome so we can get out of here after the game."

Agreement was mutual among the threesome, though Cosell wasn't above using his favorite whipping boy to take one last shot at the crowd before the drive concluded. After Newhouse was upended for a modest gain on second-down, Cosell said, "Thank heaven he didn't fumble. [The crowd] would've booed him."

Perhaps Cosell was a better judge of human character and emotion than he was given credit for. The boos that he alleged to have been stored up for the next Cowboys' miscue landed instead on the ears of Dallas' popular quarterback. Just moments after being nearly knocked senseless on a touchdown scramble, Staubach received the brunt of the audience's displeasure when a short pass to Jean Fugett on third-down came up short of the yardstick. And when Fritsch, on the next play, booted a 31-yard field goal try through the uprights to give Dallas a 10-3 lead, all he got for his efforts was a smattering of mock applause.

It only got worse. As if belittling the athletes on the field wasn't enough, the crowd soon turned its attention to the game officials.

To begin Kansas City's next possession, Livingston directed a pass over the middle to Barry Pearson, the Chiefs' wide receiver whose first impactful play of the game reached an abrupt end when he was body-slammed by Cliff Harris. Harris was penalized, turning an 18-yard gain into one of 33 yards, prompting the voices of displeasure to rise in unison yet again. "The way these people are booing it's starting to sound like Philadelphia," observed Cosell.

The scorner's corner soon found another Cowboys' figure to ridicule. A Harris recovery of a MacArthur Lane fumble had given Dallas possession of the ball at their own 3-yard line. On first-down, it was Preston Pearson sidling to his left looking for an opening, fighting for yardage. Suddenly, the ball popped loose from the pack and bounded backwards into the end-zone. Reaching it a step ahead of Pearson was defensive end John Matuszak, who smothered the ball to score the touchdown and tie the game. "It's the first time I've fumbled in two or three years," moaned Pearson.

Newhouse provided a much-needed moment of lightheartedness on the ensuing drive, restoring a spirit of conviviality among the masses. Anxious to re-take the lead they had just squandered, Dallas needed only two plays to move from their own 27 to the Kansas City 38-yard line, Staubach using passes in the middle of the field to Jean Fugett and Golden Richards. Working from the left hash, Landry called for another pitch right to Newhouse, and was rewarded with a thunderous 18-yard gain. With only six carries, Newhouse had already accumulated 45 yards rushing.

"And again," Gifford told his television audience, "Howard gives a salute to the capacity crowd, and he blows them a kiss. I wish you could see this, ladies and gentlemen."

"I only hope," responded Cosell, trying to stifle a laugh, "that [Newhouse] doesn't fumble. I said it before, they'll boo him out of the stadium... So far we've had a critical fumble by Dennison and a critical fumble by Pearson. So Newhouse is excelling tonight."

What was shaping up to be a career night continued for Newhouse two plays afterwards, when he burst through the line on a delayed handoff and covered ten more yards.

Cosell: "I hope I've inspired the young man. But you know what Tex Schramm told us."

Gifford: "You better be careful."

Cosell: "Aww, no. He said he'd like two Bobby Newhouses, one standing on the other one's shoulders. Then he'd look like Calvin Hill."

A monster thus far with the ball, Newhouse became just as dangerous without it. On a third-down play, Staubach's play-fake to Newhouse sucked the defense in and allowed the quarterback to deliver a cross-field bullet to Richards. Working from right to left, Richards was able to reach up with his left hand and tip the ball, before leaping and snagging it while falling to the turf. Such an incredible catch it was that even Landry couldn't resist a pump of the fist and a slap on the back of Richards.

There was additional satisfaction among the throng in realizing that Newhouse's strong performance made the scoring play possible. Without a per-carry average of nearly eight yards, Kansas City wouldn't have been nearly so willing to step up and defend against another Newhouse scamper. Newhouse, almost singlehandedly, had put the Cowboys ahead once again.

His virtual stomping ground the first two quarters, the game turned into a nightmare for Robert Newhouse in the second half. With one spasm of pain and another moment of truth, Newhouse played himself off the pedestal of heroism he had built for himself, joining a long line of culpable Cowboys who directly contributed to a most maddening of Monday night defeats.

There to laugh last and loudest was the same antagonist who had provoked an entire region into anger by laughing first. A memorable night in Texas Stadium was plotting its way toward an infamy so deep and so dark as to pronounce Howard Cosell the only winner assembled.

The evening wore on, making one thing quite apparent. The Kansas City Chiefs were not going away. Another fact of equal significance was that the Dallas Cowboys would not let them. Every time Dallas looked poised to gain the upper hand, they would offer up a free gift and a helping hand to keep the game close.

Doug Dennison fumbled a kickoff return, allowing Kansas City to take a 24-17 lead. Later in the second quarter, Golden Richards dropped a perfectly-placed bomb from Staubach down the left sideline that would have tied the game. Richards atoned for his mistake with a sensational over-the-shoulder scoring grab of 47 yards with 8:31 remaining in the third quarter to draw Dallas even at 24-24. But another Stenerud field goal had the Cowboys in chase mode yet again.

As he had throughout the second quarter to such success, Landry called Newhouse's number to get the ball moving again. But instead of running right, the Cowboys were going left, Staubach in front on a college-style quarterback option. The play looked out of sync from the beginning, Staubach having to wait for Newhouse to catch up before making a precarious pitch to him. Newhouse's knee was hit hard by the helmet of Emmitt Thomas, requiring team doctors to come out and attend to him. With pain etched on his face, Newhouse limped slowly to the bench area.

And when Charles Young joined him there shortly after with a limp of his own, Landry had little choice but to insert Scott Laidlaw into the lineup. Due to Preston Pearson's rise up the depth chart, and a nagging knee injury of his own, Laidlaw had been relegated to kick-coverage duties in recent games, failing to crack the offensive stat-sheet since Week 4. But, upon the offense getting a first-down, Landry figured to put the rookie to good use while he was in the huddle. After taking the snap from center, Staubach rolled to his right and began fading...fading...fading. Just when it looked like the defense would bury him for a momentous loss, Staubach turned, jumped in the air and threw back across the field to the waiting Laidlaw, who did his part by rumbling all the way to the 1-yard line. Laidlaw's 25-yard catch-and-run set up a simple quarterback-sneak from Staubach on the ensuing play that awarded Dallas the lead for the third time in the game.

But the third time would not work its charm on this night. The Cowboys simply couldn't hold a lead against the Chiefs. A Stenerud miss from 53 set the Dallas offense up with prime field position. Charles Young, back from a short stay on the sideline, was there to fumble the ball back to Kansas City at the 30-yard line.

The Dallas defense did their job once again, causing Livingston's tenth incompletion in his last twelve pass attempts and another punt. That's when Newhouse declared himself fit for battle, and walked back into the huddle for the first time since his injury, and the last time for the game.

Taking a handoff and going left, Newhouse was stood up in the backfield and stripped of the ball by Matuszak. If not for a hustling tackle by Ralph Neely at the Dallas 41-yard line, Thomas would have taken the runback the full distance.

As inexplicable as Newhouse's fumble was, things only got stranger for the Cowboys. Livingston's first-down pass was batted into the air by a charging Ed "Too Tall" Jones. Four Cowboys' defenders and one Chiefs' receiver had a chance at grabbing it in the middle of the field.

Lee Roy Jordan looked to be in perfect position, as the ball landed in his hands at the 24. But before he could fully gather it, Brunson knocked the ball from his grasp and then caught it himself while falling down. Jordan argued that the ball had hit the ground before the catch, but to no avail. Instead of a Dallas interception, the Chiefs had a 17-yard pass completion of their own, and were looking for more.

Three plays later, the Chiefs cashed in on Newhouse's fumble when Podolak caught a short pass in the left flat, turned inside of Jordan and walked into the end-zone. Kansas City now led 34-31.

The beat continued for the Cowboys, right to the very end. Two fourth-quarter interceptions by Staubach – making seven Cowboy turnovers in all – gave Kansas City a three-point victory, and provided Howard Cosell the perfect opportunity to emphasize, what to him was, the critical turning point in the game.

Speaking to a Houston-area columnist after the game, Cosell said, ""Newhouse is a pedestrian runner who, if he makes an 18-yard run, [fans] think he is Red Grange incarnate. But they were hoist on their own petard. Sadly, it was his fumble that gave Kansas City the game. I only hope that the fans do not turn on the lad."

It was with joy that north Texas bade Cosell farewell that night. The three hours of fun he had experienced at Texas Stadium was the last time he would be calling a Cowboys' game for the rest of the season.

But with the disappearance of ABC's traveling caravan over the distant horizon, the city was confronted with a startling question. With the loss to the Chiefs, their beloved Cowboys had fallen a full game behind Washington and St. Louis in the standings, and admittedly, were playing a poor brand of football of late.

Did the team have it in them to make it up, or would they be sitting out of the playoffs for a second year running?

CHAPTER 20

GETTING BACK ON TRACK

"It was a real smart play on my part."
- A sarcastic Roger Staubach, while explaining the events that led to him suffering an arm injury against New England.

On the morning after Dallas' three-point home defeat to Kansas City, a stone-faced Tom Landry stood in front of the projector screen and, with the entire team assembled, calmly pointed out the good and the bad from their performance of the night before. As usual after a loss, Landry's tendency was to harp on the negative, effectively squashing any ego in the room that might have entertained illusions of having played well. Seemingly no one received a passing grade from the head coach after this game.

Lee Roy Jordan overran this play. Burton Lawless' poor footwork led to a missed block on that play. Mitch Hoopes could have kicked better here. Golden Richards should have caught that pass there.

The list went on and on.

When nearly an hour had passed Landry called an end to the meeting, and the team separated into positional groups. Presiding over the meeting of the defensive linemen was coordinator Ernie Stautner, and the message he had to deliver to his unit was equally as unsavory as Landry's seemed only a minute before. But while Landry focused primarily on Xs and Os and certain rudiments of fundamental football, Stautner had to address – and even question – the emotional desire of the entire defensive line.

A Hall of Fame lineman in his own right from a 14-year career with the Pittsburgh Steelers, Ernie coached the game with the same passion in which he played it, all-out all the time. And when he sensed that his players weren't giving back that same effort, he coached them even harder.

Players knew when Stautner was angry during meetings because he would begin writing so hard on the blackboard while stuttering over his words that the chalk would break in his hands. But there was to be no chalk episode on this day. The Cowboys had just allowed 30 or more points in consecutive games for the first time since 1963, a fact that Stautner believed rested squarely on the collective shoulders of an under-performing defensive line.

Stautner acknowledged that opponents, in recent weeks, had been using different tactics to block the Cowboys. Early in the season, offensive tackles would drop back in pass protection and allow edge rushers Harvey Martin and Ed "Too Tall" Jones to either use their speed and quickness to turn the corners, or pin their ears back and overpower them to get to the quarterback.

Of late, blockers were attacking Martin and Jones. Rather than backing up, offensive tackles were stepping up to meet them before they could get their momentum started. With additional blocking help in the backfield by a running back or a tight end, and a steady increase in play-action passes from the quarterback, opponents appeared to have frustrated Dallas' potent pass-rushers into a mid-season submission that Stautner could not tolerate. He also took into account the fact that Jones was playing with a broken hand and Martin with a sprained ankle.

The first order of business for Stautner moving forward would be to simplify matters for his young stars. "Too Tall" Jones was a 6-9 up-and-comer at his position, yet still showed signs of inexperience that belied his status as a second-year pro. Going up against a wide variety of blocking formulas had caused Jones to struggle from information overload in the preseason. Rather than simply reacting and playing football, Jones had found himself thinking too much about pre-snap "keys." If Jones, the No. 1 overall pick in the 1974 draft, could be overwhelmed by the playbook at this point in his career, then it was just barely possible that Randy White, Cal Petersen and others were too. Especially in light of report cards from recent games.

"Everyone has been consistently [grading] low," said Stautner. "You can point to the fact that we have inexperience, but still the greatest part of pass-rush is the desire to get there. It's man-on-man and we just haven't been defeating our man.

"The most noticeable thing is the jump we've been getting off the ball. I take the blame here. It's just not what it should be. This is my fault. Maybe because we haven't been concentrating on it that much. But you can see the difference and I've got to make that change."

The manifestations of change became plainly evident on the following Sunday afternoon at Schaefer Stadium when Stautner made the simplest of adjustments to inject some confidence back into the Dallas defensive unit. A pass-rush grown stale over the last month received a shot in the arm with a surge of reinforcements, as the blitz-heavy Cowboys overwhelmed the Patriots on the field, and on the scoreboard.

It is a good thing indeed that Randy White's heart wasn't tied to playing one particular defensive position in the NFL. Though he certainly harbored personal preferences about where he lined-up on the field, White was a team-first player and willing to go wherever the Dallas coaching staff wanted him.

This willingness, combined with his athletic flexibility, paid huge dividends for the Cowboys during the stretch run of the 1975 season as they attempted to rally in a tightly contested race for the NFC East crown.

White grew up watching the Green Bay Packers as they stormed through the NFL during the better part of the 1960s, and discovered an especial admiration in seeing hard-nosed linebacker Ray Nitschke pummel ball-carriers on Sunday afternoons. Someday, if all the pieces fell together, he hoped to be a marquee linebacker at the professional ranks. Someday, White hoped to be just as good as Nitschke.

By the time he finished his four-year term at Maryland, White figured that dream to be a fragment of wishful thinking. The winner of college football's *Outland Trophy* in 1974, White found himself an established menace along the defensive line as he prepared to graduate to the NFL ranks, and expected nothing less than to be given the opportunity to build upon that reputation as a professional.

Then the Cowboys grabbed him in the draft, with the hope that he could develop into a game-wrecker behind their vaunted defensive front. Randy White, so they told him, would be the second-coming of Lee Roy Jordan at middle linebacker for the Cowboys. Randy White the linebacker was about to re-emerge on the football scene.

Or was he?

Personally, White viewed being drafted by the Cowboys as one of the best things that could have happened to him coming out of college. In Dallas, he would be coached by the great Tom Landry, an innovator and defensive genius whose name was regarded in high estimation by everyone along the Atlantic coast. If there was any one man in the National Football League who could help White re-acclimate himself to playing linebacker after a highly successful stint as a defensive end at Maryland, then surely it would be Landry.

His first visit to Dallas shortly after the draft convinced him he had found the perfect home. The city loved its football, and its team. Landry was everything he had heard; an articulate teacher and a patient one. The uniforms were cool. And the cold beverages were second to none! White was so ecstatic upon finding Coors beer in Dallas that he brought an entire case of the adult drink back with him to campus in Maryland.

After up and moving to Dallas later that spring, White put away the beer and hit the playbook hard. Hours upon hours of study, numerous meetings with coaches, and a lot of help from Lee Roy Jordan supplied White with a quiet confidence that he could make a seamless transition from an All-American defensive end to a standout middle linebacker in Tom Landry's Flex defense.

Heading toward training camp, the Dallas coaching staff couldn't have been happier with their top pick. Here they had a 6-4, 250-pound physical specimen with legs growing out of a pair of enormous shoulders, just waiting to receive the passing of the torch from Jordan in the near future.

But what looked perfect on paper failed to serve the process of practicality on the football field. White never could acclimate himself to middle linebacker, too often filling the role of the prototypical dumb football player, inclining more to wasted action than to calculated forethought. Though not performing poorly, White undoubtedly looked out of position throughout the preseason schedule, being plagued constantly by a poor combination of indecision and over-pursuit. He wasn't terrible, but he wasn't comfortable either.

The steady progression of Bob Breunig in the middle made it easier for Landry and Ernie Stautner to begin experimenting with White at different positions. What else were they supposed to do? White was too gifted an athlete to let sit on the bench and go to seed. If he couldn't play at middle linebacker, then why not somewhere else? Through the first eight games of his rookie season, Randy White played six different positions along the defensive front-seven. Middle linebacker. Strong-side linebacker. Left defensive end. Right defensive end. Left defensive tackle. Right defensive tackle.

White, as the coaching staff learned quickly, was a natural wrecking-ball at the line of scrimmage, with sufficient strength to overpower blockers in the middle and enough speed and quickness to get around the edge. By mid-season, his duties as strong-side linebacker remained the only ones in which he could be found standing up at the snap of the ball. And even from that position, White rushed the passer more often than not.

Much of White's contributions during the first eight games was done in a reserve role. But when Harvey Martin was relegated to almost exclusive spectator status with a bum ankle for Dallas' Week 9 game, White stepped in and played the part of a wily veteran from his defensive end spot, leading the defense in big plays against the New England Patriots while helping the Cowboys get back to their winning ways.

For the second time in five games in 1975, Schaefer Stadium welcomed a sellout crowd, as nearly 60,000 filed through its gates for the inaugural visit of the Dallas Cowboys to Foxboro. Four years had passed since the two teams had last met, a 44-21 Cowboy triumph that opened Texas Stadium. Now on a cool, clear day in Massachusetts, fans gathered to watch the highly-popular Cowboys bury what had thus far been a forgettable season for the hometown Patriots.

Coming off a 7-7 season with second-year head coach Chuck Fairbanks, the Patriots fostered hopes during the spring months of mounting a playoff run in 1975. The team lost its way, however, toward the close of preseason when quarterback Jim Plunkett landed on the injury list with a shoulder injury.

While their team leader was busy rehabbing, winning football games took a backseat to taking a hard-line stance toward league management. Less than two weeks away from their regular season opener, the Patriots went on strike, and came back from it a few days later a very different football team than they were expected to be.

Beginning with a surprising loss to the Oilers on opening day, New England dropped five of their first eight games, while displaying numerous signs of ineptness. In the days leading up to the Dallas-New England contest, Frank Luksa offered this observation on a season gone wrong for the Patriots in the *Dallas Cowboys Weekly* magazine. Wrote Luksa: "Without Jim Plunkett, [the Patriots] seemed to think their best chance was to lead a strike. They were right. When you can't beat a Houston, you are better off carrying a sign."

The grating sounds of negativity continued on game-day with the Cowboys in town, as the New England faithful greeted Plunkett with a chorus of boos during player introductions. So engrossed in their heckling of the former Heisman Trophy winning quarterback were fans that they failed to notice a key omission in the Patriots lineup.

Mack Herron, a diminutive running back of unquestioned talents, had walked out of the tunnel in full uniform and then quickly gotten himself lost in the crowd of bodies on the sideline. At 5-feet-5-inches tall, that wasn't particularly hard for Herron to do. When considering that "Mini" Mack was the newly-crowned record holder for all-purpose yards (2,444) in a single season from a year before and a crowd favorite in Foxboro, it was also equally certain that he couldn't hide for long.

The 3-5 New England Patriots would need Herron's services were they to pull off an upset against the Cowboys. But Herron, due to what Fairbanks later described as "unsatisfactory contributions" to the team, never stepped onto the field. Nor would he again. Mack Herron, a budding star in the league, was released from the team three days after the Cowboys came to town for what was eventually discovered to be a drug-related problem.

Without the speed of Herron to concern themselves with, the Cowboys' defense turned into a relentless monster, harassing Plunkett in the pocket on nearly each passing play. With Dallas crowding the line of scrimmage, Plunkett and the Patriots failed to record a single first down during first-quarter action as Dallas parlayed an early Cliff Harris interception into a 10-0 lead.

A slew of defensive penalties against the Dallas defense allowed New England to tie the score later in the second frame, a 29-yard chip-shot field goal and a short touchdown rush by Plunkett providing the scoring. The mock applause that accompanied Plunkett's first scoring play of the season didn't last for long. The Cowboys struck back quickly on the right arm of Roger Staubach, a development which failed to surprise Fairbanks on the New England sideline in the least.

In game-planning for the array of offensive weaponry that the Cowboys possessed during the week, Fairbanks realized that sitting back and playing a straight-up scheme gave his defense no chance of success.

Fairbanks was the first NFL head coach to use the 3-4 defense, bringing it over with him from the University of Oklahoma. The system, using many of the same philosophies of the modern-day Cover 2 defense, was predicated upon stopping the run, while preventing the big play. Where the Flex was based upon pre-snap "reads," the Patriots simply reacted as each play developed. And while the Flex offered the possibility, according to Tom Landry, of the middle linebacker making every tackle, Fairbanks' 3-4 made it advantageous for *two* inside linebackers.

In Fairbanks' two-gap system, it was paramount to have big, strong physical linemen willing to take the punishment, rather than the glory. If the nose-tackle could occupy the center and a guard, it would free one, or both, of the middle linebackers to clean up the play. The same could be said for the ends. If one of the ends occupied a tackle and guard, then theoretically both inside backers could be free to make the tackle.

The Patriots implemented this philosophy on a weekly basis in attempting to stop the run. Based on recent returns, a "theory" that many initially doubted would translate to the professional game had been tried and proven in a very short period of time. A year after finishing last in run defense, the Patriots finished first in the AFC in stopping the run in 1974.

Fairbanks found no reason to believe he couldn't shut down the Cowboys and their three-headed rushing attack of Pearson, Newhouse, and Dennison. But in the event that Dallas called a pass play... what then?

New England's defensive backfield, the acknowledged weak link of the defense, was already littered with bullet holes from early-season encounters with Joe Namath and Ken Anderson. And only a few days before in San Diego, a young Dan Fouts had ripped them to shreds with 329 passing yards on 25 completions. To sit back and play coverage against a dual-threat quarterback of Staubach's capabilities would be a direct invitation to an even longer day for the Patriots' defense.

The only hope for a suspect New England secondary to slow down Staubach and the Shotgun was for the Patriots to blitz early and often, and pray that someone broke through and reached the quarterback before a receiver flashed open downfield. Attacking a quarterback the caliber of Staubach was a risky business. But Fairbanks didn't see any other way to go about it. Not, that is, if he expected to have any chance of upsetting the favored Cowboys.

With the score knotted 10-10, the Patriots attacked the line of scrimmage in force and numbers. The Cowboys were ready for it. With the pass-rush closing in around him, Staubach lofted a downfield pass for Drew Pearson who was behind the man-to-man coverage of Ron Burton. The 31-yard touchdown bomb put Dallas back in front going into halftime.

Staubach and Co. continued their butchering of New England's 3-4 defense after the break. After a Staubach-to-Preston Pearson pass went for 27 yards, the Cowboys used five consecutive running plays to cover the remaining distance to pay-dirt. Doug Dennison's 6-yard scoring burst, his first touchdown romp since Oct. 19 versus Green Bay, gave Dallas a 24-10 advantage.

And when Randy White chased Plunkett down from behind and forced a fumble that D.D. Lewis scooped up and scooted with to the New England 21, the Cowboys were poised to put the score out of reach. But a poor play from Staubach gave the ball right back to the Patriots, and resulted in an injured shoulder for the Dallas quarterback besides.

Scrambling out of the pocket, Staubach showed poor judgment in trying to stiff-arm 260-pound defensive end Julius Adams. In getting smashed beneath the imposing form of Adams, the Dallas quarterback landed hard on his right elbow, jamming his arm and shoulder. He also lost his grip on the ball, and found himself pinned to the turf a helpless spectator as Sam Hunt recovered the fumble for the Patriots.

Whereas Cowboys' penalties opened the door for a first-half New England comeback, injuries in the Dallas secondary presented the same opportunity in the second-half. After missing the entire Kansas City game with a virus, Mel Renfro was removed from the game by team trainers with a foot ailment.

And on the first series of the third quarter, Mark Washington joined him on the bench with an injured neck.

To compound this sudden shortage of cornerbacks was an injury to strong safety Charlie Waters, who was in and out of the lineup for most of the second-half. Where the Cowboys before had three established veterans in their defensive backfield, they now had Benny Barnes playing alongside rookies Rollie Woolsey and Randy Hughes.

It didn't take long for the Patriots to cash in on this inexperience. Just six plays after Staubach's fumble, Plunkett spotted rookie tight end Russ Francis running free in the secondary and duly found him with the pass for a 37-yard touchdown. A game that, moments earlier, had seemed about over had now tightened up considerably. With less than a minute remaining in the third quarter, the Dallas advantage had dwindled to 24-17.

Over on the Dallas sideline, Staubach was grimacing noticeably. That shoulder of his was becoming more of a problem than he had originally thought it to be. While hanging loose by his side, Staubach's arm throbbed with pain, and when he followed through with a warm-up toss on the sideline, his shoulder felt as if it was being wrenched from its socket.

To himself, Staubach wondered if he would be able to complete another pass. To the trainers and coaches, he said his shoulder was fine and for them to stop their worrying. Nothing was going to stop him from going back into the game.

Landry knew that his quarterback had been shaken up on the previous series, but with him coming back onto the field Landry merely figured it to be a matter of Staubach getting his bell rung. Consequently, the offensive philosophy remained the same for the Cowboys. If the Patriots blitzed, then Staubach's job was to attack them with deep passes.

Wrenched arm and all, Staubach did just that when he hurled a bomb into the end-zone for Golden Richards, another tormentor of Burton's in the New England secondary. The 41-yard touchdown toss elicited a dismal cry of pain from the quarterback upon delivery. As certain as the Cowboys were now up again by fourteen points, Staubach realized unequivocally that he was dealing with something more troublesome than just some momentary discomfort. Staubach was hurt, a fact which he couldn't hide from his Head Coach, who immediately told Clint Longley to start warming up.

Longley struggled mightily off the bench, completing only 1-of-6 pass attempts for 8 yards, while opening up the door for a late-game comeback by New England. After a 26-yard field-goal from Toni Fritsch made the score 34-17, Plunkett and the Patriots caught fire and tore through Dallas' patchwork secondary, scoring two touchdowns in a matter of four minutes.

A Dallas pass-rush led by Randy White (three sacks and two forced fumbles) and Larry Cole looked gassed in the final minutes, as Plunkett picked on Rollie Woolsey with cruel relentlessness while moving the offense down the field in huge chunks. After tossing a 13-yard touchdown to Darryl Stingley, he went back to his preferred wide receiver to complete the next series, a 5-yard scoring pass that drew New England within three points, 34-31, with just over a minute remaining.

The Cowboys avoided a three-game losing streak and a collapse for the ages by recovering the Patriot's onside kick and running out the clock. In a game that felt like Dallas outplayed its opponent by a wide margin, Tom Landry was able to take a deep breath after his team squeaked by with a three-point victory.

When approached during his post-game meeting with the media about the struggles of Woolsey at cornerback, Landry displayed the diplomacy you would expect from the victorious head coach. "I'd say he had a typical day for a rookie in such a spot for the first time," said Landry, a former NFL defensive back himself. "I was there once and I remember you tend to get beaten pretty badly when you first get out there…

"We did show some improvement in defense out there," Landry continued, "although I know it didn't look like it. But if the defense can continue to improve, then we have a chance. If it doesn't, we have no chance at all. St. Louis gets by with giving up a lot of yards and a lot of points. But they manage to pull out those close ones. We'll have to do the same or really start cutting down on the points we give up.

"We can't give up 90 points in three games and expect to win enough from here on in to find ourselves in the playoffs."

It was Staubach, after throwing for 190 yards and three touchdowns on 10-of-14 passing, who offered up the most vital news update of the postgame interview session, telling reporters what he knew of the extent of his arm ailment.

"It's pretty sore," he said of the arm, "but I don't think it's anything serious, probably just a muscular. I'll have X-rays to make sure. It will be a problem and I won't throw for at least a couple of days, but I think it's all right."

But Roger Staubach's right arm wasn't all right, a sobering development that caused fans more than their usual share of anxiety during the next week, while forcing Landry to significantly alter the playbook for the Cowboys' next game against Philadelphia.

CHAPTER 21

THE CURSE OF THE CAKE

"They used finesse. That's the Dallas game and they do it well."
- **A disdainful Bill Bradley, after the Eagles safety watched his defense get outthought at every turn by the unpredictable Cowboys**

"It was physical but not pugilistic. That in itself constitutes an upset where the Cowboys and Eagles are concerned."
- **Randy Galloway, columnist for the Dallas Morning News**

The city of Dallas began its work week on Monday morning with cries of foul play emanating from Washington D.C. The Redskins, a team riding an emotional high only a few weeks before after beating the Cowboys in overtime, were now speculating upon the likelihood of being placed under some sort of plague. Who can but say that they were justified in their speculations.

Since celebrating a momentous victory over Dallas on the afternoon of Nov. 2 with a giant victory cake, the wheels had begun to come off the Redskins' caravan in the strangest of ways. Keep in mind that Tex Schramm had been of the hope that Allen would choke *on* that particular cake. He never mentioned the possibility of them choking *from* it. Yet it didn't take a devious mind very long to come up with enough ironies in the wake of that Redskins' victory to find cause for belief that Allen's victory cake was perhaps something more than cursed.

On Friday, a mere five days after Washington outlasted Dallas by a 30-24 final, place-kicker Mark Moseley reported with a staph infection on his kicking leg. He played on Sunday against the New York Giants, but was finally admitted to the hospital on Tuesday.

The next day, return specialist Larry Jones was hospitalized with a foot ailment caused by a bacterial infection, the same germ that had negatively affected Moseley. Jones, who also played wide receiver when not returning kickoffs and punts, was admitted to Arlington, Va. Hospital with what the team physician described as "an infection in his left foot with lymph angitis and lymph adenitis." Doctors said Jones was hospitalized in order to accelerate the healing process and isolate the Redskins' players. Jones' symptoms soon spread to other parts of his body. While in the hospital, Jones started experiencing pain in his groin and had to be fed intravenously.

This wasn't the first time a mysterious disease had made entry upon the Redskins' camp. Three years prior, before their 1972 playoff game against the Green Bay Packers, a virus infection hit the team hard, causing doctors to require the healthy players to wear surgical facemasks during meetings.

The club took preventive steps in a similar fashion this time around. A professional outfit was brought in on Thursday to spray the locker room, showers, and even the telephones with disinfectant. All wet laundry was treated chemically. Surgical soap was being used by some players. Players were encouraged not to leave wet towels laying around and that any cut or pimple that looked suspicious be immediately reported to trainers.

A team on edge all week then was provoked into a state of paranoia by game officials on Sunday afternoon in St. Louis. During the latter stages of a first-place showdown with the Cardinals, the Redskins found themselves protecting a 17-10 lead as Jim Hart and Co. mounted one final drive. With the ball on the six-yard line, Hart fired a pass toward Mel Gray in the corner of the end-zone. Gray caught the ball while in the air, bobbled it on the way down, and landed with both feet out of bounds. Allen emphatically signaled incomplete. The referee, perhaps encouraged by the biased opinions of the home crowd, saw it a different way, and awarded the touchdown to Gray and the Cardinals.

Allen blew his top there on the sideline, and was even angrier during his postgame press conference after St. Louis won the game on an overtime field goal. The rulebook had always required the receiver to have two feet in bounds with possession of the ball for it to be considered a legal catch. Gray had neither. Allen cursed the NFL rulebook which prohibited public criticism of officials by tearing into the referee and his crew for all he was worth.

With the loss, Washington dropped into a second-place tie with Dallas at 6-3 in the NFC East. The curse of the cake was working its magic, keeping the division-favorite Redskins jumbled up in the middle of the pack, while giving Dallas time enough to gather their bearings and make a late-season run at the crown.

As the Cowboys prepared for a rematch with the Eagles at Texas Stadium, news filtered through the locker room that the Dirty Dozen had lost one of its own. After playing through the pain of torn knee cartilage for the better part of a month, running back Scott Laidlaw finally waved the white flag on his rookie season and accepted the recommendations of team doctors that he be placed on injured reserve. Surgery was scheduled for the following week.

To fill his place on the depth chart, Tom Landry reached out to Walt Garrison in the hope of convincing the veteran running back to make a comeback. Now fully recovered from his off-season rodeo accident, Garrison agreed to join the team for an eleventh season and told Landry to have Tex Schramm draw up a contract.

Schramm nullified what would have been a highly popular reunion by reminding Landry that the deadline for signing veteran free-agents had already come and gone. Thanks to a mid-season congressional ruling, NFL teams were still allowed to sign free agents off of WFL rosters. As of late-November, NFL free-agents were off-limits. Per league rules, if the Garrison Gallop was to make a return to the Cowboys, it would have to be in 1976.

Landry's attention then turned to the defensive side of the ball. With Bob Breunig likely out for a few more weeks with a foot injury, Thomas Henderson ailing from several minor injuries, and Randy White busy along the defensive line, the Cowboys were in need of help at the linebacker position. At the suggestion of scouts who had followed the World Football League, Landry offered the open position on the roster to former Birmingham linebacker Warren Capone. Capone was everything that Landry had hoped he would be. A speedster with a knack for sticking his nose into a pile, Capone looked to be a natural fit on the Cowboys' kick-coverage units, and quickly ingratiated himself to new teammates by making the tackle on the opening kickoff against Philadelphia.

For Dallas restaurateur George Cook, eating, drinking, and making merry was more than just an admirable model for the game of life. He also claimed it to be a hallmark of a winning football team.

With an establishment situated in close proximity to Texas Stadium, Cook had been afforded several opportunities to serve a meal to the visiting team before a game, and came to an implicit realization of the inherent magic of a well-rounded meal. In August, he watched the Oakland Raiders pile off the team bus and consume a hearty midnight snack consisting of 100 pounds of hamburger and 125 pounds of barbecue ribs. The following night, the Raiders went out and beat the Cowboys.

On the afternoon of Dallas' Monday night tilt with Kansas City in early November, Chiefs defensive end John Matuszak put away the following: a 14-ounce steak, a slab of ham, seven slices of bacon, six scrambled eggs, and eight pieces of toast – before pausing to order four more eggs, fried over hard. When Matuszak and his teammates walked out the door, Cook shocked his staff by predicting a Chiefs upset later that night. He was right.

So it happened that, on the Sunday before Thanksgiving, Cook watched Eagles quarterback Roman Gabriel amble into the restaurant just hours prior to squaring off against the Cowboys and order – of all things – a piece of rye toast with honey. Walking back into the kitchen, head shaking, Cook offered his game prognosis for all to hear: Fear not, today would belong to the Cowboys.

In his last start against the Eagles on Oct. 26, Roger Staubach had saved the day with his arm by orchestrating a pair of scoring drives in the final minutes. It took every one of 49 pass attempts from Staubach for the Cowboys to triumph at Veterans Stadium.

That was October.

Options in November were not so plentiful.

There was no thought given to having Staubach throw that many times in Dallas' Week 10 rematch in Irving. Due to a shoulder injury suffered against New England which had since transformed into a "sore arm," Staubach had not thrown a single pass during the entire week of practice, as coaches were of the hope that rest would cure what ailed him. The time off certainly helped Staubach, but it didn't completely heal him. After going through warm-ups nearly two hours before kickoff, it was determined that he could play against Philadelphia, but only while operating from a limited playbook. Deep passes were out of the question. Staubach, very simply, couldn't throw downfield for the pain it would cause him.

Because of Staubach's limited range, the screen pass, once a staple in the Dallas offense that took advantage of the open-field skills of runners like Don Perkins, Duane Thomas, and Calvin Hill, was about to re-surface. Tom Landry had dug deep in his playbook during the week and come up with a few new twists to an old play.

The fundamental precept of any screen play is to invite the pass-rushers up-field before having the quarterback dump it off short on one side to a running back with blockers in front of him. The more common this play became in the 1960s, more defenses got wise to it and began stopping it, requiring offensive coordinators to disguise the play in several different fashions.

"I used to have about the same screen pass to Calvin Hill," said Staubach. "But then I'd look to one side, pump and then spin around and throw to Calvin on the other side. Teams were playing that one, waiting for me to spin. So we changed it. [Robert] Newhouse went to one side and I just looked at him, as though I might throw a flare. Then I dropped the ball off to Preston [Pearson] on the other side."

Tackle Rayfield Wright would try to cut the defensive end, or block him to the inside. The guard and center on that side pull to set up an alley for Preston to pick his way through the defense. In the Eagles zone defense, the linebackers retreat about 10 yards on pass plays, allowing runners to catch the dump-off passes, and the blockers a chance to get organized.

The Eagles never seemed to catch on to this new strategy from the Cowboys. In the first quarter, Staubach dumped it off to Pearson on third-and-8, and he took off for 18 yards to the Philadelphia 8, leading to a short Toni Fritsch field goal and an early Dallas lead.

Later, the same play worked for 40 yards after Pearson zigged and zagged his way through the Eagle defense, breaking two tackles along the way. That big-gainer was the catalyst on Dallas' second touchdown drive of the game, and provided the Cowboys with a fourteen-point margin heading into intermission.

Fritsch's third quarter field goal from 30 yards was set up by a 21-yard catch-and-run by Pearson. The final touchdown drive of the game for Dallas was sparked by Pearson's 13-yard gainer on second-and-14 from the Philadelphia 34-yard line, giving him four receptions for 109 yards for the game. "Preston is just great in the open field," said Landry. "He knows how to use his blockers. He isn't a power back, but boy can he find those holes."

"Those were some of the first screens we got off this season," remarked Blaine Nye, "but that Preston Pearson can really run that thing. That was sweet."

The screen passes seemed to take the fight out of a normally aggressive Eagles defense who, on this day, appeared to be having trouble finding the ball-carrier behind the cavalry of big blockers in front of him. "They used finesse," Philadelphia safety Bill Bradley said, a hint of disdain in his voice. "That's the Dallas game and they do it well."

When not scheming the Eagles to frustration with screen passes, the Cowboys were pounding them into the turf with tough running. Robert Newhouse, who had been hampered by injuries in recent weeks, had a 21-yard scamper on his way to leading all Cowboys' runners with 82 yards. Doug Dennison had another strong output, totaling 65 yards on the ground, 21 of which came on one play, and scored his second touchdown in as many games.

Collectively, the Cowboys rushed for 208 yards against the same team that had held them to only 78 yards a month earlier, and averaged 4.3 yards-per-rush. The team's best rushing day of the season came with little fanfare, as the 58,900 in attendance seemed preoccupied in either consciously saving their energy to cheer on Bob Lilly's induction into the Ring of Honor at halftime, or in keeping a close eye on the health of their quarterback. That there was a game going between two division rivals seemed to be lost on the majority of the fans for much of the afternoon.

Even while completing over seventy-five percent of his passes, it was hardly a perfect game for Staubach. Twice he ignored the pain in his arm and tried to force a pass downfield. He was intercepted each time. On another play, Staubach turned the wrong way on a handoff. The arm injury that robbed him of strength failed to rob Staubach of his quickness. His second-quarter touchdown run of 1-yard that put Dallas ahead 17-3 came after he followed a fumble near the goal-line and into the endzone.

Staubach didn't get away completely unscathed on this day. In the fourth quarter with the ball on the Eagles 13-yard line, he was blind-sided attempting to throw and was down on the turf afterwards for several seconds. "I got hit in the neck," said Staubach, "and my whole life passed before me. We had a timeout, then I called the wrong formation on a handoff to Newhouse. Philadelphia's rough. They always give me trouble."

With the Cowboys executing at a near flawless pace on the offensive side, the Eagles were proving to be very, very mortal on the other side. The Eagles' offense, a unit that did quite a bit of trash-talking going into the game, had a horrible first half, and were so pathetic in certain moments as to endear sympathy from the crowd. On one particular play, two running backs collided in the backfield, and Roman Gabriel piled into them. "No way that kinda stuff should be happening," said Eagles' Head Coach Mike McCormack. "We run into each other, we're jumping off-sides, we're getting caught in motion. Those plays were put in during training camp. We've run 'em ever since then. It's just stupid."

They also couldn't catch a break when on defense. On Dallas' second touchdown drive of the first half, an interception by John Outlaw was waved off by a late flag for interference on Drew Pearson. The Cowboys' final touchdown was aided by a holding call in the end zone. McCormack disputed that the holding infraction should have been ignored since it occurred after Staubach had already been knocked down.

When the Eagles weren't running into each other, they were colliding with Cliff Harris. The Dallas safety put a big first-quarter lick on tight end Charlie Young in the end-zone that prevented a touchdown. Before the Philadelphia kicking team could put the Eagles on the scoreboard for the first time, Harris had to be helped from the field. Harris' hit on Young had helped his team, while also rendering the defender unconscious. Harris returned to the game, but had no recollection afterwards of anything preceding his jarring collision. "I hope I played well," he said.

The Dirty Dozen

Harris was one of many outstanding performers for a Dallas defensive unit that made life miserable for Gabriel and the Philadelphia passing offense. Charlie Waters and Mel Renfro each tallied an interception. Bill Gregory and a rejuvenated Harvey Martin notched a sack each. The ineffective Gabriel was benched in favor of Mike Boyrla late in the third quarter having completed just 13-of-26 passes for 113 yards, an especially satisfying event for the defensive line. "Oh, we hit Gabriel more times in the first half than we did the whole game in Philly," said Martin. "We were ready, fired up. It was just all five of us, all six of us, getting together, deciding we could do it."

Boyrla nearly rallied the Eagles, leading two fourth-quarter touchdown drives to make it interesting. But with the score 27-17 and the ball resting on the Dallas 6-yard line in the waning seconds, Boyrla's luck ran out as he was taken down in the backfield by Martin and D.D. Lewis to snuff out the threat.

Above the hallowed hole in the roof, evidence of evening's firm grip was fast becoming evident. A sun brilliantly set against a backdrop of purest blue dipped, and finally disappeared, below the horizon, effectively signaling the conclusion to a picture-perfect day in north Texas.

More than two hours had passed since patrons filed out of Texas Stadium after watching their Cowboys improve to 7-3 on the season with a convincing victory over a fading Philadelphia team. Inside the stadium's press lounge, the festivities continued. Led by Cowboys' play-by-play radio announcer Verne Lundquist, a group of Metroplex media types gathered around a television set to cheer on the Raiders in their tussle with Washington. Picking sides in the press-box during a game was considered taboo among Northeasterners. But among friends, a postgame party in Texas that concentrated on rooting against the Redskins was more typical than anything else. It was a common understanding that the only thing better than a Cowboys' victory, was basking in the mutual pleasure of a Redskins' loss.

The gathering had formed under the most positive of circumstances. The Raiders, behind three Pete Banaszak touchdown runs, were leading 20-9 at halftime. But with the second half came a new flavor of intensity in the room, as Oakland began turning the ball over with regularity, leading to a late Washington charge.

Everyone in the room knew that only the division winner and a wild-card could qualify for the postseason from the NFC East, meaning that between the three quality teams at the top (St. Louis, Washington & Dallas) one would be left home at the end of the regular season. A Redskins' loss to John Madden's Raiders would leave them a game behind Dallas for second-place in the East with four games remaining.

Groans of derision could be heard in the group as Billy Kilmer mounted another fourth-quarter comeback and tossed a 33-yard touchdown to Frank Grant to force overtime. Now things were getting serious. The first team to score in the extra period would walk away as the winner. Lundquist and the others didn't like Oakland's chances to help the cause of the Cowboys. After turning the ball over five times, the Raiders' offense was in shambles and their defense gassed. If momentum was as important as some people believed it to be...

But in overtime the tide turned. Ken Stabler, a misguided miscreant for the previous two quarters, suddenly found his touch again, and marched the Raiders down the field and into scoring position. At the 7:13 mark in overtime the aging George Blanda, who only last December parlayed his final career passes to a victory over Dallas on national television, booted the Cowboys into second-place in the NFC East with a 27-yard field goal to beat the Redskins, provoking a chorus of whoops and cheers from Lundquist and others.

As things stood with four games remaining, the Cowboys were in the playoffs. The curse of the cake was alive and well!

CHAPTER 22

A GIANT VICTORY

"Jethro was all over the place. He was running down screens, trapping the quarterback, stopping draws, stopping sweeps...what else can you ask of a defensive lineman?"
- **Cowboys tight end Jean Fugett describing Jethro Pugh's performance against the Giants**

Since 1966, the Dallas Cowboys and Thanksgiving Day had been an American tradition that highlighted everything there was to love about life: family, food, and football. But a 7-2 record for Dallas on Turkey Day proved cause for jealousy from other owners, who claimed that the Cowboys gained an unfair advantage every season by hosting a mid-week game.

In true democratic fashion, NFL commissioner Pete Rozelle responded to these complaints by pulling this holiday rug from under the Cowboys' feet and spreading it over the hearth of another popular franchise – the cardiac Cardinals of St. Louis. So, in 1975, for the first time in a decade, the parking lots at Texas Stadium were strangely empty as players, patrons and pom-pom girls celebrated the fourth Thursday in November with the familial warmth of home and fireplace.

What was perceived to be a victory for the NFL in the arena of fair-play backfired loudly over the airwaves of national television. The Cardinals, playing in a snowstorm on their home turf, were bowled over by O.J. Simpson and the visiting Buffalo Bills 32-14. Winners of seven of their last eight games, St. Louis had entered the eleventh week of play a full game ahead of Dallas in the NFC East race. With the loss to Buffalo, they now faced the reality of having to sit back on Sunday afternoon and hope for a Giants' upset in Irving that would prevent them from being dragged into a first-place tie.

Such was the tale of irony that gladdened the hearts of the football faithful throughout north Texas. No matter how hard the league tried to flip the script, the Cowboys always seemed to emerge from the Thanksgiving Day festivities as the unequivocal winners of professional football.

Game day finally came to Irving, and with it a chance for the hometown Cowboys to join St. Louis at the top of the standings. For the second consecutive week Dallas was hosting a divisional foe under their half-finished roof. But unlike the previous game against Philadelphia, there were no health precautions linked to the right arm of Roger Staubach.

Another week of rest had worked wonders on Staubach's wrenched arm, and left him in the perfect frame of mind to continue a recent trend. The Dallas offense had begun to show signs in recent weeks of shedding the label of being a slow-starting unit. One week after playing the uncomfortable role of game-manager, Staubach was all too ready to come out of the gates and throw bombs all over Texas Stadium's crowned surface. The resulting 14-point first-quarter outburst against the Giants was Dallas' best of the season.

The first touchdown play came from the Shotgun formation. The Giants were in a defense that called for double-coverage on both outside receivers, Drew Pearson and Golden

Richards, leaving Jean Fugett one-on-one with strong safety Charlie Ford.

"The route was to Golden but the weak safety (Jim Steinke) slid over toward Golden and I knew that Fugett would be open," said Staubach, who later in the game surpassed the 10,000-yard career passing mark.

Fugett ran under a perfect throw at the New York 17, jerked away from a tackle by Steinke who had come over to help, and carried Ford into the end-zone, spiking the ball while Ford was still on his back to complete the 54-yard touchdown play. Said Steinke: "That was a Mickey Mouse play...something you make up on the street...a hook and go. He drew me off and I made a stupid mistake."

Later in the quarter, Tom Landry dialed-up another play for Richards, and this time Staubach went to his speedy wide receiver with the pass. On second-and-5 from the Dallas 30, Staubach faked a hand-off to Doug Dennison and completed his drop-back. When his vision focused downfield he saw Richards splitting and separating from Ford and cornerback Clyde Powers. The pass from Staubach landed in the arms of Richards at the Dallas 20, and he stumbled his way to the 8 before finally falling to the ground. "I picked him up a little late or we'd have scored," acknowledged Staubach afterwards.

Richards' loss turned out to be Dennison's gain. The Dallas runner scored his third touchdown in as many games when he ran over from four yards away moments later to give Dallas a 14-3 lead. The offense had done its part to give the Cowboys control of the game. Now it was up to the defense to protect it.

The Dallas defense entered the game having yielded an average of 28 points per contest during the month of November, while displaying numerous inconsistencies. A non-existent second-half pass-rush doomed them against Washington. Poor run defense contributed to a home loss versus Kansas City. And in victories over New England and Philadelphia, it was second-half letdowns that allowed the opponent to make a game of it in the latter stages.

Tom Landry had spent the previous two weeks deflecting criticism by insisting that the defense was improving and that a complete performance would come with time. That time finally arrived on the final day of the month against the visiting New York Giants.

A crowd of 53,329 came out to see an aerial battle of one-time quarterbacking teammates. The Craig Morton vs. Roger Staubach angle had been pumped-up all week by local sports writers, who were desperately trying to invoke some interest for a game pitting a 7-3 playoff contender against a 3-7 bottom-feeder. In the end, the hype and expectations fell flatter than the Giants' playoff hopes. After a fast start from the home team, offensive football became a complete anomaly, causing some in the crowd to start booing in the direction of the Giants' bench, where an especially beleaguered quarterback could be frequently seen worrying over his troubles. "Instead of returning to Dallas a conquering hero with the New York Giants, Morton gave his critics and Roger Staubach worshippers a chance to gloat," observed Randy Galloway in his Monday column for the Dallas Morning News.

But it was even worse than Galloway indicated. Not only was Staubach the winner of this highly-anticipated showdown, Morton made himself out to be the goat of a dubious Giants' defeat. Morton distinguished himself in the art of inefficiency with unforeseen fluency against the Cowboys, completing only 8-of-24 passes for 102 yards. Much of his struggle could be attributed to a persistently swarming Dallas defense, which intercepted the Giants quarterback three times and sacked him four other times.

One of seven linebackers kept on the Dallas roster coming out of training camp, Cal Peterson had seen an increase in playing time in recent weeks while Bob Breunig recovered from a toe injury. It was Peterson who provided the Cowboys with a golden opportunity to put the game away midway through the second quarter. With Dallas already leading 14-3, Peterson stepped in front of a Morton pass for Walker Gillette and returned it 19 yards to the New York 7-yard line.

In what was to be the beginning of unending struggles for each passer, Staubach immediately gave the ball back to the Giants with a poor pass near the goal-line. On second-down, Staubach faked a run to the left, and instead, rolled out to his right looking for Robert Newhouse. He hesitated for a fraction of a second, before attempting to force a pass to Newhouse at the flag. Cutting underneath the pass was Steinke, who made a two-handed grab for a return-the-favor interception. "That was an awful play, which kept us from having a much easier time," said Staubach. "They had both safeties on that side. I thought one was going with Fugett. I didn't see Steinke in time."

It wasn't to be Staubach's last run-in with the New York safety. Late in the first-half, Roger completed an evasive move around a defender in the backfield before trying to hit Preston Pearson with a short pass across the middle. Steinke was there waiting on it, and deftly snagged his second theft of the game.

With that scoring threat snuffed out, the game settled down into a series of exchanges. New York's Dave Jennings kept the field tilted all afternoon, averaging 53 yards on six punts. Mitch Hoopes, on the other hand, struggled for the Cowboys. Hoopes' poor game was rendered mute by the strong play of the Dallas defense.

To counter Steinke's role of persistent pest on the New York side was Dallas defensive tackle Jethro Pugh. Pugh was a force to be reckoned with in the Giants' backfield from start to finish, unofficially recording 2.5 of the Cowboys' four sacks for the game. On two separate occasions, Pugh broke through the line to nail running back Doug Kotar for a loss.

When he wasn't pummeling Morton behind the line of scrimmage, Pugh was using his veteran instinct and field awareness to prevent a big play. On one particular play, Pugh chased down Larry Watkins from behind and tackled the runner for a five-yard gain on a play that could have gone for 20 yards...or even longer. "It was one of my better games," said Pugh in the dressing room. "It was a must game for us and we knew the defense was going to have to come together and start playing well if we're going to do any good. And I just wanted to do my share. I had a lot of help, though."

That he did. Pugh's defensive line mate, Ed "Too Tall" Jones, made the play that stopped the only Giants' threat of the second half. A Danny Buggs' kick-off return of 43 yards to begin the third quarter and a penalty on rookie Pat Donovan for roughing the punter had the Giants on the march. From there,

Morton moved the offense to a first-and-goal at the Dallas 9-yard line.

Two good plays from Pugh left the Giants facing a third-down from the 7. Ernie Stautner signaled for a safety blitz, which called for Cliff Harris to rush and Jones to drop off and cover the running back. "I dropped back but he went inside," said Jones, referring to the running back. Instead of coming back toward the middle of the field, Jones leaked out into the flat, never dreaming that Morton would actually throw a pass to the outside for Gillette. "Then I saw the ball coming and I jumped up and got it. It kind of scared me."

The Giants never got close again, as Dallas' pass-rush nullified every Morton attempt at a comeback. Dallas had an opportunity to extend their advantage to fourteen points, but watched that fall by the wayside when Toni Fritsch skied a 37-yard field goal attempt so high that the ball fell short of the crossbar.

A bad day for the Dallas kicking game only got worse in the fourth quarter. With less than two minutes to go the Cowboys were on the Giants' 36-yard line, with every intention of punting the Giants deep in their own end. And then Mitch Hoopes started running wild again. He ducked under a tackler, then threw incomplete. It was the fourth time on the season that Hoopes had bailed on the scripted plan. "Some guy came in from the left,' Hoopes related, "and I thought he could get to it. We were on their 36 and there wasn't much time left, so I just wanted to sidestep to the left. He spun me around, and then I thought I had to get a first down." He admitted the thought also crossed his mind, "Oh, spit, here we go again."

"Really I just wanted to kick on the run," Hoopes said of his sprint to the right. "Then I saw Randy Hughes open...and I bounced it to him. Heck, he was an ineligible receiver anyway...I don't know if it was my fault until I see the films."

When asked if anyone on the Dallas coaching staff said anything to him when he came off the field, Hoopes said, "No, and that's a bad sign. I'll probably get chewed out. They'll probably say I could have gotten the kick off."

Hoopes' prediction came true in the postgame press conference when Landry pointedly criticized the entire specialty unit for their performance against the Giants. "Our kicking game was very poor," said Landry. "We let them return one about 45 yards (second-half kickoff), didn't get a punt off when we should have (Mitch Hoopes), then let the ball roll when we should have caught it (Golden Richards)."

But not even a worry-wart like Landry could wallow in the muck of mistakes for very long. Not with what next awaited his team. The two game home stand had apparently healed what ailed the Cowboys. Their quarterback was healthy again. The defense was back to playing tough for all four quarters. And they had reclaimed their spot on top of the NFC East mountain.

Now, with a date looming large in St. Louis followed by a home tilt versus Washington, Landry's young team would be charged with the task of staying there. Now was the moment of truth. Now was the time for the Cowboys to claim what they had come for.

"It's in the stretch run," said Jethro Pugh, "and we've got to let it all out."

CHAPTER 23

BLOWOUT

"That Metcalf is something. One time I KNOW I had him and then... he just wasn't there." - **Jethro Pugh, marveling at Terry Metcalf's big day for the Cardinals**

"We didn't stop the big play, the little play, and not much in between."
- **D.D. Lewis, after the Cowboys' 31-17 loss in St. Louis**

With the turning of the calendar came even more drama surrounding the Washington Redskins. This time in the form of a court appearance.

A group of concerned Redskins' fans, masquerading as ambitious lawyers, had filed a suit against the National Football League, requesting that U.S. District Court Judge George Hart issue a temporary restraining order and prevent any scheduling of playoff games until the court made a ruling on the controversial call that led to Washington's overtime loss to St. Louis in Week 9.

To review the dramatic play: St. Louis quarterback Jim Hart's fourth-quarter pass from the 6-yard line hit a leaping Mel

Gray in the hands. Before Gray's feet ever touched the ground, defensive back Pat Fischer knocked the ball from his hands. What looked like a simple incompletion quickly turned into something far more complicated. A debate among officials developed into a two-minute conference that resulted in a ruling that Gray had legally caught the ball for a Cardinals' touchdown, despite video evidence clearly showing that Gray had lost control of the ball before landing with both feet on the ground. The touchdown tied the game at 17-17, and St. Louis eventually pulled it out in overtime.

According to one of the plaintiffs, a certain George Morse, the suit asked that Judge Hart either return the teams to finish the game from the point just prior to the controversial touchdown pass or to declare the game "no contest" and divide up percentage points as if it were a tie. "We are simply asking the court to hold that where the rules of the NFL itself have been violated there is redress."

The likelihood of Hart granting a "do-over" of the final stages of the fourth quarter were smaller than zero. Whichever team lost would just start complaining all over again, this time about the unjustness of concluding a game a month after its regularly scheduled date.

Should the judge declare a tie, in the event that the case actually went to trial, it would have a marked effect upon the current landscape of the NFC East race, drawing St. Louis and Washington into a dead heat at 7-3-1, one-half game behind the 8-3 Cowboys. That scenario would be especially pleasing to the Redskins, who would own the tiebreaker over St. Louis with the opportunity of sweeping the season series with Dallas still in front of them. Either way, this case was a big deal for each team at the top of the division.

On Monday Dec. 1, the suit was brought before Judge Hart for a preliminary hearing, at which a representative of the NFL was also present. After listening to presentations from both sides and taking into account the human element of officiating that – per league rules – was allowed no aid in the form of video replay, Hart tossed the case out altogether. Hart acknowledged that the officials had made a mistake, but failed to see any reason to waste tax dollars over it while bemoaning the fact in court.

Mistakes were, and always had been, part of the game of football.

"The court deems the suit to be frivolous," commented Hart. "There is no just issue."

Get out! And get over it!

Muffs and mittens were out in resplendent display on a cold, windy afternoon at Busch Stadium, as fans filed through the gates in high spirits. The biggest game of the year in the NFC East had come to St. Louis, where the Cardinals and Cowboys would tussle for the outright lead in the division. The playing surface had been cleared of snow from earlier in the week, but with temperatures in the low 40s and wind-chills at or below the freezing mark, the artificial turf promised to feel more like a cheese grater for the players than the proverbial field of dreams.

The Cowboys, sporting their dark blue jerseys for the first time all season, came prepared for another close battle, much like the one they had with St. Louis at Texas Stadium in Week 2 when a Roger Staubach-to-Billy Joe Dupree pass won it for Dallas in overtime. The Cardinals, on the other hand, arrived at the ballpark determined to avenge their earlier loss in Dallas with a show of power. They wanted to blow the Cowboys out of their own building.

Don Coryell's game plan on offense was simple; get the ball in the hands of his playmakers and let their speed do all the talking. And in St. Louis, there was no better playmaker than Terry Metcalf.

Metcalf had been enjoying a sensational 1975 campaign in a Cardinals' uniform. His touchdown reception against the Bills on Thanksgiving Day was the fifth different way in which he had scored on the season. Metcalf had also scored via rush, kickoff and punt return, and passing.

The Dallas defense combined with the excessive Texas heat to do a number on the 5-10, 180-pound running back during their September meeting, holding Metcalf to 46 total yards. Coryell vowed that this time would be different.

On the game's opening drive, Metcalf took the handoff from Jim Hart and went around right end for 15 yards. Then, behind devastating blocks from the threesome of center Tom Banks and guards Dan Dierdorf and Conrad Dobler, the speedy Metcalf turned the corner on the left side for 17 more yards. When the ball reached the Dallas 30-yard line, Coryell threw a change-up and called for Metcalf to stretch his legs on a deep pass pattern.

Metcalf's route took him directly into a coverage sandwich of Mel Renfro and Cliff Harris. Hart didn't think twice about throwing it up, a dubious decision when considering that his intended target was the shortest of the three players in the vicinity. Renfro jumped up at the goal-line to make the interception just as Metcalf turned and stumbled. The ball went right through Renfro's hands, and stuck in the gut of a falling Metcalf for a Cardinals' touchdown. The game was less than three minutes old, and Metcalf had already touched the ball three times and given his team the lead. "I tell you I thought that catch had to be an act of God," said Renfro.

The Cardinals continued to run to the strong-side of the defense, where they pushed Dave Edwards and the defensive end around at will. Whether it was Metcalf taking the handoff or Jim Otis doing the honors, St. Louis got what they wanted when they wanted it with their rushing game against a passive Dallas defense.

Otis would finish the game with 88 yards on 21 carries. Metcalf tallied 86 yards on only 14 attempts, a stat line that Charlie Waters attributed directly to a Cowboys' defensive unit playing with the star runner in the open field like a cat plays with a mouse. "You can't do that," said Waters. "You have to go ahead and take a shot at him, hope you can knock him off-balance and that the pursuit will help you."

The Cardinals' second possession concluded with a 49-yard touchdown bomb from Hart to Mel Gray, who had raced past a surprised Renfro down the sideline. "I'm not gonna knock Mel Renfro," opined a smiling Gray in the postgame locker room, "but let me say this – there's not a defensive back in the league that Mel Gray can't beat deep."

The circumstances that led to St. Louis' next score put Tom Landry on blowout alert. After the Dallas defense had finally put together a stand, Jim Baaken kicked a short field goal that extended the Cardinals' advantage to 17-3. But an official dusted off an old, forgotten rule when he flagged Thomas Henderson for jumping on a teammate in an attempt to block Baaken's kick. The video replay showed Henderson putting his hand on Jethro Pugh's shoulder while trying to get up high enough for a block. The unsportsmanlike conduct penalty gave the Big Red machine a first-down on the Dallas 2-yard line, and preceded Steve Jones' 1-yard scoring plunge a few moments later.

With the score fast getting out of hand, Landry had to try to force the action to get his team back in the game. But it was no use. This just wasn't the Cowboys' day. Leaving his offense out on the field for a fourth-and-14 play, Landry watched as Staubach's pass was batted down, giving St. Louis possession at their own 44-yard line.

Hart orchestrated the fourth Cardinal touchdown drive in response, culminating another long march with a 6-yard scoring pass to Gray in front of a chasing Waters. It was Hart's sixth pass completion in only ten attempts, giving him 140 yards through the air after one-half of play.

From merely an alert, a blowout in St. Louis had become an unwanted reality for Landry and the Cowboys, who tromped into the visitor's locker room at halftime trailing 28-3 and searching for answers. "We had plenty of people to stop them, even intercept it, on that first touchdown," commented Landry. "I don't know how, but he (Metcalf) made the play. Then we go down on a long drive but have to settle for a field goal and they come right back with the big play to Gray. That's 14 points in two series and we never shook it off. "I think we were mentally ready, but in a game of this importance a break or two can get you doubting, cost you confidence. And once that confidence is shaken it doesn't take long to lose the concentration and then everything come apart."

The Dirty Dozen

Their performance after the break spoke well of the Cowboys' character and leadership, but wasn't nearly enough to cover the season's largest deficit. Staubach began the second half by leading a touchdown drive out of the Shotgun formation. In an ultimate display of physical superiority on this day, the Cardinals answered back with a 17-play field-goal drive that consumed all of the remaining third quarter clock.

Randy Hughes was the lone standout on defense during a sluggish final period. His theft of a Jim Hart pass was the first of his NFL career.

The 31-17 final left Dallas a full game back of St. Louis with only two weeks remaining in the regular season, making the possibility of a division championship for the Cowboys highly unlikely.

"They just whipped us," said Landry. "They knocked us off the line of scrimmage and any team that can do that to you is going to control the football game."

A shell-shocked Cowboys; team landed in Dallas later that evening after a short plane ride back home, looking heavy with concern. A 1975 season, once so young and innocent and free of expectations, was now resting on the doorstep of pressure-packed moments and the NFL playoffs. But to get there, the youthful Cowboys had to go through George Allen's Over The Hill Gang and the Washington Redskins. The winner would earn an automatic bid into the postseason. The loser would spend the Christmas holiday sucking his thumb and moaning over what might have been.

The stage was finally set. After nearly three months of regular season action, all eyes were trained on Dallas and Washington for a play-in playoff game at Texas Stadium.

As expected, what transpired between the lines on that Saturday afternoon in front of a national television audience was of the unexpected variety, while the flavor of inherent inspiration proved to be equally so.

CHAPTER 24

THE SWEETEST REDEMPTION OF ALL

"I had rather beat them than anybody else." - **Cliff Harris, basking in the joy of a blowout victory over the Redskins**

"We got our butts kicked today. That's just the way it was." - **Washington wide receiver Charley Taylor, after the Cowboys eliminated the Redskins from the playoff race**

Tom Landry didn't bother to mince words about his team's showing against the Cardinals. It was, he admitted, extremely poor. And the timing of such a performance? Well, that was poor too. But all of that didn't mean Landry had lost confidence in the Cowboys. On the contrary, Landry found plenty of reason to be optimistic about an 8-4 record.

"For us to have gotten where we are this season, we had to make a lot of progress," Landry said at his weekly press luncheon on Tuesday. "Now, we're in a position to have a super year or an average year. It will be up to us what happens in Saturday's game. Our job this week is to get back to doing the things we do well. We've done a lot of things well this season. If we get back to doing them Saturday we have a chance. We played our best game this season in Washington. Both teams played great games. I hope this one is as good. It certainly could be."

Five of Washington's previous six games had been decided either in overtime, or by a field goal or less. That they had managed to stay so competitive with starting quarterback Billy Kilmer limping around with a broken foot was also impressive.

Though George Allen had plenty to say in regards to the NFL's 43-man roster limit, he was hardly in a position to moan over a nicked quarterback. Through the first twelve weeks of the 1975 season, only three starting quarterback – Fran Tarkenton, John Hadl, and Joe Namath – had managed to play every game without departing with an injury. Kilmer was still healthy enough to play. That was more than some teams had going for them.

Another indication of a preeminent battle between two classic heavyweights was the buildup. Tex Schramm started the ball of fun rolling early in the week when he started spreading nefarious reports suggesting that he thought Kilmer deserving of the NFC Player of The Year honors.

Supporters in Washington were a bit more than just sly. They were also artistic. Two-thousand Redskins' fans gathered mid-week for a team-sanctioned pep rally, at which the local radio station hired a sky-writer to print "Stomp Dallas" over the practice field. In addition to this demonstration, an area bakery donated an 80-pound Redskins' cake to be flown to Dallas for the inevitable party after the game. The cake had been sent from a Marriott Hotel urging them to "Bowl Over Dallas."

The only uncertainty revolving around this meeting was which Cowboys' team would show up. The young, immature one from the previous week, or the cool customers that sent the Rams packing on opening day? Not even veteran linebacker D.D. Lewis dared to hazard a guess on this front. "I've never felt so awful in my life as I did when the Cardinals tore us up,"

Lewis acknowledged. "I was in a daze four days......Before the Cardinal game, we'd had such good spirit and workouts, I thought we'd win. But then preparing for Washington, I got worried that we wouldn't do the job."

It wasn't until he was pacing the sideline before kickoff that Landry got a true sense of where his team was at on an emotional level. While milling around the bench area Landry took time to look in his players' eyes, and noticed a calm and a quiet focus that wasn't there against St. Louis. "You could feel it on the sideline, the feeling was there," recalled Landry. "There was no question about it; we were ready."

There had been a time during the life of Charlie Waters in which he thought a lengthy career in professional football might not be such a realistic option after all. Waters' athletic skill set had made for an easy transition from college quarterback at Clemson to weak-side safety with the Dallas Cowboys. His speed and his knowledge of the game made him a natural in providing coverage help for teammates in the secondary. While fellow rookie Cliff Harris served his turn at military duty, Waters tallied five interceptions while helping Dallas reach Super Bowl V, causing many to predict a bright future for Waters in Dallas.

His path to stardom took an unexpected detour shortly after when Tom Landry asked him to make a position switch to right cornerback in replacement of the newly-retired Herb Adderly. The new position demanded different things from Waters, many of which he struggled to meet. Waters was fast enough to run step-for-step alongside running backs and tight ends. Matching up against the NFL's top wide receivers proved to be another thing, a bit of news that quickly spread around the league.

In the Cowboys' secondary, Mel Renfro normally covered the receiver on the defensive left, while Waters stayed on the opposite side. In the event that the offense stacked both receivers on the same side, the general understanding was that Waters was to take the receiver farthest to the right.

When opponents figured this out, they began to pick on Waters by putting their best – and usually fastest – wide receiver across from him. Early on, Waters struggled to adapt to this strategy. During a 1973 game against Los Angeles at the Coliseum, he yielded four touchdown passes to Harold Jackson, leading to a Cowboys' loss.

Waters improved his footwork and technique over time, and had developed into a passable good cornerback by the end of the 1974 season. He was still susceptible to getting beat deep on occasion, though not with the same frequency as when he first started out. And the coaches could always count on Waters to be in position on run support.

Yet, when the opportunity arose a few months later for him to push the reset button and make another position switch, Waters didn't hesitate for a moment. After three years out on an island at cornerback where he learned the nuances of one-on-one coverage, Waters was more than ready to try his luck at strong safety.

In his first season on the strong-side, Waters rediscovered some of the magic that made him an up-and-coming prospect earlier in his career. His strength and zest for tackling made him a tough foe for any ball-carrier, and his speed a problem for even the fastest of tight ends. He ascended to the top of the depth chart in August after Cornell Green announced his retirement, and didn't look back from there, turning in some key performances on the road over the first twelve weeks.

In Week 3, his coverage of Detroit tight end Charlie Sanders was a big factor in why the Cowboys were able to sack Lion quarterbacks a league-record eleven times. And against New England, it was his fourth-quarter interception of Jim Plunkett that set up the game-winning field goal in a 34-31 contest.

But nothing he had accomplished before could ever compare with the moment when Charlie jumped out of the box and onto the national screen, and delivered the Cowboys from the clutches of elimination. Once a misplaced miscreant with a penchant for giving up the big play, Waters made himself into a hero by making the big play. In the fourth quarter of a tight game against the hated Redskins, Charlie Waters assured himself of a place in franchise lore with a game-clinching interception that assured his team a place in the NFL playoffs.

When it happened, the visionaries up in Washington wanted you to believe that Roger Staubach's plunking of Pat Fischer was the punch that sealed the Cowboys' fate as playoff outsiders. As is so often the case around Capitol Hill, such a declaration reeked of the presumptuous mind. On Dec. 13, just twelve days before Christmas, a first quarter happening at Texas Stadium turned this apparent presumption into a complete falsehood. Whereas Staubach's intentional punch led to six weeks of bitterness and frustration in Dallas, it was Billy Kilmer's inadvertent punch that gave way to an entire off-season of regrets for the Washington Redskins.

While passing on the very first play from scrimmage, Kilmer smacked the back of his hand on a helmet as he completed his throwing motion. Despite wincing in pain, Kilmer stayed in the game and helped the Redskins get off to a fast start.

Shortly after a 48-yard Mark Moseley field goal got the scoring started, Kilmer tossed a 14-yard touchdown to Frank Grant, giving Washington a 10-0 lead. But when his throwing hand began to swell…and swell…and then stiffened as a result, Kilmer's accuracy began to suffer, slowing the Washington attack to an eventual standstill.

Without that hand injury of Kilmer's, who knows but that the Dirty Dozen would have become just a blip on the radar of Cowboys' history. Who could say but that George Allen would get his first victory at Texas Stadium in his fifth attempt, and would take the largest slice from the 80-pound cake in the postgame locker room?

Because as effective as Kilmer was in the early going, Staubach was equally ineffective. Whether he was lined-up in a traditional manner under center or working from the Shotgun, Staubach had no answers to solve the Redskins' pass coverage. In a game the Cowboys had to have, the NFC's leading passer failed to complete a single first-quarter pass, as Washington ganged up on his favorite targets, Drew and Preston Pearson.

Everything changed with one throw in the second quarter. Looking in the direction of Golden Richards, who was running a deep comeback along the left sideline, Staubach fired a dart for what originally appeared to be an innocent 15-yard gain. But when Richards shook loose from the arm tackle of Brig Owens, he saw nothing but green turf stretching in front of him. Turning on the jets, Richards streaked down the sideline with his trademark blonde tresses flailing out the back of his helmet, and outran Harold McClinton and Chris Hanburger into the end-zone for a 57-yard touchdown.

Late in the first half with the Redskins still clinging to a 10-7 lead, Washington's Larry Jones muffed a deep punt off the foot of Mitch Hoopes. Diving in front of a caravan of Redskins' pursuers was Benny Barnes, who reached in and slapped the ball down the field and away from the crowd. Barnes' act of desperation worked like a charm, the bouncing ball rolling directly to Randy Hughes, and making for an easy recovery for the rookie at the Washington 16-yard line. Twelve yards later, the Cowboys were faced with a third-and-goal from the 4.

Determined to try almost anything to get his team the lead, Tom Landry dusted off the old quarterback-draw, a play the Cowboys had kept under wraps the entire season for just such a situation. Staubach received the snap from under center, but instead of looking for a receiving outlet he took off running up the middle. He cleared the wall of defensive linemen, and found that head-hunting linebacker Harold McClinton was waiting for him at the goal-line. Staubach dove. McClinton popped him hard in the ribs, and smashed him down onto the unforgiving surface. "It felt like I was shot," Staubach later admitted of his collision with McClinton.

Staubach remained down on the field, trying to catch his breath and trying to process the pain that formed in his mid-section every time he moved. An insulting statistical line thus far for the Dallas quarterback (2-of-10 passing with one interception and a smattering of boos from the home crowd) had now been compromised by what attending doctors told him might be broken ribs. Staubach stayed on the field for several minutes, before being helped to his feet and slowly escorted to the locker room.

Over on the Dallas sideline, Clint Longley began warming up, visions of another late-game conquest of the Redskins dancing in his head. He came in, threw incomplete on his first pass, not realizing that it would be his last. Staubach's painful touchdown run was the Cowboys' final meaningful offensive play before both teams headed toward their respective locker rooms for a fifteen-minute intermission period. When they reemerged from the tunnel, Staubach was among them. His ribs were not broken, though they were wrapped tightly. He was hurting, no doubt, but raring to get back on the field.

With his quarterback playing through noticeable pain, Landry relied on the Dallas running attack to churn out yards in the second-half. Using a heavy dose of Robert Newhouse and Preston Pearson, the Cowboys controlled the pace of the game and dominated the field-position battle through a scoreless third-quarter. In the opening moments of the final frame, a long march on the backs of Cowboys' runners ended with Toni Fritsch booting a 19-yard field goal through the uprights, giving Dallas a 17-10 lead.

A one-touchdown lead was soon enlarged, thanks in large part to the Dallas defense. In what Tom Landry would afterwards describe as "a super-hitting game" from both sides, it was the men in blue and silver who delivered the most impactful hits of all.

It began in the first half when Washington tight end Jerry Smith had to exit the game after being pancaked by Cliff Harris while trying to make a catch between the hash-marks. "That makes them think. They know they're going to get hit when they go in the middle," said Harris.

Busting through the line on the Redskins' initial possession of the fourth quarter was linebacker D.D. Lewis, who swallowed up Kilmer in the backfield for a sack. An instant after Lewis landed on top of Washington's veteran quarterback, Ed "Too Tall" Jones fell on top of both, separating Kilmer's shoulder in the process. "I didn't get a big hit on him," explained Lewis. "I didn't spear him with my helmet. I don't think the hit was what hurt him. He was down. I was on top of him, and then somebody slammed on top of me. That's when I heard him groan. It must have jerked his head up and his shoulder down."

Disheartened at the sight of their leader on the bench, the Washington defense watched Preston Pearson cap a 75-yard Cowboys' march with a leaping 5-yard touchdown grab to boost the Dallas advantage to 24-10.

But if George Allen entertained any thoughts of backup Randy Johnson pulling a Clint Longley miracle out of the bag with a series of late-game bombs, he was very much mistaken. With less than six minutes remaining Johnson threw wide of his intended target near the right sideline, an errant pass that Charlie Waters was only too grateful to snare. Waters broke one tackle, cut inside of another Redskins' pursuer, and followed the escort of Dave Edwards across the goal-line for a score that sent his teammates and the on-looking audience into a complete frenzy.

After spiking the ball, Waters was mobbed by a host of Cowboys' defenders – Cliff Harris, Bill Gregory, Ed "Too Tall" Jones, and a 36-year old version of Edwards who was nearly jumping out of his shoes in delight. It was as sweet of a 20-yard run-back as anyone at Texas Stadium could have imagined. Little Charlie Waters, a punching bag for George Allen's team over the years, had not only dropped the curtain on the Redskins' 1975 season, but extended that of the Cowboys. "This is my biggest individual play for me," said Waters in the locker room. "I've had a lot of things go wrong for me. A few right too. But the public has a tendency to remember the bad. I wanted this win more than any of my career, which is why the play is so pleasing to me. I've got about 18 Redskin scars on me and this is great medication."

The 31-10 final guaranteed the Cowboys a spot in the NFC playoffs, most likely as a Wild-Card. Were the Cardinals to drop both remaining games against Chicago and Detroit and the Cowboys win their finale against the New York Jets, then Dallas would claim the NFC East crown. All of which was secondary information in a very jubilant Cowboys' locker room.

Harvey Martin was tooting the horn of a Cowboys' defensive unit which had limited Washington to a season-low output on the scoreboard. "It was an overall defensive game," said Martin. "People been talking all week about if the offense could outscore them, then we could beat them. I think that gets a guy thinking. I was tired of reading how weak we [the defense] were."

Fellow lineman Larry Cole credited the victory to the team's mental toughness and never-say-die attitude. Cole had seen the Cowboys crumble a season before when faced with an early deficit, but had nothing but praises for the way the team bounced back after a rough first quarter. "Reminded me of the Rams' game," said Cole. "Everybody was quiet. We were concentrating...determined. That's what happened to us last week...everybody got too emotional and when that happens you can't execute. We knew we were 10 points down and we were going to come back. Then came that big play on the pass Richards caught and turned into a touchdown and that helped. We did not think at any time that we were out of it."

Wearing a devilish smirk in front of his locker, while smoking what was clearly intended to be a victory cigar, sat the disheveled figure of Cliff Harris. His black hair was mussed. His jersey was torn. Droppings of cigar ash were staining his pants. Cliff didn't care, though. Through no fault of his own, he had lost out on a party when the Cowboys suffered an overtime meltdown against Washington in November. So he wasn't about to miss this chance at celebrating. "Oh, boy, it was great to beat those guys," he said. "I had rather beat them than anybody else."

But nobody seemed to find more joy in winning than did the Dallas Head Coach. Normally a stone-faced diplomat to the media, win or lose, Landry was bubbly with excitement while raving over what the Cowboys had accomplished in beating the Redskins. On his way down to the locker room after the game, Landry espied a writer who had been critical of his team during the week. In passing, Landry remarked with a smile, "See, sometimes you never can tell."

When in front of reporters a few moments later, Landry echoed that sentiment. Not even he could have anticipated all of this happening before the season. "We're in the playoffs and we'll play anybody," he declared, grinning. "Tomorrow, in Minnesota or in sub-freezing temperatures. We won with 12 rookies and I really didn't dream of this happening. Not because they are not good football players but because we lost so many players – like the Lilly's, Green's, Garrison's and Hill's. So this is a great season for us under the circumstances. We're real happy."

"Happy?" questioned *Dallas Morning News* columnist Sam Blair the next day. "Landry may have been more than that. Doctor, get that man's temperature."

Yes, Tom Landry had the playoff fever. And, as America was soon to find out, his team did too.

CHAPTER 25

RUMORS & REACTIONS

"The bad deal is that I want to play pretty badly and I can't unless [Roger] gets hurt." - **Clint Longley**

With their blowout victory over the Redskins, the Dallas Cowboys were thought to have ended any dramatic storylines pertaining to the NFC playoff race. With a 31-10 final score on Saturday, the 9-4 Cowboys assured themselves of owning the tiebreaker over 8-5 Washington with one week remaining on the regular season schedule, thus securing the fourth – and final – playoff spot in the National Conference.

Yet, by the time Wednesday afternoon rolled around, the four team playoff field of Minnesota, Los Angeles, St. Louis, and Dallas appeared to be anything but set in stone. In one of the strangest news releases in recent memory, an 11-2 team appeared to be on the verge of postseason disqualification on the merits of a single eye-popping health report.

Amidst a very trying season for former Heisman Trophy winning running back John Cappelletti, the second-year pro found himself not only buried on the depth chart and forgotten behind Lawrence McCutcheon, but suddenly ostracized from the rest of his Rams' teammates when doctors diagnosed him with mononucleosis and strep throat.

In an effort to keep the sickness from spreading through the locker room, Head Coach Chuck Knox ruled Cappelletti out for the regular season finale against Pittsburgh and quickly sent him home to recuperate.

The NFL, meanwhile, was faced with the dilemma of what their reaction would be in the event that an epidemic did strike the Rams' camp. Would they disqualify Los Angeles from the postseason and allow their playoff opponent (likely St. Louis)) to advance to the conference championship game? It wasn't in the nature of commissioner Pete Rozelle to allow a payday to slip through the league's fingers, but it was certainly an option he had to consider. The more likely alternative was to replace the Rams with the NFC's first team out of the playoffs. That, of course, was none other than the Washington Redskins.

John Crittenden perfectly captured the thought of every sports conspiracy theorist in Texas when he penned this query in the *Miami News*. Wrote Crittenden: "You don't think that maybe George Allen spiked the drinking water, do you?"

With the folding of the World Football League in late October, the local press began to pepper high-ranking Cowboys' officials with questions about which players could possibly be making a return to the team. Both Tom Landry and Tex Schramm tried to remain non-committal on this subject, reminding reporters that the earliest players could come back from the fallen league was the start of the 1976 season.

But still the queries came their way. Every week someone wanted to know something. Would Calvin Hill come back? Did the Cowboys own the rights to Duane Thomas?

One of the questions that Landry seemed more receptive to answering centered around the status of Danny White. A third-round pick of the Cowboys in the 1974 draft, White had been one of the many who had joined the WFL, and saw extensive playing time as the quarterback of the Memphis franchise. Landry clearly thought highly of White's abilities, and assured everyone that he would not be treated like a rookie when he reported to camp the following season.

What seemed to be an innocent remark from the head coach was received as a threat by White's chief challenger. So far in the 1975 season, Clint Longley had enjoyed the typical existence of a quarterback who finds himself stuck behind a legend on the depth chart. He was rarely seen, and never heard from. And until conversations about White started bouncing off walls in Dallas, he had been perfectly fine with that.

Clint was like any old cowboy of the west, who fretted over any enemy he couldn't see. Up until now, Danny White had been but a shadow. But when expectations were applied to that shadow, Longley began checking for his hole card. It didn't take him very long to discover that he didn't have one.

Outside of what many deemed to be a fluke performance on Thanksgiving as a rookie, Clint's allotment of meaningful action as a professional boiled down to a few simple handoffs and a couple of meaningless throws. Playing well in a preseason victory over Pittsburgh had helped his resume somewhat, but not enough to cover the shame of being replaced by Staubach in an earlier game versus a bad Houston team.

As the Cowboys chased a playoff berth during the stretch run of the 1975 season, Longley began fretting over his personal insecurity. He watched other quarterbacks on television, and marveled at the injustice which circumstances had burdened him with. Why, he could play better than a lot of those guys!

Why then did he have to get stuck behind this immovable object named Staubach? He already knew the history of every ambitious quarterback who had designs on the starting job. And Clint had no intentions of becoming the next Craig Morton. "No, I couldn't sit around like this for a few more years," he said in December of 1975. "I have goals but I don't want to talk about them now. You can't tell what might happen. Roger came along, got a little experience and then challenged and won the job. The bad deal is that I want to play pretty badly and I can't unless he gets hurt. I'd hate to see him get hurt, so what can you do? Nothing."

Nothing except wait until Roger gets hurt, which is exactly what happened to Staubach against Washington. In spite of finishing the game out, Roger couldn't dodge from the medical report that followed. He had severely bruised ribs. More importantly, they were the same ribs he had busted in August of the previous year.

Team doctor Pat Evans informed Landry that Staubach was healthy enough to play in the finale against the Jets. But warned him that an injection of medication would have made the quarterback sore for another three days. With that, Landry decided to go with Longley.

It was an easy decision, by all accounts. With their win on Sunday, St. Louis had already wrapped up the division, and so Dallas would be playing virtually a meaningless game. There was no reason to put the franchise quarterback needlessly in harm's way. A week's rest would do Staubach some good, no doubt. And it would give Clint Longley a chance to release some of the frustration that had been building within him.

So it was settled. For his first career start as a pro, this Texas gunslinger named Longley was headed to Broadway, where Joe, the Jets, and the Shea Stadium gusts would give him all he could handle.

With his team stuck in a 14-14 tie coming out of the halftime break, Longley went to work and authored the game-defining drive. To begin a march that started at the midfield stripe, Longley knifed a pass through a cold wind for Drew Pearson that gained 23 yards. After the running back trio of Robert Newhouse, Doug Dennison, and Preston Pearson carried the offense to the ten-yard line, it was Longley rolling right and finding Pearson again for the touchdown.

And when Randy Hughes intercepted a pass from replacement Jets quarterback J.J. Jones in the final minute and returned it 33 yards for a touchdown, Longley walked off an NFL field as the winning quarterback of record for the first time. By completing 6-of-15 pass attempts in miserable conditions and leading Dallas to a 31-21 victory, Longley had accredited himself well. Suddenly, his portfolio was looking better all the time.

For the first time in weeks, Clint Longley slept like a baby.

Whether in politics or football, life very often moves in cycles. The America of the mid-1970s was learning this lesson the hard way. Just as 1974 was a bad year for the office of President, 1975 was proving to be just as forgettable for NFL referees. Thirty-seconds of altered recordings bought Richard Nixon a fame he could have lived without. He was responsible for cheating the system, and paid with his job.

On the merits of two late-game blunders, NFL referees were being accused of cheating the game. Based on the outburst of the throngs, an innocent bystander might have come to the conclusion that a few particular zebra-shirts might just pay with their lives.

The outbursts had started earlier in the season when officials controversially awarded St. Louis' Mel Gray a fourth-quarter touchdown that ultimately led to a Washington defeat. These complaints were renewed with all vigor during the Christmas shopping season.

On the very day after Dallas secured the NFC's final playoff spot with a Saturday afternoon thumping of those same snake-bitten Redskins, linesman Jerry Bergman threw a decisive monkey-wrench into the AFC playoff picture. Late in a game between Miami and Buffalo, the Bills thought they had recovered a Mercury Morris fumble deep in Dolphins territory. Once down 21-0 in the first-half, Buffalo had rallied to within three points, and were trailing 24-21 at the moment. With the fumble recovery, the upstart Bills looked poised for the upset.

But before the pile around the ball could disassemble, two things happened to dampen the party atmosphere. One official mistakenly ruled that Morris was down before the fumble occurred. Another official, Bergman in this case, dropped a yellow hankie onto the field and charged defensive end Pat Toomay with unsportsmanlike conduct. (Toomay, you will remember, was shipped from Dallas to Buffalo early in training camp after falling out of graces with the coaching staff and requesting a trade.) Toomay, it seemed, had bumped into

Bergman during the fracas for the ball. Toomay said he was merely attempting to recover the ball. Bergman dubbed him an ineffective liar, and duly walked off 15 yards in favor of Miami.

Two plays later the Dolphins scored the deciding touchdown, knocking Buffalo from the playoff race. After the game, Bills owner Ralph Wilson blew up in front of the media, verbally marking the officials with every shade of incompetence and thoroughly lacking in late-game manners. Wilson's frustrations were seconded by a handful of coaches around the league, who claimed that video replay had become necessary to overcome the human tendency toward error.

The NFL front-office didn't take kindly to this frontal attack on the integrity of their game, and quickly lowered the boom on Wilson, fining him a grand total of $5,000. And just in case Wilson's punitive contribution didn't get the point across to everyone else, the league threw their full support behind the striped-shirts by sending Bergman north to Minnesota for the opening round of the playoffs, where the Cowboys, officially the No. 4 seed after doctors cleared Los Angeles to participate in the postseason, would try to pull off a monumental upset.

Bergman's surprising assignation gave him a VIP date with history, and a birds-eye view of one of the NFL's iconic plays. More than perhaps anyone else on the Metropolitan Stadium field, Bergman saw it all, the start and the finish of a moment that turned the playoffs upside down.

He called fair. The crowd called foul. The cries of the visiting Cowboys tended toward joyous yelps of disbelief.

CHAPTER 26

THE HAIL MARY GAME

"The ball hit right in my hands. Then he hit my arm and the ball slipped but stuck between my elbow and hip. I just pulled it up and ran into the end zone." - **Drew Pearson, on his game-winning touchdown catch against the Vikings**

"You get guys like Drew and Roger and they just believe they can do it. They've done it before and expect it to happen." - **Tom Landry**

    Graced with companionship customary for the time of year, a day reserved for miracles dawned upon the cold, unforgiving hearth of Minnesota Vikings football. Everywhere a body looked within the epicenter of Minneapolis' Sunday marquee on the morning of Dec. 28, 1975, there could be seen someone doing an ordinary job in an ordinary way for – very likely – ordinary wages. Enshrouded in a thick fogbank and with icicles hanging above them from the upper deck facade, grounds crew members inside Metropolitan Stadium worked steadily to prepare for a Noon kickoff between Minnesota and Dallas in an NFC Divisional playoff game. The temperature was hovering around fifteen-degrees, and was projected to rise to about 25-degrees by game-time.

Up in the stands, seats were cleared of snow with brooms and concrete walkways relieved of treacherous ice patches with square-point shovels. Down where the action would be, snow from earlier in the week was either piled behind each bench or removed from the stadium altogether.

The tarp covering the playing surface was then removed, revealing a field in surprisingly good condition. The grass was green, and the footing better than expected. Space heaters were distributed near each bench to take some of the chill out of the air, turning the sideline areas into a mixture of slush and mud. Dimensions and markers were reemphasized with an extra coating of white paint, while the true artists of the crew took time in the cold, damp conditions to make sure that the NFL logo emblazoned at midfield would resonate during the game with TV viewers from across the nation. A dab of blue, a dash of red, and a splash of white did the trick. By the time a few players straggled out onto the field for warm-ups at around 10 a.m., the field was fully prepped and ready. The only thing remaining now was the game itself.

A typical winter morning in Minneapolis was complete, and now awaited the embrace of an afternoon whose fate was founded on the atypical, and whose legend would forever be linked with the divine.

Long before the "frozen tundra" of Lambeau Field was ever immortalized by legendary NFL Films narrator John Facenda, it was Minnesota's Metropolitan Stadium that seemingly overpowered unsuspecting opponents with its brutally cold temperatures and fierce winter winds. No habitat in professional football during the 1970s was more revered for its alleged climactic impact upon meaningful late-season games than was the Vikings' open-air castle in the North.

Having won seven division titles over the last eight years with Bud Grant at the helm on the sideline, the Vikings had played host to more than their fair share of playoff challengers, the majority of whom were consecrated by historians as postseason road-kill. As of 1974, no team in the NFC had played in more Super Bowl games than Minnesota. While many coaches and players around the league acknowledged the quality of the Vikings roster, they also claimed that Grant's team benefitted from the best home-field advantage money could buy.

Tom Landry was of a much more pragmatic mind on this subject. To the Cowboys' head coach, cold temperatures and frigid winds were certainly a factor in Minnesota's recent run of success, but not because of any advantage that the Vikings may have had. To Landry, weather was the great equalizer, not a pendulum that swung in the home team's favor. Inclement weather created a level playing field, of sorts, and an assortment of opportunities. The Cowboys, despite being seven-point underdogs and despite the pervasive skepticism of sportswriters far and near, would have their fair share of chances against the Vikings.

The first thing Landry's team had to do was slow down the Minnesota offense. Even for one of the league's better defensive units, that was easier talking about than actually doing. The Vikings' offense operated primarily on a ball-control philosophy, one that ground out tough yards on the ground and moved the chains with short, precise passes.

Quarterback Fran Tarkenton was especially fond of throwing to running backs Chuck Foreman and Ed Marinaro. Between the two backs, Tarkenton had completed 127 passes in 1975, nearly half of all his completions for the season. Foreman's 73 receptions set a new league record for a running back. Stu Voigt had also figured in Minnesota's short passing game. The sixth-year tight end had hauled in a career high 34 catches of his own on the season.

The Cowboys had played against this style before when they hosted the Vikings for their annual Salesmanship Club game back in August. What they had not seen was a Vikings' team with the big-play capabilities of John Gilliam on the outside. When Gilliam was playing for Chicago in the World

Football League, the Vikings were picked to be either a No. 2 or No. 3 seed in the NFC playoffs, depending on whom you asked. With him back in purple after the franchise folded in September, Minnesota became a likely favorite for back-to-back Super Bowl berths.

Gilliam's presence was a game-changer for a Minnesota offense that could lull a defense to sleep. Now, in addition to their precise short passing game, the Vikings had a legitimate deep threat who could stretch the field with his speed. In 14 games in 1975, Gilliam had averaged 15.5 yards on fifty receptions.

Landry's defensive strategy going into their playoff meeting was simple. The Cowboys were going to crowd the line of scrimmage and try to close off all running lanes. By lining up closer to the action, Dallas safeties and linebackers would be in better position to clamp down on the Vikings' short passing game.

The poor tackling which had plagued the Cowboys in their preseason meeting with Minnesota was, in Landry's mind, attributable largely to a lack of confidence. At the time, Dallas was coming off a pair of disheartening losses to start the exhibition schedule, and the younger players were beginning to second-guess themselves on the field. With his team still bubbling with enthusiasm from their dismantling of Washington on Dec. 13, Landry had no such concerns of a repeat performance.

Landry, of course, was gambling that his pair of cornerbacks could prevent the big play from Gilliam and Jim Lache on the outside. In Grant's offensive system, the Vikings would line Gilliam up on either side of the formation, meaning that both Mark Washington and Mel Renfro would be tested at times during the game.

Landry had no second thoughts about leaving Renfro on an island. The 33-year old veteran was still one of the better cornerbacks in the league, injured foot notwithstanding. Renfro sat out the last two regular season games against the Redskins and Jets, so would be fresh and ready to go.

Mark Washington was another story indeed. Since early in the season, opponents had treated Washington as the weak link in the Dallas defense, attacking the first-year starter relentlessly. Washington had fared well against teams' No. 2 receiver. But when offensive coordinators started switching formations and attacking him with the No. 1 wide-out, holes in Washington's game began to appear, forcing Landry and Defensive Coordinator Ernie Stautner to swing an array of coverages over to his side of the field as protection. Help for Washington would be minimal against Minnesota. A good cornerback in his own right, Washington needed to be great for the Cowboys to have a chance.

Everything Landry could have hoped for transpired to start the game. Foreman had nowhere to run inside, and Tarkenton's flairs in the flat were put to rest with sure tackles from Charlie Waters and others. Even the deep balls weren't landing. On Minnesota's first drive, Tarkenton overthrew an open Gilliam, who had a step on Washington down the right sideline. The NFL's fifth-ranked offense was stuck in neutral.

Dallas' early efficiency on defense was accentuated by a stroke of good fortune on the offensive side. Two plays after a penalty on Minnesota for roughing Mitch Hoopes extended a Dallas drive, Roger Staubach's inside handoff was fumbled by Robert Newhouse, after All-Pro defensive tackle Alan Page reached in and poked it out. The ball caromed into the backfield, setting off a mad scramble for positioning. By diving in at the opportune moment, Staubach was able to swat the ball farther downfield and away from a chasing Page. The ball rolled between the legs of linebacker Jeff Siemon before Blaine Nye pounced on it for the Cowboys at the 28-yard line. A loss of eight yards hurt, but not nearly so much as a turnover would have.

A friendly bounce in the first quarter gave way to an evil carom off the foot of Neil Clabo early in the second frame. Another Vikings' possession had just gone awry on a pair of Tarkenton overthrows to Gilliam, and Clabo was faced with the task of pinning Dallas deep in their own end. His kick was high, deep, and angling toward the right side, prompting return-man Cliff Harris to signal for a fair-catch near the 5-yard line.

Whether or not Harris actually meant to field the ball so close to his own goal-line is uncertain. But while giving a healthy impression of doing just that, Harris ran into a two-man blockade consisting of Benny Barnes and Autry Beamon.

The ball, instead of landing in his arms, was ruled to have deflected off Harris' leg, and rolled back toward the middle of the field, an unfortunate fumble there for the taking. Cowboys' rookie special-teamer Pat Donovan was the first player to catch up with it, reaching out for the ball between the hashes at the 3-yard line. But when he couldn't control it, Fred McNeil was there to pounce on it for the Vikings at the 4.

Harris confronted officials in a heated manner off to the side, insisting that Beamon had interfered with his attempt at fielding the punt. The official told him that Beamon had been blocked into him by Barnes, making any contact inconsequential. Harris listened, but didn't care for the explanation. He cared even less when video replay showed Barnes doing just what the referee had suggested he did – shoving Beamon directly into him.

The first break in the game had put Dallas between a rock and a hard place, a short twelve feet from yielding the game's first points. In response to Minnesota's jumbo package, the Cowboys sent in their run-stopping unit, with savvy, veteran linebackers D.D. Lewis, Lee Roy Jordan, and Dave Edwards.

On first-down, it was Jordan crashing into Foreman and stopping him at the 2-yard line. A second-down quarterback sweep to the right ended with Harris taking Tarkenton down at the 1. On third-down the Vikings went back to Foreman, and the 215-pound bruiser went over the pile and through Jordan to break the scoreless tie.

The remaining 11:49 of the second quarter was filled with wasted opportunities for the Cowboys. Immediately after Minnesota's touchdown, the Dallas offense penetrated inside the Vikings' 20-yard line for the first time that day. But back-to-back sacks of Staubach stalled the drive, leading to a 49-yard field goal try from Toni Fritsch, which he duly hooked to the left.

A few moments later, Mel Renfro's theft of a sideline pass while falling out of bounds gave Dallas possession at the Minnesota 49. Consecutive completions to Golden Richards out of the Shotgun moved the ball to the 34. When Doug Dennison was stopped a foot short on a third-and-1 play, Landry was faced with a familiar dilemma.

While pacing the muddy sidelines in conspicuous black combat boots, Landry pondered one of football's ageless questions: The offense or the kicker? With only a foot to go and seven points to make up on the scoreboard, Landry's decision was a relatively easy one. As he had on multiple occasions throughout the season, Landry left his offense on the field for fourth-down. This time though, the big Cowboys' offensive line was pushed back, clogging up Dennison in the backfield and ending another drive in emptiness and frustration.

A game that the Cowboys were dominating on the field in virtually every category witnessed them going into halftime trailing 7-0 on the scoreboard. It was the first time since Week 5 versus Green Bay that Dallas had been shut out in the first half which, ironically, was the last time they had played against a team from the NFC Northern division. That game, more importantly, had resulted in the Cowboys' first loss of the season. Would a poor first-half output in Minnesota lead to their last?

The fourth quarter clock showed 2:20 remaining. Outside Metropolitan Stadium, patches of fog joined forces with snow and ice to make for treacherous conditions for drivers. Inside, where all 46,000 fans were still bundled in their seats, the situation was startlingly clear. A game and a season had come down to one play for the Dallas Cowboys.

A display of misplay through the first two quarters, this playoff game between two proud franchises from the NFC broke out into a battle of football heavyweights in the second-half. With the grit and determination that had become synonymous with their season, the Cowboys rallied from their halftime deficit to take a 10-7 lead early in the fourth quarter. The Vikings, as you would expect of the conference's defending champions,

The Dirty Dozen

came back with a long scoring drive of their own to re-claim the lead, setting the stage for some late-game drama.

A nine-play, 72-yard drive, highlighted by a 17-yard catch-and-run by Billy Joe Dupree, concluded with Dennison's 4-yard touchdown off left tackle. A blindside sack of Tarkenton on a third-down play by Randy White forced another Minnesota punt, and preceded another long Dallas march. This time the drive stalled at the eight-yard line, setting up Fritsch's 25-yard field goal that put the Cowboys ahead for the first time.

A series of breaks then served to keep the Vikings within striking distance. Video replay of the ensuing kickoff return showed that Ed McLanahan fumbled while falling to the ground after being hit by Randy Hughes, leading to a Dallas recovery. But instead of awarding the ball to the Cowboys, the officials ruled that McLanahan's knee was already on the ground when the fumble occurred.

Following Clabo's sixth punt of the game, Roger Staubach's third-and-11 Shotgun bomb to Golden Richards down the left sideline was on the money. Richards had beaten cornerback Bobby Bryant by nearly two full steps, and had designs on the longest scoring play of his young career. But Richards, as he had in the second-half against Kansas City, watched the ball bounce off his shoulder pad, through his hands and fall harmlessly to the ground.

On the very next play from scrimmage by the Vikings, Tarkenton's deep pass for Gilliam on the right side was dropped by a well-positioned Mark Washington. Seconds later, D.D. Lewis stripped Foreman of the ball in a crowd. The ball bounced straight to a Vikings' lineman. Tarkenton then salvaged the drive by completing a 16-yard pass to Foreman on third-down, and the Vikings were off and running. Eight plays later, McLanahan capped the 70-yard drive with his one-yard scoring burst through the arm tackles of Cliff Harris and Lee Roy Jordan to put Minnesota back in front 14-10.

Now, as fans watched the home team try to put away the Cowboys for good, Landry and the Dallas defense used its first timeout of the half before a critical third-and-2 play from the Cowboys' 47-yard line. If Dallas couldn't stop Minnesota from picking up a first down on the next play, then the Vikings would be able to milk nearly all of the remaining time from the game-clock. In the event that Dallas forced a punt, their offense would still have to drive the length of the field in less than two minutes against the league's top-ranked pass defense. Either way, their chances looked about as bright as the Minneapolis skyline.

Minnesota had relied on the legs of McLanahan on the two previous plays. But when they broke the huddle on third-down, their plans were a bit different. Rather than running inside with either of their backs, the plan was for Tarkenton to execute a quick rollout to the right and find Stu Voigt or Steve Craig with a short pass. If neither receiver was open, then Tarkenton would have the option of either throwing the ball away or scrambling for the yardage required.

A blitz off the edge from strong safety Charlie Waters blew the play up before it ever had a chance to develop. With Tarkenton rolling to his side, Waters went around the block of Chuck Foreman, grabbed the 35-year old quarterback by the jersey, and slung him to the ground for a one-yard loss. By the time Richards downed the punt from Clabo at the Dallas 15-yard line, the clock showed 1:51 remaining.

Eighty-five yards away from a touchdown and victory, it was acknowledged by everyone in the building that the Cowboys needed more than just a drive. They needed a miracle.

It is the poet's nostalgic mind that provokes him to pen the darkest-hour phenomenon on the fertile grounds of faith and selflessness. For your average football player, whose emotions are tied to an unforgiving scoreboard and a sixty-minute clock, the moment of no return is often accompanied by a sense of frustration and doubt.

Even the most stalwart of teams have trouble avoiding this inherent drawback of human nature. For the 1975 Dallas Cowboys, a team that had shared a common sense of belief, trust, and purpose on the way to winning ten games and earning an improbable playoff spot, their story while looking down the steel barrel of elimination was no different. "It looked pretty grim," admitted Tom Landry of the scene on the Dallas sideline before their final drive. "I was feeling sorry for our defense, for the team really, because everybody had played so well." Sensing the mood of Cowboys' players and coaches, one security guard tried to console Robert Newhouse on the bench, telling the Dallas running back, "Nice game, nice game."

Pro Bowl invitee Rayfield Wright, the Cowboys' veteran offensive tackle who had been on the field for several dramatic comebacks over the years, had no sub-conscious forewarning of the destiny that awaited. He, better than almost anyone else in the stadium, knew that marching 85 yards in less than two minutes was possible, but also the highest degree of improbable. It was a sobering reality that convinced Wright his time would be best served focusing on his immediate job than any likely outcome. "Sure, you have to feel you can win if you have the football and there's any time on the clock. You can't give up. But frankly, I was thinking mostly about giving the cat (Staubach) time to throw the football…"

Perhaps the most depressed member of the Cowboys was wide receiver Drew Pearson, who took to the field for the final time while wallowing in a mire of frustration and self-pity. Through the game's first 58:09, the Cowboys' leading receiver on the season had failed to catch a single pass, leading to some disgruntlement as the game neared its end. "It had been frustrating all day," reflected Pearson. "He hadn't thrown any passes to me. My team was losing, the season was about to end… And I was a little upset I hadn't made the All-Pro team again."

It is a good thing that Pearson's competitive streak didn't allow him to mentally check out of the game because, after looking elsewhere all afternoon for yards through the air, Staubach would be coming his way early and often on Dallas' final march. Just like they had earlier teamed up to steal a victory from the jaws of defeat at Veterans Stadium against the Eagles in Week 6, it would be the Roger & Drew show, for better or for worse.

On first-down, Staubach threw a short sideline pass to Pearson, who was open against a soft Vikings' coverage bent on preventing the big play. The pass went for nine-yards, and advanced the ball to the 24-yard line. Two plays later, Staubach scrambled in the backfield long enough to find Pearson working from right-to-left at the 31, giving Dallas a first-down and a sense of momentum.

There to compromise the comeback effort was the unexpected figure of John Fitzgerald. The Cowboys center, who had gone the entire regular season without an errant snap, had started missing his target in the backfield earlier in the game on several plays from the Shotgun formation, and even botched a traditional snap in the third quarter. When this problem reared its ugly head again in the waning seconds, Landry was forced to consider a line-up change.

Fitzgerald's first-down snap that landed at the feet of Staubach left the Dallas quarterback with no other alternative but to eat the ball and get swallowed up for a sack. After the whistle blew, Staubach slammed the ball down in frustration.

Incompletions on second and third downs brought up a fourth-and-17 play for Dallas with 44 seconds remaining. It also brought a change at center. Rookie Kyle Davis, who normally served as the team's deep-snapper on punts and field goals, was inserted into the lineup during a called timeout to replace the errant Fitzgerald.

With Minnesota likely employing a prevent defense that called for only three or four pass-rushers, the Cowboys had little worry of the young Davis missing a blocking assignment. His first and most important duty on the field was to get the ball back safely into the hands of Staubach to start the play. A rookie who had caught the scouts' eyes in college while operating under Barry Switzer's Wishbone offense was now seeing his first meaningful action as a professional as the center in Tom Landry's vaunted Shotgun offense.

While in the huddle, Staubach asked Pearson what route he had been getting open on. Pearson said that a corner route might work. Staubach nodded, and told him to give it a try. Staubach, assuming the snap from Davis was decent, knew exactly where he was going with his next pass.

With the ball resting at their own 25-yard line, the Cowboys broke the huddle knowing their season was officially on life-support. To extend their season beyond this fourth-down play, they needed 17 yards.

The snap from Davis was spot-on, the blocking in front of Staubach adequate. From a perfectly-formed pocket, Staubach stepped up and launched a frozen rope to Pearson deep along the right sideline. Seeing that the ball was slightly underthrown, Pearson flattened his route a bit and reached up with both hands. Securing the ball firmly, the 5-foot-11-inch target was able to tap both feet in bounds at the 50-yard line, before being pushed out by Nate Wright. The 25-yard gain left Dallas with a ray of hope, but only 37 seconds on the clock.

Back in the huddle, Staubach asked Pearson if he could run a streak pattern. Staubach felt confident that the Vikings would be expecting a deep-post from Pearson in that situation. Pearson thought the suggestion a good one, but asked his quarterback to give him a play to catch his breath and to get over the pain of a newfound bruise on his leg. It seems that after being knocked into the sideline crowd on the previous play, Pearson had bumped into a security guard who was so pleased with Pearson having extended the game that he gave the Cowboys' receiver a hearty kick on the shin.

Staubach agreed to wait a play, and promised to throw to Golden Richards instead on first-down. But when Richards was blanketed by double-coverage downfield, Staubach looked short for Preston Pearson, who had slipped out of the backfield unnoticed by the defense. The pass was too far in front of the awaiting running back, leading to Staubach's fourth incompletion of the drive.

With only 32 seconds showing on the game-clock, all 46, 425 fans in the building knew that Staubach must go long. And with his trusted receiver now rested and ready, Staubach knew who his second-and-10 pass from the midfield stripe would be aimed toward.

From his backfield station in the Shotgun, Staubach received another accurate snap from Davis and surveyed the scene downfield as he finished his customary drop-back. He set, pumped left towards Richards – who was running a deep-post – and let sail a high, arching pass that, according to locals, must have touched the heavens. The first "Hail Mary" pass in NFL history, a desperate prayer of a throw that the Cowboys' Catholic quarterback authored with a silent submission to the Holy Mother for heavenly assistance, went up into the slate-grey sky as an impossible hope that no rational mind could attach their faith to. And as the ball reached its peak and started on its downward flight, its chances of being completed to a Dallas wide receiver looked even bleaker. The pass was wobbly and, on top of that, short of the streaking Drew Pearson.

Pearson hesitated to let the ball catch up, while jousting for position, like a basketball player, with Nate Wright. Pearson shoved a bit. Wright shoved back. And just when it appeared that the Minnesota defensive back would make a game-ending interception, Wright fell down and left Pearson alone to reach out, make the catch and walk in for the touchdown. The same receiver who had been shutout for the game's first 58 minutes, had caught all four of Staubach's completions on the final drive and given the Cowboys a 17-14 lead with 25 seconds remaining. The 50-yard touchdown play gave him 91 yards receiving on the day, to lead all receivers.

When he crossed the goal-line, Pearson fired the ball at the scoreboard in celebration, before being mobbed by a host of jubilant teammates. Golden Richards and Billy Joe Dupree got there first. Then came the rest of Troop Cowboy. Like young boys having just completed the last day of school, Kyle Davis and Burton Lawless sprinted all the way down the field to give Pearson his dues – a hearty pat on the back and a good-natured slap on the helmet. There to help them were others off the bench- Jethro Pugh, Toni Fritsch, and even Clint Longley. The happy mass of Cowboys basked in their good fortune before slowly making their way back to the Dallas sideline. Robert Newhouse went in search of the security guard who had offered his condolences earlier, but he was nowhere to be found.

While Cowboys' players danced and paraded in the endzone, the Vikings were arguing with linesman Jerry Bergman over what they deemed to be pass-interference on the part of Pearson who, they claimed, had shoved Wright down in order to make the catch. When questioned about it later, Pearson acknowledged, "We were both jousting, trying to get inside for the ball. They could have called it on either one of us."

Bergman had jumped into a hot pool of controversy by throwing the flag in the Buffalo-Miami game. Now he was getting roasted for not throwing one. Sometimes it's just hard to please these people!

Safety Paul Krause argued his case respectfully. Bud Grant came over and offered his opinion a bit more forcibly. Through it all Bergman listened. But when the air became filled with the curses of defensive lineman Alan Page, Bergman finally dropped the yellow hankie – not for interference on Pearson, but for unsportsmanlike conduct on the part of Page. Page responded by leaving the field altogether, an All-Pro performer overcome with shock and frustration.

The emotions of the fans boiled over into much more than mere words. After Ed "Too Tall" Jones took down Fran Tarkenton for a 14-yard sack on first-down, what had been a few harmless oranges flying onto the field turned into a barrage of liquor bottles. One bottle smacked Armen Terzian on the forehead, dropping the field judge as if he had been shot and causing a stoppage in the game. Terzian was removed from the field after a couple of minutes, a $5,000 reward posted by Vikings owner Max Winter for the discovery of the mysterious fan who had tossed that particular pint-bottle, and the Cowboys squeezed the remaining seconds from the clock to savor a most satisfying of victories.

"Just two more to go," yelled defensive end Harvey Martin in the locker room. "Two more, one at LA, and then one at Miami, and we are the world champs."

That night in north Texas, nearly 5,000 delirious Cowboys' fans gathered in a corridor of Dallas-Fort Worth Airport. Children, the elderly, poets, and rednecks were all assembled to greet and cheer their conquering heroes. They wore jackets and sweatshirts, they wrote poems, held up banners, and drank beer. It was a Texas-sized gathering to honor Texas' No. 1 football team.

One sign read "Tom Terrific." Another said "Super Bowl Bound. Rest Stop in LA." A third sign said "Killer Cowboys will ram those Rams."

The poems that could be seen above the crowd did justice to the emotionally-charged state that most fans were in. One poem read "Doomsday Defense they thought was dead, but ask the old Vikings to feel their heads."

Those too excited to read took solace in distributing and downing cans of beer that a few zealous fans had brought. A couple of kids who were obviously too young to partake held up their own sign in support of the new hero, Drew Pearson, which said, "He's All-Pro to us."

After three hours of waiting and basking in the mutual admiration of all things Cowboys, the crowd exploded in a thunderous chorus of cheers and whistles as the players and coaches emerged from inside the plane. The loudest cheer of all came when Thomas Henderson walked through the crowd wearing a Viking helmet with one of the horns broken off.

Without a doubt, Roger Staubach's Hail Mary pass to Drew Pearson had set off an epidemic in Dallas. The playoff fever had come to north Texas. But how long would it stay?

On the following Tuesday, it was brought to Tom Landry's attention that, though marvelous and extraordinary as it was, the Cowboys weren't exactly strangers to these playoff miracles like the nation had witnessed against Minnesota. A Hail-Mary ending had also saved them in the 1972 postseason. That was the day that Roger Staubach came off the bench in relief of Craig Morton and led the Cowboys to 17 unanswered points to beat San Francisco.

A certain reporter wanted to know if Landry's team would be able to come off their emotional high of beating the Vikings in time to avoid an NFC Championship letdown of the 1972 variety, when Dallas followed up their comeback over San

Francisco with a 26-3 loss on the road at Washington. Could the Cowboys gear themselves up to play the role of spoiler again?

"We came from behind and beat San Francisco two years ago but it was a different victory,' Landry said. "The 49ers whipped us all over the field and let it get away. We just couldn't come back mentally and got whipped the next week.

"Now, we deserved to beat Minnesota," he continued. "We outplayed them. That's a big difference. Sure, we had to come from behind with a shocking play but we deserved it. We also expected to win when we went to Minnesota."

Depending on who you asked, the road to Super Bowl X in the NFC was supposed to have run through Minnesota and the vaunted Purple People Eaters' defense. With the Vikings now eliminated, the Los Angeles Rams became the overwhelming favorite to go the distance, having dispatched St. Louis by a wide margin over the weekend.

The Cowboys, while certainly a feel-good story, were thought to be more lucky than good. Odds makers and sportswriters gave them absolutely zero chance of going west to the Coliseum and stealing a game from the Rams.

Whether it was a streak of youth showing through their armor, or just a plain case of stubbornness, Cowboys' players thought they had as good a chance as any to be NFC champions. And they weren't about to forget the whipping they had put on Los Angeles to start the regular season. That game, more than anything else at the moment, was a reminder of the potential inside the Dallas clubhouse. The Cowboys, though perceived to be going into a lion's den of Rams, were going there for the kill.

Reflecting on his team's mood heading into their showdown with Los Angeles, Landry said, "We were confident. We were going to Los Angeles to win."

CHAPTER 27

WILD CARD WONDERS

"It was the most perfect football game we ever had as Cowboys." - **Roger Staubach, reflecting on the 1975 NFC Championship victory over Los Angeles**

"That was one of the best games that Roger Staubach has ever played." - **Tom Landry**

Leading up to a big prize fight, trainers often spend weeks – even months – lecturing their pupils on the fundamental art of getting in the first good punch. There is no advantage, they say, quite like the first one. So go ahead and get it in before your opponent does. It often is the first step toward victory.

Special teams' coach Mike Ditka saved such a one-on-one conversation with Thomas Henderson for the moments just prior to the Cowboys taking the field to receive the opening kickoff of the NFC Championship Game. Ditka had a special liking for the young rookie linebacker. Not only was Henderson an exceptional athlete who could run with the wind, but his fundamental instincts for the game made him a weapon unlike any other Ditka had come across.

Ditka saw every day on the practice field how Henderson grappled with, and occasionally rebelled against, the stringent rules of Tom Landry's Flex defense. He saw firsthand the teaching sessions that Landry or Dave Edwards or even Lee Roy Jordan had with the youngster off to the side, trying to convince Thomas to pay more attention to his technique and craftsmanship.

The technical aspect of playing defense did not carry over in the same way to the special teams' units. Running downfield at full speed and crashing into your opponent had more to do with will and desire than an abundance of artistic maneuvering. It didn't take very long in training camp for Ditka to find out that this was the perfect style of play to unleash all of Henderson's untapped potential.

Outside of Rollie Wolsey, the rookie speedster who often played gunner on the outside, Henderson was the fastest player on the Cowboys' kick-coverage unit. And there was an ongoing debate between Thomas and Rollie about just who was fastest. Henderson claimed that he hit the hardest of anybody, though he was willing to make an occasional exception in the case of Randy White.

The fact that Henderson could run so fast from the middle of the field disrupted so many returns that Ditka finally gave him a free hand on the play. No longer did Thomas have to stay in a prescribed running lane like everyone else, but could use his instincts and superior speed to track down the ball-carrier using whatever pursuit angle he deemed necessary.

His ability on Cowboys' returns was second to none, as well. He could block like a crazed monster. He could even return kickoffs. That Henderson did it all with that trademark devil-may-care attitude reminded Ditka of his own playing days as a tough, rugged tight end in Chicago, where the legend of "Iron Mike" was spawned.

As a player, Ditka had always raised his performance level in playoff games. He expected nothing less than that from young Thomas. A few seconds before the players were called onto the field, Ditka leaned over and whispered a few special instructions to Henderson. *Forget about blocking, Thomas. Forget about returning. Just go rough up the kicker.*

One of the NFL's premier talents at his position, Tom Dempsey was a standout kicker as much for his withered arm and metal, prosthetic foot as for his long, booming kicks. Dempsey once booted a 63-yard field goal in a game, an NFL record. Ditka knew that a weapon like that could turn a close game in the Rams' favor. So he told Henderson to go knock down the pudgy three-point artist, preferably with an emphatic flair.

Henderson nodded his head in understanding and walked out onto the luscious green grass of the Memorial Coliseum. It was a perfect day in southern California for 82,000 fans to watch a pair of football heavyweights square off for the championship belt of the National Football Conference. It was a perfect moment for Thomas Henderson to set the tone for what was to transpire over the next three hours.

Under cloudless skies, Dempsey approached the ball with head lowered and kicked it into the air. When he looked up an unexpected guest clobbered Dempsey in the chin with his helmet, dropping the victim on the spot. "He went down like he was dead," Henderson gloated afterwards.

Dempsey picked himself up off the grass, before wobbling over to the sideline, bells ringing in his head. Henderson went back to the Dallas bench and gave a full report to Ditka.

In a game that nobody had given them a chance to win, the Cowboys had landed the first punch. Postgame reports marveled at the evidence confirming the notion that the Rams never had a first of their own.

The Dirty Dozen

When the Cowboys last saw James Harris, he was biting his fingernails on the Texas Stadium bench, a perfect picture of misery after being yanked in the second half of the Cowboys' 18-7 Week 1 victory. Nearly three months later, the James Harris they saw in the huddle at the start of the NFC Championship Game was just coming off the bench.

Harris' second season as the Rams' starter had taken off in a big way, just as soon as the team plane landed back in Los Angeles after the Dallas game. Beginning in Week 2, Harris orchestrated a ten-game winning streak that had the Rams sitting atop the conference.

But his glass house of cards began to show signs of teetering when head coach Chuck Knox placed him on the injured list after a shoulder ailment began to affect his performance. With Ron Jaworski in the lineup, the Rams closed the regular season strong, and then destroyed St. Louis in the Divisional playoffs.

A precocious vote from locals claimed that Jaworski was the no-brainer candidate to start the next game against the Cowboys. Knox thought otherwise, and when Harris proved himself healthy enough with a strong mid-week workout, the coach re-anointed him as the Rams' starting quarterback.

Harris walked into the huddle for the first offensive series with a "Let's Go, Rams!" chant from the crowd echoing throughout the stadium. It wasn't very long before Harris had the audience up in arms and chanting four-letter words that sounded nothing like "Rams."

The game-plan coming in was a relatively simple one for the Dallas defense. Prevent the big play to Harold Jackson on the outside, and slow down running back extraordinaire Lawrence McCutcheon. Against the Cardinals a week before, McCutcheon had singlehandedly carried Los Angeles to victory, carrying 37 times and piling up 202 yards.

The Rams were a team that loved to pound McCutcheon on early downs, believing the big back would wear down opponents over the course of a game. It had worked to perfection against St. Louis, when the Rams ran 21 times and averaged 5.3 yards-per-carry. But the Dallas defense was a different monster entirely, as the Rams soon found out.

On first-down, McCutcheon took the hand-off from Harris and went straight ahead and into a two-man wall of Jethro Pugh and Ed "Too Tall" Jones. After the pile disassembled, McCutcheon noticed that he had gained all of two yards on the play.

If McCutcheon thought that running to the inside was going to be tough against the Cowboys' Flex system, then his first taste of what life was like trying to get to the outside gave him nightmares of an impossibly long day ahead of him. Going right on a sweep, the Rams' workhorse was accosted in the backfield by Dave Edwards, who grabbed him by the sleeve and slung him to the ground for a loss of three yards. Things were getting worse, and fast.

It wasn't until Los Angeles' second possession that things began to snowball in a bad way. After a first-down carry from McCutcheon netted seven yards, the Rams thought it time to dust off the right arm of their quarterback. Looking in the direction of John Cappalletti to the left, Harris hesitated in the face of pressure from a leaping Harvey Martin then threw late to his target. The off-target throw went straight to D.D. Lewis, who then returned the ball 11 yards before being tripped up at the 18.

"The wolves are howling at James Harris," aptly noted Vin Scully on the CBS broadcast, as murmurings started spreading throughout the crowd. Rams' fans had seen this act from Harris against the Cowboys before, only that was on television. It looked far worse in person. If ol' Coach Chuck didn't do something about this – and quick – the Rams wouldn't stand a chance of going to the Super Bowl.

But as Knox and everybody at the Coliseum soon learned, the Rams didn't stand a chance with or without Harris on the field. With the energy and emotion from their miracle win over the Vikings still spurring them on, the Cowboys were a machine that simply could not be stopped on this day. Their defense was impeccably overpowering. The kicking game was superb. And the play of Preston Pearson, well, that was the best of all.

On a hot, September evening at Texas Stadium, Preston Pearson stood alone in a crowd, knowing full well that his time in Pittsburgh had come to an end. A reserve running back for the Steelers behind Franco Harris and Rocky Bleier, Pearson didn't play at all in the preseason finale against Dallas, a good indicator that the team was prepared to release him after the flight home.

This didn't surprise him. He had almost been expecting it. What did catch him unaware was the lack of interest from other teams. After being let go by the Steelers, Pearson cleared waivers without getting a single phone call from an interested party. Surprise quickly turned to frustration. Pearson had worked hard during the off-season, running and lifting weights, and was in excellent physical condition. If not with the Steelers, Pearson was certain he could contribute for some other club out there.

A seven-year NFL veteran, Pearson had benefitted from the tutelage of coaches like Chuck Noll and Don Shula, and developed into a serviceable do-it-all running back. Pearson was a pro at reading blocks and allowing plays to develop. He understood pass-protection assignments, and how to pick up the blitz. Perhaps a byproduct of his days as a basketball player at the University of Illinois, Pearson also owned a special knack for making himself available for his quarterback on short, underneath throws against zone coverage.

A well-rounded player at his position, Pearson had determined by mid-week that his NFL days were behind him, and duly started planning for an entry into the business world. When he relayed this news to his family, five-year old Greg almost threw a party on the spot. Greg had never been thrilled with his Dad playing a game for a living. Games were for kids. Business was for adults.

In Greg's undeveloped world, a business card was the ultimate of status symbols. Prosperous men sold insurance or sat behind a big desk. And never, ever did they have to work on weekends. They could go fishing instead, or play with their kids in the yard. Or why not both?

For the first time in his life, Greg was really, really proud of his Dad. Proud enough to give him a big hug. And even proud enough to go to school the next day and inform his classmates that Daddy Preston was finally growing up and going to work. "My Dad's going to be a businessman," he told everyone.

But Greg's Dad fell prey to temptation when the phone rang on Thursday and discovered that the Dallas Cowboys were on the other line. Tom Landry, the voice said, was in need of a reliable veteran to help fill the void created when Calvin Hill followed his rainbow to Hawaii and the World Football League. Preston said he would be in Dallas on the following morning.

When Preston told his son the news, Greg cried. Greg's mother tried to explain that some people were meant to do certain things in life at certain times. *"Mama, does that mean that Daddy grew up to be a cowboy?"* *"Yes, son,"* Linda said, *"that's exactly what it means."* Greg could accept that. Like businessmen, cowboys had their own unique attractions too.

One of the perks of being a Cowboy was giving out birthday presents on television. The best gift Greg ever got was on his sixth birthday when he watched his Daddy celebrate like a little kid after helping the Cowboys beat the Minnesota Vikings in the Divisional playoffs. One week later, Linda blew out the candles on her own cake while watching Preston turn out the lights on the Rams with an NFC Championship Game performance for the ages.

The boos were still piercing the backside of James Harris when Preston Pearson followed Roger Staubach and the offense onto the field. Dallas was preparing to begin their third possession, but it had already been a long day for Pearson, who was so apprehensive about the game that he woke up at 5:30 that morning and spilled his guts out onto the floor. When he couldn't go back to sleep, Pearson grabbed his playbook and made sure that he knew all of his assignments. "I don't think I've ever been as worked up before a game as I was about this one," Pearson said. "We were all excited."

Pearson was still a bundle of nerves at kickoff, but had settled down enough by the time D.D. Lewis made a spectacle of James Harris. On first-down, Staubach lined-up under center with split-backs behind him, Pearson to his right and Robert Newhouse opposite. Staubach faked an inside handoff to Pearson, before feigning another give to Newhouse, who had cut across the formation to the right. Staubach then faded back and tossed a soft pass to an awaiting Pearson on the left side. With good downfield blocks from Burton Lawless, John Fitzgerald, and Blaine Nye, Pearson had an open alley to run in and plenty of wiggle room to elude the grasp of Bill Simpson at the 5 and dash in for a touchdown.

The Dallas defense chased Harris from the game on the next series by forcing a punt after three plays. Harris retired from the action having missed on both pass attempts, giving him a combined one-completion in twelve-attempts and four interceptions from both encounters with the Cowboys.

A Staubach interception and subsequent return of 37 yards by Simpson gave Los Angeles their first scoring opportunity later in the first quarter. It also provided Thomas Henderson a chance to reacquaint himself with an old friend.

As Tom Dempsey lined up to kick a field-goal of 34 yards, Henderson yelled for everyone to hear, "I'm gonna take Dempsey *out!*" Henderson proved better than his own word by replacing injury with insult and blocking the kick, giving the ball back with their 7-0 lead still intact. Dempsey's day of misery continued on the next series when he missed a second field-goal.

While Henderson cackled in delight on the sideline, Staubach and the rest of the crew rediscovered some of their earlier magic. A nine-play, 76-yard scoring march was sparked by Staubach's bomb of 42 yards to Golden Richards on a deep post pattern. Quarterback and wide receiver then capped the drive with a simple pitch-and-catch touchdown of four yards with 9:50 remaining in the second quarter. In celebration of the score, Richards gave the ball to Ralph Neely, who spiked it with a gusto befitting a big offensive lineman. "Ralph has done so much for me in the past and he's taught me so many things that I wanted to do something that I wanted to do something for him," said Richards. "Ralph's done just about everything possible in

11 years of pro football. But we were talking one day, and he said he had never spiked the football......Ralph almost forgot about it. I had to yell for him to come back and spike it."

In less than two quarters of play, the Cowboys had already surpassed the per-game average of 11 points that the Rams' defense had allowed all season. But that didn't stop them. With Staubach and Preston Pearson leading the way, Dallas was about to run away with the NFC crown.

During the week of preparation, Tom Landry had devised an intricate game-plan for Staubach that was specifically designed to take advantage of a simplistic Rams' defense. By watching what defenders the Rams sent in from the sideline, the Dallas quarterback was able to determine with uncanny precision exactly what defense Los Angeles was going to be in. Staubach would then change the Cowboys' play accordingly.

The entire plan, according to Landry, was to "go around the corners." He said: "It's tough to run against LA. That's one of the toughest run-defense teams in pro ball. So with our swing passes, screens, and rolls we tried to work on the corners...to move outside of what we believed to be their strength."

A screen play had already worked for one touchdown. Late in the second quarter, Staubach opted to try his luck with a swing pass to Pearson from the Rams' 15-yard line. Staubach's drop-back from center was straight, his pass down the right sideline was long, and Pearson's last-instant leap was true. With his body hanging in the air parallel to the ground, Pearson managed to gather the ball in and pin it to his stomach before he finally came crashing down. The line-judge standing behind Pearson never saw the ball touch the ground from his vantage point, nor did a Rams' player or coach argue the point. The play went down in the record books as a touchdown, giving Dallas a 21-0 lead.

Dallas opened the second half with another long procession down the field. When the offense reached the 19-yard line of Los Angeles, Landry dialed up the old shovel-pass to attack the edge of the defense. The Cowboys had used the shovel-pass in their earlier meeting with the Rams, when Scott Laidlaw burst through the left side for 24 yards. This time, Landry thought to try it with Pearson. And why not?

The Dirty Dozen

Calling out signals from his backfield station in the Shotgun, Staubach received the snap from John Fitzgerald, ran to his left, and then pitched the ball to Pearson who was sliding across the formation a few yards in front of him. Pearson turned up-field and followed Fitzgerald for a few steps, before cutting hard left and outracing the defense the rest of the way. "That was a big drive and a big boost for us," said Richards. "We came out and held the ball for something like five minutes. Then we made it 28-0, you could tell that the Rams became very frustrated. That's when we buried them."

The defense kept the pressure on to the final whistle, intercepting Jaworski on two occasions, and rendering Lawrence McCutcheon an afterthought. A week after wowing the league by running roughshod over the Cardinals, McCutcheon ran up against a buzz-saw in the Cowboys, managing only 10 yards on eleven carries. If not for a 34-yard pass-interference penalty against the Cowboys, the Rams might not have scored at all.

Three Toni Fritsch field goals supplied the final Dallas points in this 37-7 thrashing that made the Cowboys the first Wild-Card team to ever qualify for a Super Bowl. A season many had written off in August was still going...going...going all the way to Miami to meet the defending champion Pittsburgh Steelers in two weeks.

But for now, Sunday-afternoon recognition for Staubach, Pearson, and the Dallas defense was in vogue. "I didn't think anyone could score four touchdowns against the Rams," said All-Pro defensive end Jack Youngblood. "And I didn't think anyone could hold us to zero points through three quarters." Like any good coach after a big win, Landry gave all the credit to his players while standing in a joyous Cowboys locker room. "The best game-plans in the world don't mean much if the players don't execute," he said. "I've had what I thought was a good plan in the past and they didn't always work."

For Preston Pearson – the only Cowboys' player on the roster who had ever played for another team – it was a rare afternoon in the national spotlight. His three touchdown receptions tied a conference championship game record, and the press afterwards wanted to know how he did it. "Individually speaking, it was the biggest day I've ever had," said Pearson.

"...It wasn't great individual effort that got those touchdowns. You can't do anything without those blockers. On the screen pass and the shovel pass, that was all blocking. I think I had one guy to beat on both of them, and I think I can do that most of the time.

As for the catch in the right corner of the end-zone, I think that was primarily luck. Roger put it out there, and I was going to go after it no matter what. But it was luck that I held on to it." In two games, the Cowboys had outscored the Rams by a combined score of 55-14. And no matter what some of the Ram defenders may have thought about the Shotgun, there was no questioning the fact that in each game they had been torn to shreds by the gunslinger named Staubach. "Staubach threw about as well as I've ever seen him,' said safety Dave Elmendorf after the game. "He made a big difference."

The biggest difference of all though was something that so few outside of Dallas had anticipated. What was thought to be an average group of Cowboys coming out of camp, were proving themselves, in some of the season's biggest moments, to be anything but. Dallas hadn't run the table in the playoffs on the merits of just their star players. This had been a collective effort, a fact that Chuck Knox acknowledged willingly at his postgame press conference. "Dallas has some fine players," he stated. "I said in preseason Staubach was a great quarterback. But he didn't beat us. A great team beat us."

That great team was now headed to Miami with the daunting task of proving themselves Super.

CHAPTER 28

THE BUILDUP

"I really hate Dallas. They try to fool folks instead of trying to out-physical them. The game shouldn't be played that way. Personally, I think what Dallas does is garbage. When I was a kid, the Cowboys were my favorite team, but I can't stand them now." - **Glenn Edwards, the Pittsburgh Steelers' safety who intercepted Roger Staubach's last pass in Super Bowl X**

The aftermath of the Cowboys' thirty-point drubbing of the Rams revealed a tale of two cities whose moods could not be more different. Miffed at watching their team come up short in the playoffs for the third consecutive season, Los Angeles cursed their luck and cursed the day that fate dropped James Harris on the Rams' roster. With nothing better to do, and a long off-season period staring them in the face, fans occupied themselves in numerous ways, such as hanging their quarterback in effigy. Some of the less militant followers simply called in to the team's offices to proclaim their displeasure with Harris. A few season-ticket holders even phoned to announce their intentions of boycotting the team should "that black quarterback" be the starter for the next season. The support system around James Harris continued to disintegrate over the next several months.

It was a different tune being sung back in north Texas. More than 10,000 screaming fans gathered in sub-freezing temperatures at Dallas' Love Field airport to welcome home the victors on Sunday night. No beer was reported at this gathering, perhaps due to recommendations from airport officials who had trouble with rowdies blocking the runway after the Minnesota game. But the folks still came armed with big smiles, large banners and witty signs. One banner draped along the runway fence read "Smile, Landry." Another said "Taunts for Howard Cosell." Nobody ever missed a chance to poke fun at Howard.

One proclamation even had a religious connotation, declaring "Hail Mary Full of Grace, Roger Takes Us To First Place."

"Roger will like that, he's Catholic," one fan pointed out.

A middle-aged woman wrapped from head-to-toe to ward off the cold said her son fell and broke his arm during the Cowboys' send-off on Friday. However, he was in the car waiting for their victorious arrival. She went on to say, "We even put our church services back 15 minutes so everyone could watch the game. But I'm not going to tell you what church it was."

At about 11 p.m. the Cowboys landed in front of their expectant audience. Thomas Henderson, sporting a Rams' sun visor, was the first to alight from the chartered plane. As to be expected where two fan-favorites were concerned, Roger Staubach and Lee Roy Jordan received warm ovations when they were spotted coming down the tarmac. Before reaching the airplane door, Staubach proclaimed over a waiting microphone that the game in Los Angeles was "better than the Army-Navy game of '63." But the loudest cheers of all were reserved for

Preston Pearson, whose seven catches and three touchdowns stole the show against the Rams.

By the time the players were walking along the fence on their way to a nearby parking lot, the crowd had packed the corridor from the lot across six lanes of Lemmon Avenue, blocking traffic for 30 minutes as the Cowboys drove through. It wasn't until church bells were chiming midnight that the party broke up and everyone went home.

This warm greeting at the airport was just the first of many examples over the next several days that the city of Dallas was once again in love with the Cowboys. By noon Monday, about 100 people had gathered at Moody Coliseum on the campus of Southern Methodist University to purchase Super Bowl tickets, which were scheduled to go on sale for Cowboys' season ticket holders the following morning at 7 a.m. Some were wrapped in blankets to ward off the cold, others were bundled in sleeping bags. One bystander remarked, "It looks like an Indian powwow."

In preparation for a long, cold night ahead, one man yelled to a departing friend, "Tell the wife to send me more clothes. I mean a lot of clothes."

June Turner and Juanita Moore, who had sat in line for each of the Cowboys' two previous Super Bowl trips, said they left their husbands behind in a warm house. "They said they'd furnish the money, but we'd have to do the sitting," Mrs. Turner said. Also doing some sitting were several children, who kept a spot in line while their parents were at work. They were well compensated for their time, some kids being paid as much as $100 each to brave the elements.

Ricky Westbrook of suburban city Garland showed a bit of southern ingenuity to ensure himself a ticket to the Big Game. He had arrived late to the gathering, but that still didn't prevent him from getting ahead of the crowds. Dismayed by the long line in front of him, Ricky bought tickets to the professional mixed-doubles tennis tournament being played at the coliseum. No, Ricky didn't give a hoot for tennis. He wanted the tickets merely so he could park some 100 yards closer to the Super Bowl ticket office.

On a nearby sidewalk, two young paperboys stood with their afternoon editions flapping in the breeze. *Cowboys going to the Super Bowl! Read all about it!* Then one of them turned to the other, and said, "I told you, smart mouth, that we had the best defense in the history of football."

The afternoon wore on, with welcome news along the way. Braniff International relieved thousands of prospective ticket buyers across the state by announcing they would provide as many flights as needed to deliver fans to the big game. Braniff employees were passing out flyers among the crowd advertising an unlimited number of seats for newly-created weekend excursion flights. Not to be outdone, Eastern Airlines added three jumbo L1011 jets to Miami for Jan. 16, the Friday before Super Bowl Sunday.

Moody Coliseum officials then warmed the hearts and toes of the frozen crowd by promising to allow fans to spend the night inside after the conclusion of the tennis matches later that evening. The news was received in the same spirit it was offered, though one fan did admit, "I can guarantee you, if we had to stay outside all night, we'd still be here."

By dinnertime the crowd of 100 had swelled to more than 1,000, attracting a fair share of ticket scalpers. Scalping without a license had become legal in Texas on Jan. 1, just four days prior, making some businessmen bolder than ever before. One man from Dallas who said he had invested $75,000 in Texas Stadium bonds for 102 season tickets, was purchasing 30 Super Bowl tickets with the aid of two friends.

"I've already been offered $100 (for the $20 tickets) and I expect the price to go up to $200," he said. Then in the spirit of a true entrepreneur, he went on to say, "This business of airline tickets being sold out is a bunch of garbage. I've got 20 extra tickets and I've already made $75 on one."

The excitement on the streets was nothing compared to the tidal wave of interest swamping the Cowboys' offices. Doug Todd, the team's assistant public relations director, said, "Our telephone hasn't stopped ringing. People are asking about tickets, about travel, you name it, they're calling in. A lot of people have telephoned just to give their congratulations. I've been here five years and I've never seen anything like it."

Less than 24 hours after his team had shocked the world and the Rams, Tom Landry had the Cowboys out on the practice field going over some preliminary preparations for their looming battle with AFC champion Pittsburgh. Normally, the players receive the day off after a game. But Landry wanted his team conscious of the fact that there was still more to accomplish in front of them, and to prevent them from being caught up in the city's hoopla. The players, likely still riding the emotional wave of their big win the day before, took the quick turnaround in stride.

"There's nobody who works any harder on the team than Coach Landry, so we don't mind," said Robert Newhouse. "Coach Landry has had red eyes all year, and you know it comes from work. He doesn't drink."

The ball coach then surprised his players after practice by giving them Tuesday and Wednesday off. For just one moment amidst cheers and yells, the spirits of Cowboys' players rose even higher, if that was even possible. Two days off, and the Super Bowl just around the bend. Life didn't get much better than this!

On Monday, Jan. 12, the Dallas Cowboys' charter jet touched down at Fort Lauderdale-Hollywood International Airport. There to greet them was the Fort Lauderdale mayor, who presented Tom Landry with the traditional key to the city. But there was much more than just a token gift of appreciation. The first wild-card team to ever qualify for the Super Bowl was to be treated in a manner fit for royalty.

The team checked out their flashy waterfront hotel accommodations at the Galt Ocean Mile, some 30 miles north of Miami. From there, they would enjoy a 20-minute commute to Fort Lauderdale's Yankee Stadium, the spring training home of the baseball Yankees, for practices during the week. Even as touchdown underdogs, the Cowboys arrived in Florida with all the pomp and support of defending champions of the football world.

The actual champions, Pittsburgh's blue-collar Steelers, had arrived in Miami earlier that morning. Their first taste of South Florida had been a bit more subdued, and much more becoming to a team enthralled with brute toughness over stylish perks. They checked into an "ordinary" hotel, the Miami Lakes Inn, which was only a short distance away from the Miami Dolphins' practice facility at Biscayne College. After unpacking and getting situated, head coach Chuck Noll then boarded everyone on a bus for a quick practice session. In true Steelers fashion, the players grabbed their lunch-pails, jumped aboard and went to work.

To be honest, the Steelers were a bit put out by having to face the Cowboys. Many players had anticipated a Super Bowl rematch with Minnesota, allegedly a far superior team than Dallas, and one which played a familiar brand of football that could never be confused with the Cowboys' fancy Shotgun offense and Flex defense. But instead of a tough Vikings' squad, an uprising bunch of Cowboys with twelve hairy-faced rookies trying to act the part of grown men stood in their way. This was a major-league letdown to the defending champs. Pittsburgh believed in unions. Dallas promoted free enterprise and rich bankers. The Steelers ate clam chowder. The Cowboys didn't know what a clam was.

The Steelers were a team that perceived themselves as a tough, working-class unit that pulled together to get the job done every day with grit and superior determination. The Cowboys, on the other hand, were nothing but soft-bellied squeezers, who sponged on the intellect of their head coach and used numerous gimmicky formations to make a surprising run through the playoffs. They were frauds.

Why, the Cowboys actually tried to out-think opponents on the field, a despicable practice in a game founded on the precepts of brute force and manly toughness. They trained in California during the summer, gobbled up headlines in the fall, owned every nationally-televised game in the winter, and forever

The Dirty Dozen

sported that infernal star on the sides of their sleek, silver helmets.

Pittsburgh also felt put out by the Cowboys' interpretation of divine assistance. The Steelers were the first and greatest team to have been aided by the Holy Mother. Their Immaculate Reception against the Raiders in 1972 had ignited their run of recent success, ultimately leading to a Super Bowl in 1974. The Hail Mary may have been miraculous, but it certainly wasn't Immaculate.

These two teams sharing polar opposites in views, customs, and habits began a war of words leading up to the game, with reporters serving as intercessory agents. The Steelers questioned the Cowboys' toughness, and called them a team that relied on "gadgets." Cliff Harris responded by issuing veiled threats toward Lynn Swann, the Pittsburgh receiver who was still questionable to play after being concussed in the AFC Title game versus Oakland. Said Harris: "I'm not going out Sunday to intentionally hurt anyone, but getting hurt has to be in the back of Swann's mind."

While noting the Cowboys' spiffy hotel accommodations next to the ocean, Pittsburgh linebacker Jack Lambert declared, "I hope a shark bites Staubach's arm off!" He claimed he was only kidding.

A day later, Harris promised to make life tough on Terry Bradshaw, should the Steelers' quarterback try to scramble. Ironically, Harris insisted he was dead serious.

From these musings of players erupted a debate about which team had the smarter quarterback. Was it Pittsburgh's Terry Bradshaw, an ignorant "blockhead" from Louisiana who called his own plays, or the former Naval officer Roger Staubach, a "highly intelligent" player who wasn't allowed to call plays for the Cowboys?

Steelers head coach Chuck Noll explained it this way: "What is the criteria for intelligence? Just now educators are discovering they haven't been teaching kids how to read. They've been doing it wrong. Some people say a high forehead is a sign of intelligence. If that is so, then Tom Landry is smarter than I am, but Terry is a heckuva lot smarter than Roger."

The verbal warfare died down on Thursday when the players were made off limits to the media. Behind closed doors, the spirit of antagonism remained simmering, just waiting to boil over on Sunday afternoon.

Tales about Super Bowl Week night-life are often hard to come by, and even harder to clean up. More likely than not, such scarcity is a good thing. Full disclosure under these circumstances could ruin many reputations. Like they suggest in Las Vegas, what happens here is best left here.

But there is one story from that week-long Bicentennial Bash in South Florida that's family-friendly and well worth the telling. Nearly forty years after the fact, Randy White took the stage at the *Winspear Opera House* in downtown Dallas for the taping of a CBS-TV series dubbed "Glory Days." There, beside former teammates Roger Staubach, Drew Pearson, Mike Ditka and others, White told of some of the fun that the Cowboys had in the week leading up to Super Bowl X.

"Hollywood Henderson was dating one of the Pointer Sisters, so we got to meet the Pointer Sisters, which was pretty neat," White said. "We're at the bar and I'm sitting next to Joe Namath. That was about as good as it gets…"

But when the party in that Miami nightspot began to get too hot, Cowboys' players sought to make their escape. Randy and Burton Lawless were offered a ride in a police car. As they were getting in, Randy noticed that there was someone already in the backseat. A prisoner, if his appearance meant anything. "Scraggly, long-haired guy, a mess," said White. "I wanted no part of him. So I sat in front and told Burton to go back there with him."

The police car rolled along, and it became apparent that their backseat friend had just as little interest in getting to know Lawless. Completely ignoring the Cowboys' starting guard, the guy spent the ride tapping White on the shoulder. White tried to ignore him, but finally turned around. "Randy," the guy said, "I just wanted to tell you, I'm a big fan."

"Turns out," White told his audience, "the guy in the backseat was Willie Nelson."

Willie and Randy hit it off like old pals and, later that week, shared a tune together at a local honky-tonk. Whether or not this new friendship extended to sharing Willie's stogie, known for its special brand of weed, remains unknown.

Field conditions were a hot topic during the week leading up to the big game. Super Bowl X was to be the last time that a meaningful football game took place on the Orange Bowl's razor-thin, moth-eaten, green-painted poly-turf. The surface at the Orange Bowl had long been noted by media personnel as one of the league's fastest tracks. Players often compared it to a hair-trigger mouse trap that could reach out and bite with the least provocation.

With their home games at Texas Stadium and Three Rivers Stadium respectively, both the Cowboys and Steelers were accustomed to playing on artificial surfaces. But they would be in for a whole new experience on Super Sunday, said Miami Dolphins' wide receiver Nat Moore. Especially if it was raining.

Moore, a regular frequenter of the Orange Bowl with the Dolphins, penned an open letter early in the week to Roger Staubach and Terry Bradshaw that was published by the *Miami News*. "If either of you believe in divine assistance," Moore advised, "pray for a bright, sunshiny day, because if it rains you're in big trouble."

Moore knew from past experience that puddles formed on the field's outer fringes, from the 20-yardline toward each end-zone. When this happened, Moore claimed that the footing in those areas were nearly impossible for runners attempting to make a cut. Of equal difficulty to navigate were the spots where the turf was completely matted down. According to Moore, a wet field would favor the team with a strong straight-ahead running attack, because an offense relying on pulling guards and trap plays would have trouble with footing.

When dry, the turf was "still in terrible shape," wrote Moore. "There are bumps and rips and patches and drop-offs and seams that have worn through to the concrete. If you're not careful, you might catch a cleat in one of those seams or rips, and turn an ankle. Or worse."

Footing was such a concern that both teams were prepared to use part of their allotted time at Saturday morning's walk-through practice just to experiment with different shoes. In some ways, grip had become more of a concern than execution. So what kind of weather should players and coaches be expecting come kickoff on Sunday?

A full seven days before Super Sunday, Ray Biedinger of the National Weather Service said, "In January during daylight hours, there's only a fifteen-percent chance of precipitation in Miami." Biedinger had no response to the monsoon-like rain that struck the Miami area at midday on Thursday. Nor could he contend with the forecast that predicted more rain on Friday and Saturday.

The credibility of meteorologists had been dealt a serious blow. Sunday's weather, on the other hand, remained just as big a mystery as before.

CHAPTER 29

SUPER BOWL X

"I'm proud of the way this team played, especially with the number of young people." - **Lee Roy Jordan, assessing the Cowboys' performance in Super Bowl X**

"They used single coverage on me all day, which really surprised me. I had the same guy on me all day – they didn't rotate their coverages or anything. We just worked it to our advantage." - **Pittsburgh wide receiver Lynn Swann reminiscing on his MVP performance against the Cowboys**

In a sparkling tribute to God, Country, and football, the very best that Florida had to offer promenaded at the Orange Bowl on the afternoon of Sunday, January 18, 1976. A new week had invoked a new forecast, allowing no chance of rain for the city's highly anticipated Super Bowl matinee. Where dark thunderheads were once feared, a bright sun shined down brilliantly, its backdrop of purest blue only enhanced by a few light, wispy clouds.

A new year required a new standard in celebrations. Red, white, and blue balloons were in abundance throughout the stadium during a very patriotic pre-game demonstration that honored America's bicentennial anniversary. At different intervals, a command would result in a pack of these colorful balloons being released, giving way to a helium-induced flight that carried them much higher than even eagles.

And speaking of eagles, Old Glory had never looked so regal at a sporting event, the pure colors and white stars twinkling – if not smiling – on the festivities below.

High above the playing surface the press boxes were filled to overflowing. More than 1,700 media personnel, from San Diego to Nova Scotia to Timbuktu, had filed for press credentials, a Super Bowl record. Pens hurriedly scratched on notepads in a frantic attempt to verbalize the flavor of the moment.

Hollywood was well represented down on the field. As a part of their sports terrorism-themed movie *Black Sunday*, Paramount Pictures' filmmakers were present on the sidelines recording the sights and sounds of not only the game, but the television broadcast as well. In the movie, which earned the Best Motion-Picture Award for 1978, would be heard the voices of Pat Summerall and Tom Brookshier. Also making a cameo appearance in the film was Miami Dolphins owner Joe Robbie.

While Hollywood set a stage which highlighted a worst possible scenario at a sporting event, camera operators for CBS-TV and NFL Films were busy capturing the spirit in the stands, where fans for both teams were well represented. With an accent peculiar to this southeastern melting pot, Steelers' supporters pounded their chests and prophesied to those in ten-gallon hats that back-to-back Super Bowls was an inevitability for their team. Sporting cowboy-cut jeans and an unmistakable strut which only accentuated their Texas drawl, Cowboys' fans reminded their good-natured antagonists that Cinderella's glass slipper was not a one-size-fits-all piece of merchandise that could be bought on past credit. Dallas had beaten the very best that the NFC had to offer, so why couldn't they do the same with the AFC?

This verbal jousting continued until nearly the end of pre-game warm-ups when a disturbance broke out in the stands at one end of the field. Unlike most National Football League stadiums, the Orange Bowl was not equipped with a net behind the end-zones designed for catching the footballs before they fly into the seating area. This became a problem for Pittsburgh place-kicker Roy Gerela, who ran out of his allotment of practice balls when a few testy fans refused to throw them back onto the field.

Gerela wasn't known for acting on emotional impulses. Rumor had it that he was incapable of emotion. The AFC's scoring leader in both 1973 and 1974 while with Pittsburgh, Gerela started his career down in Houston with the Oilers, where he once made five field goals in a single game. But a change in the Oilers front-office resulted in him being waived and picked up by the Steelers. "I asked the new Houston coach, Ed Hughes, why he let me go," Gerela recalled. "He said I didn't show sufficient emotion toward the game. Imagine that. If you miss one, are you supposed to throw your helmet on the ground and prove you're a jackass? Who can't handle situations?"

The situation that arose in the moments before Super Bowl X caused Gerela to consider his options. He could throw his helmet at a few deserving fans, but what good would that do? He could sit idly by and accept the cards that were dealt with him. In the end, Gerela chose neither of those options.

Determined to make the most of his practice time, Gerela instead went up into the stands to retrieve a ball or two. Or three. While there, he had a confrontation with one gentleman who had tucked a ball under his jacket. The two were rumored to have exchanged words, possibly even a shove or two. When the crowd started to press around him, Gerela figured it was time to leave before any tempers began to rule the scene. Picking his way through the crowd, Gerela re-joined his teammates on the field. Without a football to work with, Gerela became a bystander for the remainder of warm-ups.

It would not be the last time the 27-year old would hear of the incident. (A few days after the Super Bowl, the alleged ball-thief filed a suit against Gerela.) Nor would it be his last confrontation for the afternoon. As an auspicious beginning to Super Bowl X, Gerela would also have a run-in with a Cowboys' player on the sideline, a full-speed collision which left a ripple effect so large as to open the door for a Dallas upset.

Blackie Sherrod was a strange man, with an even stranger way of expressing himself. A longtime Dallas-area sportswriter who now worked at the *Dallas Times-Herald*, Blackie had a habit of shutting himself off in his office for hours and then suddenly emerging with an obscure question about history, or poetry, or politics, or some other topic out of left field. A man wise far beyond his calling, Blackie wrote with a dry, caustic sense of humor that was intensified by his world-renowned wit and charm.

His vocabulary was as deep as an artesian well, overflowing with catchy terms and innuendos that, rather than overwhelm readers, only made them appreciate his work all the more. Back in the day, it was every young journalist's dream to flip through one of his many personal notepads, if only to catch a glimpse of what made him so unique. Nobody could make a point with a pencil quite like Blackie.

Blackie's most notable declaration in 1975 had come from within the pages of Dave Campbell's *Texas Football* magazine, where the 55-year old predicted during the spring months that the Dallas Cowboys would win nine games and go to the playoffs. With this prophecy, Blackie once again distinguished himself. He may have been the only sportswriter across the entire nation that deemed the Cowboys capable of winning more than eight games in 1975. Dozens of writers had the Cowboys only breaking even at 7-7. *Poor Blackie! The realist is turning into an optimist.*

Blackie in no way rescinded these comments later that summer when the team waved goodbye to longtime standouts Bob Lilly, Bob Hayes, Walt Garrison, and Cornell Green. No sir! He was sticking to his guns, no matter what anyone else thought.

When the smoke cleared from the regular season action in December and the Cowboys sat at 10-4 and owners of a wild-card playoff spot, Blackie's legend only grew. Surely, he alone knew the true state of the Cowboys. And two weeks later in the days leading up to Super Bowl X, it was his prediction more than anyone else's that counted among the press.

While other Texas sportswriters around him like Frank Luksa of the *Times-Herald*, Bob Ostrum of the *San Antonio Light*, and Dan Cook of the *San Antonio Express* jumped on board the local bandwagon and picked the Cowboys, Blackie leaned the other way and picked the Steelers to triumph 17-10.

Reasoned Sherrod: "All Super Bowl losers are down-rated two cuts lower than a Cub Scout, much more maligned by the public than a team that finished with an 0-14 record. Such is the unhappy fate of any runner-up. But the Cowboys, should they lose to Pittsburgh, won't have to accept that stigma because nobody expected them to reach Miami in the first place. The Cowboys are the sentimental favorites the country over, because of their surprising, dramatic late surge. But if indeed Super Bowls are won on defense and experience – as all coaches vow – then Pittsburgh seems to have the edge."

It was hard to deny Blackie's logic, even if you were a member of the Cowboys' coaching staff. Straight up, it did appear that Pittsburgh had the advantage. That's why Tom Landry and Mike Ditka had stressed the importance of special teams so much to their players during the week. If the Cowboys could make an impact play or two in the kicking game, then that might be enough to off-set their shortcomings in other areas.

So with Blackie and the rest of the record-setting media contingent watching from the press-box above, the Cowboys began Super Bowl X with a stylish step in the right direction. As they had in Los Angeles against the Rams, Ditka called on rookie Thomas Henderson to do the honors. This time, instead of trying to decapitate an unsuspecting kicker, the Cowboys called for a reverse handoff that would make Henderson a runner on the play. Henderson had scored a touchdown on the same play versus St. Louis in Week 2. Ditka was hopeful that, by beginning the game with it, the Cowboys would catch the Steelers unaware.

As he had against the Cardinals, Henderson started the play running forward, showing every intention of blocking for return-man Preston Pearson. Then he curled back, took the handoff from Pearson at the 10-yard line and went galloping down the left sideline, chewing up huge chunks of yardage with each long stride. Earlier in the week, Henderson had promised that, should he score a touchdown in the Super Bowl, he would dunk the ball over the goal-post with both hands. Just for a moment, it looked as if the athletically-gifted linebacker would have a chance to do just that.

Taking advantage of good blocking in front of him, Henderson ran more than 30 yards before a defender even got close to him. At the midfield stripe, Henderson attempted to cut wide of Roy Gerela, who had the angle and was trying to force the runner out of bounds. Henderson envisioned using fellow rookie Randy Hughes as a pick, but Gerela dove under Hughes' attempted block and tripped Henderson up near the Pittsburgh bench at the 45-yard line.

Leaping to his feet, Henderson ran over to the other side of the field, grinning from ear to ear. On the way over, he even managed to sneak in his best Oscar Robertson imitation. The play's result didn't call for a two-handed jam, but a jumper was still pretty good.

Nearby trainers immediately came to the aid of Gerela, who was grimacing in pain on the ground after making the tackle. After helping him over to the bench where they could further examine him, doctors told him he had a cracked rib. Gasping for breath, Gerela said he believed it. "I didn't have any wind after that tackle," Gerela said. "Anytime I'd take a deep breath it would hurt. I was hurting the whole game."

Pittsburgh's special teams woes continued. Dallas punted the ball away to the Steelers after a sloppy set of plays to start. An equally slow start from the Pittsburgh offense compelled them to give it right back. But on fourth-and-4, Steelers' punter

The Dirty Dozen

Bobby Walden dropped the snap and was smothered at the 29-yard line by Warren Capone, Randy White, and others. Walden came away from the play with his health intact, though it is likely he had a bruised ego after a short conversation with Head Coach Chuck Noll on the sideline.

The Dallas offense sought to make quick work of the short field in front of them. On first-down, the Cowboys confused Pittsburgh's mighty Steel Curtain defense with numerous pre-snap shifts that resulted in Drew Pearson running free down the middle of the field. Catching Roger Staubach's pass at the 16-yard line, Pearson angled to the corner at full-speed and ran untouched into the end-zone. "The Cowboys went into four different sets on that play," said Steelers safety Mike Wagner, who had just watched his teammates get scored upon in the opening quarter for the first time all season. "We were on our third set when the play started. We were one set behind them."

In the blink of an eye, the underdog Cowboys had turned a special-teams miscue into a 7-0 lead. Up in the press-box Blackie Sherrod marveled at the sudden turn of events, tantalized by the Cinderella story unfolding in front of him, yet ever mindful of the Steel Curtain, a unit with such might and power as to grind glass slippers into dust, and dreams into ashes.

Cliff Harris had made his point quite clearly. During the week, the Cowboys' safety had been more than fluent in his opinion that Pittsburgh Steelers' wide receiver Lynn Swann would be better off lying in bed between nice, soft cotton sheets with his head on a goose-feather pillow than running around on the aged playing surface of the Orange Bowl. Harris could have worn the week away with his assortment of veiled threats and vague prophecies if players from both teams had not been shut off from media access on Thursday. Still, even then, Harris felt satisfied that he had made his point to the world. And to Swann.

Harris would have likely been brushed off by the press as just another arrogant trash-talking football player, if not for the overall concern that surrounded this very topic. There was, after all, more than one doctor that shared his opinion. *Swann would be a fool to tempt the unforgiving fate of Harris' vicious in-game nature and suffer a second concussion in as many weeks. The brain was a delicate mechanism, so why run the risk of inflicting further damage over a silly meaningless football game?*

Swann heard all of the talk that centered around his availability, and inwardly yearned to one-up the Cowboys' bombastic safety on Sunday afternoon. But first, he had to go through a week of practice with team doctors watching his every move. He would only play with their medical clearance. It wasn't until Swann proved, late in the week, that he could function under a normal work-load at practice that doctors finally give their stamp of approval on his participation in Super Bowl X.

Swann smiled at the news. Harris shrugged. Game on.

In a game that began in such a topsy-turvy manner, it was the Pittsburgh offense that stayed true to form. Even down 7-0 to an offensive juggernaut such as Dallas, the Steelers came out running the ball on their second possession. Splitting handoffs between Franco Harris and Rocky Bleier, Pittsburgh needed only four plays to cross the midfield stripe.

There, from the 48-yard line, Terry Bradshaw dropped back for his first pass attempt of the game. With good blocking in front of him, Bradshaw set his feet and lofted a pass down the right sideline in the direction of Lynn Swann and Mark Washington. Playing with confidence following strong performances against John Gilliam and Harold Jackson, Washington had anticipated Swann's out-and-up pattern perfectly, and was even running a step in front of the Pittsburgh wide-out.

How it was that the Dallas cornerback faded away from the ball as it approached its landing will always be something of a mystery. While Washington faded out of bounds, the trailing Swann leaped and reached in front of the defender to make the catch just before Harris pummeled him to the turf. The 32-yard gain put the ball on the Dallas 16-yard line, and had Washington wondering what just happened.

The Dirty Dozen

Harris, on the other hand, opted for a familiar shrug of his shoulders. The Cowboys' safety had been a step late. Oh well. Better luck next time.

Pittsburgh punctuated an impressive march with a bit of trickery of their own. Normally, when close to its opponent's end-zone, the Steelers used guard Gerry Mullins as a third tight end on inside running plays. But this time Chuck Noll used a variation that was called simply 333.

Rather than hand off to one of his backs, Bradshaw rolled right and tossed a soft seven-yard touchdown pass to Randy Grossman all alone in the end-zone. The eight-play 67-yard march, made possible by Swann's acrobatic catch over Washington, tied the game 7-7.

Using traps and a 16-yard draw from Robert Newhouse, the Cowboys marched 52 yards to the Steelers' 14 by the end of the first quarter. By changing ends Dallas also seemed to change their luck. A once-promising drive stalled out after an off-sides penalty and a third-down pass from Staubach went awry. Even so, Toni Fritsch converted the subsequent 36-yard field goal to put the Cowboys back in front 10-7.

From there, the game settled down into a bitter defensive struggle with plenty of hitting, pushing, and shoving after the whistle. The Shotgun, a terror unto the Steelers for one quarter, fell apart under the relentless attack of the Steel Curtain pass-rush that had Staubach bailing-out and looking for greener pastures. When they weren't taking the Cowboys' quarterback down for one of their Super Bowl-record seven sacks, Pittsburgh had Staubach scrambling for his life.

After one such scramble, Steelers' safety Glen Edwards yelled at Staubach, "Hey, Roger, you come near me again I'm gonna break your neck!" "Yeah, cheap shot, that's just like you," Staubach responded.

Edwards was spoiling for a fight the entire game. A Cowboys' fan while growing up, he found it distasteful, if not unethical, to implement such high-falutin' deceptive schemes into a weekly game-plan as Tom Landry did. The Shotgun. The Flex. And all of that pre-snap motion on offense. Bah! If negative words counted as saliva, then Edwards spit on all three of those Cowboys' trademarks.

So strong was his dislike for Dallas that he made it his personal duty to destroy the Cowboys before, during, and after the play. After a first quarter punt return ended near the Dallas bench, Edwards got into a shoving match with the toughest guy he could find. Officials quickly broke up the scrum before Randy White was provoked into dismembering the Steelers' safety altogether.

Though feisty in his own way, Edwards didn't hold a candle to the passion which flowed through the veins of Jack Lambert. Though only in his second NFL season, Lambert had already cornered the market on pure-dee meanness. Steelers' Vice-President Art Rooney recalled the events that led to Pittsburgh making the Kent State standout their second-round selection in the 1974 NFL Draft. "We'd seen films of him beating up everybody. Biting them. Kicking them.

He was super intense," said Rooney. "We figured he'd help us on special teams for sure, and he wound up starting. We had been thinking about another kid but we saw that kid duck his head a few times. Jack Lambert never ducked."

His reputation followed him into the NFL. When "Mean" Joe Greene reported to training camp in 1974, defensive line coach George Perles told him, "We've got a rookie who's so mean he doesn't even like himself." Lambert tackled anything that moved, sometimes to his own discomfiture. At 23 years old, Jack was already missing his front teeth. But he knew a few ball-carriers who were missing theirs too, so it was all even.

Lambert was an ornery old cuss from his middle linebacker position who made an art-form out of cussing, kicking, clawing, and biting when on the field. And, as Cliff Harris would soon find out, Jack Lambert was equally adept in the art of body-slamming any opponent who dared to envision himself a trash-talking big-shot.

Seventy-two million people on television and 80, 187 inside the spacious Orange Bowl were watching what was fast becoming the best Super Bowl battle ever. A championship round that had delivered one yawner after another over its first nine years of existence was finally delivering the close, intense drama expected of a heavyweight prize fight. After nearly forty minutes of play, the outcome of Super Bowl X was still up in the air, Dallas holding stubbornly to a 10-7 lead.

But Pittsburgh would not go away, and, at the end of another long drive, had designs of drawing even. Roy Gerela, who missed at the end of the second-quarter from 26 yards, was now lining-up for a 33-yard attempt. It was on days like this that kickers truly earned their paychecks. Nobody had told him that making a tackle in a Super Bowl could be so painful. Gerela almost dared not breathe for fear of the pain that would grab his side when he did. For once in his life, Gerela felt like he had actually been part of the action of a football game.

Gerela approached the ball gingerly, with breath abated. He swung his right foot back, and then followed through with it, striking the ball solidly and sending it flying over the defense. He inhaled, watched the ball's flight for just a fraction of a second, and then groaned in disbelief. Drat the luck! He had missed again. It seemed as if he would never stop hurting!

Delighted with his team's good fortune, Cliff Harris approached the Steelers' shocked place-kicker and playfully patted Gerela on the helmet with both hands. "Good job. You're helping us," Harris told him.

Jack Lambert was having none of Harris' mouth. He had already heard enough crowing from Harris after watching Franco Harris get plastered on a fourth-down incompletion earlier in the game. Grabbing Harris by the shoulder pads in what the 6-5, 220-pound linebacker insisted was an act of protection for his teammate, Lambert slammed Harris to the ground without looking back.

"Harris jumped up in his face and slapped him in the helmet," Lambert explained after the game. "I thought it was unnecessary. He slapped Gerela's helmet a couple of times. I didn't say anything. I just threw him on the ground. Harris laughed in Gerela's face. When I see injustice, I try to do something about it."

Gerela saw things quite differently, and even seemed to defend the Cowboys' safety with his postgame comments. "I didn't even know Harris had hit me," he said. "He just kind of tapped me. It's excitement for him – he showed it by tapping me on the helmet and saying 'nice going' when I missed."

None of that mattered to Lambert. He threw Harris anyway. And why not? Earlier in the game, he had aimed a whistling roundhouse punch at former teammate Preston Pearson...and missed. It was about time he started getting some of his messages across.

"And then No. 39 [line-judge Jack Fette] jumped me," continued Lambert. "It was kind of a surprise. I thought he might throw me out. Then he said 'get out.' But he just meant for me to get out of the area. I changed my tune real quick. You don't help your team when you get thrown out. I got out of his way."

Down on the ground, Harris saw the official coming too. "Right after I got knocked down, I looked up and saw Striped (the official)," he said. "I knew if he didn't get Lambert, he was likely to get me."

But Harris must have been living right too, as Fette merely directed him to the Cowboys' bench and acted as if nothing out of the ordinary had occurred. The game continued, with no one the worse for wear.

The score remained the same into the fourth-quarter. Early in the final period, backed up on their own 19-yard line, the Cowboys' upset bid began to come apart at the seams. On first-down, Landry called the old flea-flicker in the hope that Pittsburgh's secondary would be caught napping. Staubach handed off to Preston Pearson who lateraled back to the quarterback. But defensive lineman Steve Furness, in the game as a replacement to the injured Joe Greene, sniffed out the trick play and dropped Staubach for a one-yard loss. "We thought that one would work for us," said Staubach of the flea-flicker attempt, "but they weren't in the defense we thought they'd be in."

On second-down Doug Dennison was stuffed after only gaining a yard. The third-down play showed more promise but, like so many before it, blew up in the face of a superior Steelers' pass-rush. Needing ten yards, Staubach espied Pearson slipping open downfield against the coverage of linebacker Andy Russell. As he set to throw to his open target, Staubach was crunched by

L.C. Greenwood for another sack at the 16-yard line, bringing about a most memorable punt.

Mitch Hoopes, on for the fifth time in the game, stood on his own one-yard line awaiting the snap from fellow rookie Kyle Davis as the clock approached eleven minutes remaining. The Steelers stacked ten-men on the line in an attempt to block the kick. Dallas took a moment to adjust their blocking up front, and then gave the signal for Davis to go ahead and begin the play.

When he did, Pittsburgh's backup fullback Reggie Harrison rushed in between center and left guard, ran over the blocking back, Rolly Woolsey, with a forearm to the chin and blocked the punt. Even had he sensed the pressure, Hoopes had no chance to run away from this catastrophe. The blocking had allowed a rusher to sneak through in the very worst place – right up the middle, leaving the punter with no other choice but to pray that his kick got through. Which, for Hoopes, it did not. The ball caromed through the Dallas end-zone for a safety, a play that Tom Landry felt was the turning point in the game.

"We just missed the block," explained Landry. "It's usually a case of the center worrying so much about making a good snap that he fails to brush his man enough. From what I could see, there was no blocking pattern at all and nobody touched Harrison. The defense was set. There are three or four different ways to block the ten-man rush, according to the call. But either the call was not made or somebody didn't get it."

The two-point play began a 14-point flurry for the defending champions, as they threatened to bury the mistake-prone Cowboys. Pittsburgh took possession at the Dallas 45-yard line after the free kick and marched to the 19 before their offense stalled. This time Gerela's aim was true, his 36-yard field goal giving the Steelers their first lead of the game 12-10.

Now trailing for the first time, Staubach went back to Drew Pearson on the very same pass play that had worked earlier for a touchdown. But this time safety Mike Wagner was ready for it and intercepted the ball at the 26-yard line, setting up another Gerela chip-shot with 6:37 left. "Both their safeties are supposed to kick out on deep coverage while Pearson comes across under them," Staubach explained. "But Wagner didn't kick. He read the play or he took a big chance. He came right up in front of the receiver and picked it off."

As the clock approached three minutes, the Steelers sought to put the knife in the heart of the Cowboys from their own 47-yard line. Looking down the right side for Swann all the way, Terry Bradshaw was able to avoid the tackle of D.D. Lewis in the backfield before stepping into a downfield throw for his favorite target. For the first time all day Swann had a step on cornerback Mark Washington. A slightly underthrown pass from Bradshaw meant another jump-ball situation had developed, something that Swann had proved himself quite adept at handling. This play would be no exception. Jumping up, Swann reached back and snared the ball out of the air at the five-yard line, before breaking free from Washington's arm tackle and rumbling into the end-zone.

Bradshaw never saw Swann's catch, nor did he join in the touchdown celebration. His nimble feet had allowed him to avoid a big hit from Lewis, but there was no avoiding the lick that he received from Larry Cole and Cliff Harris just after releasing the pass. With bells and whistles ringing in his head and ears, Bradshaw was helped to the Steelers' bench with a major-league concussion.

Bradshaw had been knocked down, much to the delight of Harris. The Cowboys, by all appearances, had been knocked out. With 3:02 remaining Dallas trailed 21-10, and Pittsburgh players were starting to relax and blow kisses to the wind over on their sideline. At long last, the favored Steelers had broken Super Bowl X wide open.

It would have been understandable had the Cowboys accepted their fate and died quietly. But such was not their way. As long as time remained on the clock, they felt they had a chance. So off the sideline the offense came trying to string together a series of magical plays. Time was short, but enthusiasm was not.

With time running out on his team's Cinderella season, Tom Landry made one final substitution in the offensive lineup. After the game, he couldn't take any credit for making the move. There wasn't any other choice he could have made. But when Landry inserted Percy Howard into Super Bowl X for the first time, the 6-4 rookie wide receiver did what no one could have anticipated. The twelfth and final member of the Dirty Dozen rookie class to see meaningful action during the 1975 campaign, Howard shocked the football world with a memorable Super Bowl catch that had the Cowboys jumping for joy and eyeing yet another miracle finish.

As the Dallas Cowboys deplaned in Fort Lauderdale on the Monday before the Super Bowl, and as Tom Landry was receiving the aforementioned key to the city, the Dillard High School band blared a brassy welcome for alumnus Percy Howard. Percy's homecoming was a highly popular one in the area. Percy Howard was back in familiar territory as a rookie wide receiver for the Dallas Cowboys, a status symbol that had no equal. He had done well in life, and had come back to South Florida nothing short of a hero in the eyes of family and friends.

The fight song was played once. Then twice. A third time? Well, why not?

Those who followed the team closely and knew Howard's impact on the Cowboys' season thus far marveled at the show of appreciation. "Percy hasn't caught a pass all season," said Frank Luksa, the Cowboys beat-writer for the Dallas Times-Herald.

"Not even in preseason?" someone asked. "Not a one."

Injuries had derailed Howard's strong training camp showing in July and kept him off the game-day roster for much of the regular season. Upon fully mending, Howard was awarded a uniform and spot at the very end of the bench. He occasionally saw action on special teams, but never at wide receiver.

That all changed in the fourth quarter of Super Bowl X. Golden Richards was bent over on the bench, the recipient of a wack on the stomach that left Dallas' No. 2 wide receiver with a busted rib. Golden was out. And now, with Dallas trailing by eleven points in the final minutes, the rookie that Cowboys' teammates called "Bird" fairly flew into the offensive huddle for the first time all season.

Beginning from the Dallas 20-yard line, Roger Staubach started the offense moving with an array of precise passes. He threw short to Charles Young for seven yards. Then Staubach found Drew Pearson for a 30-yard chunk that moved the Cowboys across midfield. An 11-yard completion to Preston Pearson was followed by the seventh and final sack of Staubach at the 34-yard line, leading to an automatic stoppage of play with 1:56 remaining.

Coming out of the timeout, Percy split wide to the left of Staubach, who stood alone in the backfield from his Shotgun position. The play started with a clean snap from John Fitzgerald to his quarterback. Staubach immediately looked to his left, where Howard seemed to be running at half-speed with Mel Blount in close coverage. Needing a quick score, Staubach decided to give his rookie a chance, and subsequently let go of a line-drive bullet in Howard's direction.

Whether it was out of surprise that Staubach actually threw the ball, or just a moment of poor coordination for Blount, the Steelers' All-Pro cornerback inexplicably tripped and fell near the goal-line with the ball in flight, leaving Howard all alone in the end-zone for his first career catch. Howard's 34-yard touchdown reception drew the Cowboys within four-points of Pittsburgh on the scoreboard with 1:48 to play.

Next in a game that was getting more compelling by the moment, Toni Fritsch tried an onside-kick from the 35-yard line. Approaching the tee with a bounce in his step from the left side, Fritsch quickly turned and squibbed the ball in the other direction. The tactic fooled no one in black. Gerry Mullins made an easy recovery for Pittsburgh at the 43.

It took another fine effort from the Dallas defense and all three of their timeouts, but the Cowboys regained possession at their own 38-yard line with 1:22 on the clock. The Cowboys had turned a similar situation against Minnesota into victory. Could they do it again?

Staubach got the drive started on a positive note, turning a low snap from center into an 11-yard gain and a Dallas first-down. With the clock still ticking down, the Cowboys rushed to the line for their next play. From the 49, Staubach dumped it off short to Preston Pearson. Rather than run out to stop the clock,

Pearson turned toward the middle of the field to try to get some extra yardage. The pass play netted thirteen yards, moving the ball to the Steelers' 38. But at what a price! By the time Dallas began their third play of the drive, only 20 seconds remained.

Fitzgerald's Shotgun snap landed at the feet of his quarterback, setting Staubach in full desperation mode. Without a timeout at his disposal, the last thing he could afford was to be trapped in the field of play. After finding the ball, Staubach stepped up through a crowded pocket and fired a downfield pass to Drew Pearson just as he was crunched in the ribs by a Pittsburgh lineman. The familiar figure of Kyle Davis ran onto the field. But after conversing with Fitzgerald for a moment, he ran back off. This was the Super Bowl. Fitzgerald wasn't coming out for anything.

On second-down, Fitzgerald's snap behind him was perfect. Staubach had time, and stepped into his deep throw down the right sideline for Howard. The high arching spiral was a thing of beauty while above the shadowed playing surface, its aesthetic qualities promoting a gambit of possibilities to the expectant Orange Bowl crowd. When a Pittsburgh defender knocked the pass away with relative ease, it was a most depressing of incompletions. Just for a fleeting moment, fans had begun to have flashbacks from a few weeks before.

With only three seconds remaining, the unmistakable baritone voice of Pat Summerall sounded across the CBS-TV airwaves giving viewers the information most pertinent for the situation. "This most certainly will be the last play of Super Bowl X, unless we have a penalty," said Summerall.

Summerall's addendum was hardly necessary. A game that had witnessed numerous scrums, punches, and even a throwdown had resulted in a grand total of two penalties, both of which were called on Dallas. Nothing short of a capital offence would induce the officials to throw a flag on this final play.

For the very last time in what had been a magical season, Roger Staubach surveyed the scene from his Shotgun position, praying desperately for a Hail Mary to land in Miami.

But the heavens were closed. Percy Howard was covered. So too was Drew Pearson. Staubach's final prayer sailed over the head of Pearson at the goal-line and into the arms of safety Glen Edwards bringing down the final curtain.

The clock had struck midnight on the 1975 Dallas Cowboys.

The Cinderella season was over.

CHAPTER 30

EVER AFTER

"The fans here have been a big part of our year. They backed us win or lose. For them to come out here on a day like today is unbelievable." - **Dallas wide receiver Golden Richards after fans greeted the team back in Dallas**

Bereavement knows no darker place than the end of the road. How much darker when that end is on the brink of nowhere.

With the season's end came a loss of purpose for the Dallas Cowboys. There was no game next week for players and coaches to prepare for, no tomorrow in sight. Losing the Super Bowl added to it a pain so sharp as to blot out even the brightest and most noteworthy of accomplishments.

Even Tom Landry, a man of unwavering faith in God, couldn't hide his disappointment from the media after the game. "If you want to look for consolations in our performance I guess you could," said Landry. "But I don't look for consolations when we lose. To have made the Super Bowl, and not win, is a tremendous heartbreak."

It was with heads hung low that the Cowboys boarded their plane on Monday for the return trip to Dallas. The short flight from Fort Lauderdale was dismally quiet, as players coped with their own thoughts and disappointments from the previous afternoon. The cloud hovering over them grew darker as the plane neared its destination, for each player knew this was goodbye until next summer. Nobody wanted the season to end. At least, not in this way.

A common sense of dread filled the aisles as the red, yellow, and blue jet touched down at Dallas' Love Field airport and wheeled to a stop. Reluctantly, almost listlessly, players each donned a coat, grabbed their bags and headed for the exit.

But the door that opened to admit the players' departure revealed a scene that no one on board had expected. There, standing in a dismal drizzle in windy, 47-degree temperatures, was a crowd of some 1,000 supporters who gave the team a resounding ovation as they deplaned.

Whether it was Roger Staubach, Lee Roy Jordan, Drew Pearson, or Thomas Henderson walking down the tarmac, the Cowboys were received with just as much enthusiasm as if they had never lost to Pittsburgh in the first place.

Amidst cheers and whistles, a small band of high school students did a take-off on Bob Hope's theme song, "Thanks For The Memories." "Thanks for all the things you've done... you'll always be No. 1,' sang the students.

This welcoming party filled with smiling faces went a long way in healing broken hearts and in provoking reminders of all that had been accomplished along the way. "It's been a miracle season," admitted defensive tackle Bill Gregory. "All these fans out here must think so too."

Not even the stoic head coach could hold back a smile. "It's amazing all these fans came out,' said Landry. "It's been a great year for us. I'm sorry it had to end the way it did. But we had a chance. It's been a satisfying season."

Indeed. Only a few days before, Landry had called his team "the most satisfying" that he had coached in all of his 16 years with the Cowboys. He praised their competitiveness, their spirit of camaraderie, and their never-say-die attitude. Those traits, even in defeat, had been on full display against the

The Dirty Dozen

Steelers. Someday soon, when the sting of this Super Bowl loss had subsided, Tom Landry would be able to sit down and recollect all of the many reasons and moments that made up a most memorable of campaigns. Indeed, it had been a satisfying season.

From the very first day in training camp when the doubters had circled and spread nefarious predictions of imminent failure, the Cowboys had bowed their head and went to work. When outsiders proclaimed that the Dirty Dozen couldn't, those twelve men listened instead to the voice of their Head Coach, who instructed them in the rudiments of how they could. When the Cowboys stumbled and were said to be done, they regrouped and started all over again. When the football gods laughed down a barrel of long odds, a Hail Mary pass provided the winning margin.

And when the team mourned a Super Bowl loss, the cheers and the faces throughout the assembled throng reminded them of an even greater victory. By braving the cold and the wind of a weekday morning, fans reminded their heroes that, even in the game of football, there are times when *giving* it all is more important than *getting* it all.

The 1975 Dallas Cowboys were never meant to be world champions. Instead, their trophy case was reserved, not for a pedestal of prominence in the public square, but a quiet place of remembrance in the human heart. A better memorial to a time and a team gone by there has never been.

The story of the Dirty Dozen will be told again and again.

Today.

Tomorrow.

And for as long as humanity embraces the plight and the spirit of the underdog.

EPILOGUE

SEASONS AFTER

The 1975 Dallas Cowboys came out of nowhere and together shared a season of fun on a field of dreams come true. But, as is so often the case in this world, the fun could not last forever. Here's a brief look at what the future held for each of the Dirty Dozen rookie class, as well as a few select Cowboy veterans.

Randy White
Randy White continued as a hybrid linebacker in 1976, occasionally flashing the potential that convinced the Cowboys to make him the No. 2 overall draft pick. Not until Tom Landry switched him to defensive tackle in 1977 did his career finally take off.
In August of 1994, after fourteen seasons, 111 sacks, and co-MVP honors in Super Bowl XII, Randy White was enshrined in the Pro Football Hall of Fame.

Thomas Henderson
The retirement of Dave Edwards and Lee Roy Jordan opened up a starting spot for "Hollywood" beginning in 1977. In each of his first two years as the Cowboys' starting strong-side linebacker, Henderson played in the Super Bowl, including his Pro Bowl season of 1978.
Henderson's time in Dallas came to an abrupt end in the midst of the 1979 campaign when the team released him due to drug abuse.

Burton Lawless
One of only two rookies to have earned a starting role in 1975, Lawless' play leveled out somewhat during his sophomore campaign, making him a backup for the majority of the 1976 season. Over his final four years in Dallas, Lawless started 10 games, and was a major contributor to the Cowboys' Super Bowl XII championship team of 1977.

Bob Breunig
After a rookie season spent primarily on special teams, Bob Breunig became a full-time starter in 1976, replacing veteran Dave Edwards on the strong side. A year later, he moved over in the middle to fill the gap created by Lee Roy Jordan's retirement. Breunig started 117 consecutive games at middle linebacker for the Cowboys, earning three Pro Bowl nods along the way. When he retired after ten seasons, Breunig was the franchise's second-leading tackler of all time, trailing only Jordan.

Pat Donovan
A special teams contributor for his first two seasons, Pat Donovan cracked the starting lineup in 1977 when Rayfield Wright went down with an injury. Playing at right tackle, Donovan helped pave the way for Dallas' run to Super Bowl XII in New Orleans.
Donovan was a standout at left tackle for the final six years of his career, participating in every game and playing in four Pro Bowls.

Randy Hughes
Randy Hughes continued to see action as a nickel defensive back over the next three seasons, and even started two games in relief of Cliff Harris during the 1976 season. Hughes' interception and pair of fumble recoveries nearly earned him the MVP honors in Super Bowl XII versus Denver, but he was nosed out by the duo of Randy White and Harvey Martin.

Hughes was a full-time starter at strong safety in 1979 as an injury replacement for Charlie Waters. In midst of a breakout season, Hughes injured his shoulder in a December game at Philadelphia. Complications from that injury led to his retirement in the summer of 1981.

Kyle Davis
The rookie long-snapper who saw action on the famous "Hail Mary" drive, Kyle Davis ran out of luck in his second NFL go-round, landing on injured reserve in the summer of 1976 and missed the entire season. Davis, who was traded before the following season, never played another down for the Cowboys.

Rolly Woolsey
1975 was Rolly Woolsey's only season in Dallas. Shortly after Super Bowl X, the Cowboys made Woolsey available in the NFL expansion draft, where he was claimed by Seattle.

Mitch Hoopes
One of the more entertaining punters in franchise history, Hoopes became expendable the following off-season when Danny White – a standout quarterback who also specialized in punting – joined the team. The first Cowboys' player to ever sport the No. 9 jersey, Hoopes was traded to San Diego for an eighth-round draft selection in the 1977 draft.

Herbert Scott
Beginning in 1976, Herbert Scott became a mainstay at the left guard position, beating out fellow classman Burton Lawless. During a ten-year career, Scott was twice voted first-team All-Pro, and was a three-time Pro Bowler.
Considered to be one of the franchise's greatest offensive linemen, Scott also owns the dubious distinction of having caught Roger Staubach's final career pass – albeit as an ineligible receiver – during a 1979 Divisional playoff game.

Scott Laidlaw
Scott Laidlaw bounced back from knee surgery as a rookie to enjoy a breakout season of sorts in 1976, catching 38 passes and scoring four touchdowns. With Tony Dorsett's arrival on the scene the following year, Laidlaw's playing time greatly diminished.

After five years with the Cowboys, Laidlaw was waived having accumulated over 1,600 yards from scrimmage and 12 total touchdowns.

Percy Howard
Percy Howard's momentous catch in Super Bowl X, unfortunately, proved to be the only catch of his professional career. A knee injury in the summer of 1976 forced him to retire after only one NFL season.

Toni Fritsch
The NFL's scoring leader in 1975, Fritsch never kicked in a Cowboys' uniform again, as he was traded to San Diego in training camp of the following year.

Jean Fugett
After catching a pass in every regular and postseason game of the 1975 season, Jean Fugett did himself a disservice a few months later by publicly complaining of his backup role at tight end behind Billy Joe Dupree. Tom Landry acknowledged his dissatisfaction by trading Fugett away to the Washington Redskins before the start of the 1976 season.

Clint Longley
Clint Longley won his first start in a Dallas uniform. Who could have known that it would be his last? The following August, a spat with Roger Staubach resulted in the "Mad Bomber"

exploding in the locker-room and sucker-punching his quarterbacking superior, forcing the Cowboys to deal him to San Diego.

Mike Pruitt & Calvin Hill
Mike Pruitt, the Purdue Boilermaker running back who wrote to Tex Schramm the previous August, saw his dreams of playing for the Cowboys shattered only a few months later when he was selected No. 7 overall by Cleveland in the 1976 draft. In September of 1979, Pruitt and former Dallas star Calvin Hill shared the Cleveland backfield as the Browns upset the Cowboys 26-7 on *Monday Night Football*.

Bibliography

The Man Inside...Landry by Bob St. John (Word Publishing, 1979)

I Remember Tom Landry by Denne H. Freeman & Jaime Aron (Sports Publishing, LLC, 2001)

Cowboys Have Always Been My Heroes by Peter Golenbock (Warner Books, 1997)

Tex! by Bob St. John (Prentice Hall, 1988)

Petrodollar Warfare: Oil, Iraq, And The Future Of The Dollar by William R. Clark (New Society Publishers, 2005)

Dallas Morning News

Dallas Times-Herald

Dallas Cowboys Weekly/Star Magzine

Time Magazine

Sports Illustrated

Dave Campbell's Texas Football Magazine

Miami News

Sarasota Herald-Tribune

Victoria Advocate

Daytona Beach Morning Journal

Observer-Reporter

Argus Press

Ludington Daily News

Lakeland Ledger

Milwaukee Sentinel

Ellensburg Daily Record

Bangor Daily News

Charlotte Observer

St. Petersburg Times

Pittsburgh Post-Gazette

Palm Beach Post

Toledo Blade

Montreal Gazette

Washington Post

New York Times

New York Daily News

Los Angeles Herald-Examiner

Spokane Daily Chronicle

Chicago Daily News

ABOUT THE AUTHOR

At the age of 18, Ryan Bush began writing a weekly column about the Dallas Cowboys for several small-town newspapers across Texas. His talent was initially recognized by H. Leon Smith, then Owner of The Clifton Record, a multi-award-winning newspaper in central Texas. After three years, his literary pursuit and passion for the Cowboys led him to write **Decade of Futility**, his first book. Ryan has just published his second book, **The Dirty Dozen**. He is currently working on additional projects about the Dallas Cowboys to be published in the future.

You may follow Ryan and his Dallas Cowboys' work online at:

Indulging in the Rich History of America's Team

Web Site - Dallas Cowboys Vault at RyanBush.biz
Facebook Pages:
    Dallas Cowboys Vault
    Decade of Futility
    Dallas Cowboys Dirty Dozen
Twitter - @rcbushCowboys

The Dirty Dozen

www.ingramcontent.com/pod-product-compliance
Lightning Source LLC
LaVergne TN
LVHW052257070426
835507LV00036B/3104